modern arabic poetry

modern arabic poetry

Revolution and Conflict

WAED ATHAMNEH

University of Notre Dame Press
Notre Dame, Indiana

Published by the University of Notre Dame Press
Notre Dame, Indiana 46556
www.undpress.nd.edu

Manufactured in the United States of America

Library of Congress Cataloging-in-Publication Data
Names: Athamneh, Waed author.
Title: Modern Arabic poetry : revolution and conflict / Waed Athamneh.
Description: Notre Dame, Indiana : University of Notre Dame Press, 2017. | Includes bibliographical references and index. | Description based on print version record and CIP data provided by publisher; resource not viewed.
Identifiers: LCCN 2016053418(print) | LCCN 2016056333(ebook) | ISBN 9780268101565 (pdf) | ISBN 9780268101541 (hardcover : alk. paper) | ISBN 026810154X (hardcover : alk. paper)
Subjects: LCSH: Political poetry, Arabic—History and criticism. | Arabic poetry—20th century—History and criticism. | Arabic poetry—21st century—History and criticism. | Politics in literature.
Classification: LCC PJ7542.P64 (print) | LCC PJ7542.P64 A84 2017 (ebook) | DDC 892.7/1609—dc23
LC record available at https://lccn.loc.gov/2016056333

∞*This paper meets the requirements of ANSI/NISO Z39.48-1992 (Permanence of Paper).*

To the most loving and inspiring parents in the world,
Nasser and Aida,

To my husband, friend, and colleague,
and the everlasting love of my life, Muhammad,

To my son and the light of my eyes, Ghassan,

To al-Bayātī, Ḥijāzī, and Darwīsh,

To all the lovers and readers of poetry,

I dedicate this book.

CONTENTS

ACKNOWLEDGMENTS

I am overwhelmed by the generosity of my family, friends, and mentors who have contributed to this book in any and every way. I would like to express my unmatched gratitude to my mentors and friends Suzanne Stetkevych and Jaroslav Stetkevych for their meticulous feedback and invaluable support and inspiration throughout the past nine years.

At the University of Notre Dame Press, I have been privileged to work with the publication team: Rebecca DeBoer, the managing editor, and the acquisitions editor, Stephen Little, for whose significant support and feedback I am thankful, and Kellie M. Hultgren for her conscientious copy editing and preparation of the final manuscript for publication. I would also like to thank Susanna J. Sturgis for her meticulous work in preparing the manuscript for submission and the peer reviewers for their insight and wisdom. I am grateful to Connecticut College for their generous financial support, such as Research Matters awards, R. F. Johnson awards, and the sabbatical leave in 2014–2015, without which I would not have been able to prepare the final version of my book.

I would like to thank my family, especially my father, Nasser Athamneh, and my mother, Aida Ajlouni, for their love, inspiration, and unmatchable support throughout the years, and for being great parents for me and my siblings: Deema, Husam, Liqa, Muhammad, Seif, and Dea. It would not be complete without dearly thanking my late grandfather Hajj Ibrahim al-Ajlouni for instilling the love for humanity and literature in me.

I would like to finally thank my husband, Muhammad, and my joyful baby, Ghassan, for their tremendous love, forbearance, and support. Ghassan was born while I was editing the book in Jordan, and he was so generous in letting me work while he slept quietly next to me. I would run to Muhammad every now and then with questions, comments, and requests for advice and encouragement. He always offered nothing but the best of all.

Finally, the lapses and shortcomings of this book are mine and mine only.

NOTE ON TRANSLATION AND TRANSLITERATION

I have followed the system of the *International Journal of Middle East Studies* in the transliteration of Arabic poetry and prose. Translations of poetry are mine unless otherwise indicated.

Introduction

Since the eruption of the Arab Uprising in Tunisia, Egypt, Libya, and Syria, scholars and students of Middle Eastern studies have been drawn to the politics and poetics of the Arab world. Poetry in the Arab world in particular and the Middle East in general has a great impact on people's lives. Arabs consider Arabic poetry one of their supreme cultural accomplishments. The Arab public has been inspired and influenced by poetry for centuries. Great poets are hailed as prophets for the key role they play in politics and society. When Arab poets express views that oppose the state, they are often dismissed from official positions, detained, or exiled.

Although many scholarly works have examined the poetry and politics of the Arab world before the 1967 Arab–Israeli war and shortly after the Arab defeat, few works have concerned themselves with the major literary directions in modern Arabic poetry beyond commitment to Nasser, Arab nationalism, and the question of Palestine in the 1950s and 1960s. This book fills that gap by exploring the development and achievement of Arabic poetry since the 1960s and the interplay between politics and poetry in the modern Arab world. After the Arab defeat in the 1967 war, the poets who stood behind Nasser's project of Arab nationalism began to question their own poetry and to see themselves as poets of a bygone era. The reason is clear: Arab poets were disappointed by the constant defeat and humiliation of their people, not only by external enemies but also by their own regimes. Modern Arab poets have tried for decades to incite their people to fight their tyrants and address their social and economic ills. Therefore, a major change took place in poetry when these poets saw no sign of revolution.

In *Modern Arabic Poetry: Revolution and Conflict* I argue that radical political changes in the Arab world inspired major transitions and new directions in the works of three prominent, modern twentieth-century Arab poets: the Iraqi ʿAbd al-Wahhāb al-Bayātī (1926–1999), the Egyptian Aḥmad ʿAbd al-Muʿṭī Ḥijāzī (b. 1935), and the Palestinian Maḥmūd Darwīsh (1941–2008). In a comprehensive and critical reading of the poetry of these three poets, the book examines the dialectical link between politics and poetry in the modern Arab world. Among the major political upheavals the book explores are the 1967 war and the fall of Nasserism, the ongoing Israeli–Palestinian conflict, and the Arab Uprising and its aftermath. *Modern Arabic Poetry* addresses enduring questions and issues from the 1950s to the present and investigates the impact of the region's past and present politics on its poetry. Enhanced by my original translations of some of the Arabic texts discussed, as well as translations published previously, this work brings twentieth- and twenty-first-century Arabic poetry fully into the purview of contemporary literary, political, and critical discourse.

Most scholars who have studied modern Arabic poetry, such as Jabra Ibrahim Jabra, Mohammad Mustafa Badawi, Issa J. Boullata, Salma Khadra Jayyusi, and Shmuel Moreh, have focused on trends and movements in Arabic literature from the mid-1950s to the mid-1970s. In this book I unveil the new directions and major transitions in Arabic poetry represented by al-Bayātī, Ḥijāzī, and Darwīsh. By examining the role of modern and contemporary Arab politics in the poetry of these three poets, I address such pressing questions as these: To what extent did the political and literary culture of the 1950s' *iltizām* (an adaptation of Sartrean "engagement") impact Arabic poetry? What happens to poets and their poetry when the regime they endorsed and praised collapses or when the regime they opposed and criticized is overthrown? How has a revolution such as the Arab Uprising influenced poetry? *Modern Arabic Poetry* answers these questions and engages the reader in its discussion and analysis of Arabic poetry in the twentieth and twenty-first centuries and its contribution to the literary canon.

This book consists of five chapters, including the conclusion. Though each of the three central chapters deals with a particular poet, the book's themes are deployed across all chapters and tie them together.

Attention to the major twentieth-century and contemporary sociopolitical events and literary movements that influenced the three poets provides further narrative coherence. The first chapter surveys the development of Arabic poetry and investigates its role in politics and society, and vice versa. Chapters 2, 3, and 4 study the lives and works of the three poets and identify new directions in their poetry in relation to key political events, revolutions, and conflicts in the Arab world. The conclusion brings the chapters together and comments on the culture of the Arab Uprising and its aftermath.

Chapter 1 introduces the politics of the modern Arab world and their impact on Arabic poetry. It introduces the book's three main theoretical concepts: commitment (*iltizām*), metapoetry (poetry about poetry), and coexistence in the Palestinian–Israeli conflict. This chapter pays close attention to the social, political, literary, and cultural movements and theories that influenced modern Arab thought, such as Marxism, socialism, Nasserism, commitment, and the free verse movement, and their roles in shaping Arabic poetry. This chapter situates the works of these three poets in the political and literary context of their time and offers an overview of the development of form and content in Arabic poetry. Understanding the key role poetry plays in the Arab world helps us understand the roots of current political events, such as the Arab Uprising, and their treatment in poetry. For example, the revolution in Tunisia was ignited by Moḥammad Bouʿazīzī, a Tunisian street vendor who was thrown into the street after his cart was taken from him, after which a verse of poetry by the Tunisian poet Abū al-Qāsim al-Shābbī (1909–1934) was chanted by demonstrators across the Arab world. In translation the verse says, "If people want to live, destiny will respond." The oppressed demonstrators and protesters found their long-awaited victory in the words of al-Shābbī. This verse united the Arab multitude around the globe and drew attention to the power of the Arab people, something they had not read or heard about since the 1967 defeat.

Chapter 2 studies the works of the Iraqi poet ʿAbd al-Wahhāb al-Bayātī and traces the transition in his works from commitment to metapoetry. I argue that al-Bayātī, one of the greatest supporters of Nasser and the 1967 war, moved beyond the commitment of the 1950s. This transition is by no means a direct one; it takes place gradually. Like his

Iraqi peer, Saʿdī Yūsuf (b. 1934), al-Bayātī did not let the political failure of Arabs in 1967 paralyze his poetry or put an end to his poetic career. Unlike other remarkable poets, such as Ḥijāzī, whose publication of poetry collections was halted by the 1967 defeat, al-Bayātī continued to look for inspiration beyond politics, which is key to his uniqueness as a poet. He experimented with free verse poetry in an attempt to disassociate himself from the language, diction, and form of 1950s commitment and its jargon.

The chapter concludes with the discussion of major poems by al-Bayātī that concern themselves with metapoetry. Al-Bayātī celebrates the unorthodox role of the Arab poet in the twentieth century as a terrorist. For al-Bayātī poetry becomes an act of terrorism and the poet a terrorist who has to find a loving home for himself in an arena of terror. The poet succeeds in finding such a loving home when he becomes a heroic terrorist, haunted by forces of change and weapons of destruction. Al-Bayātī's metapoetic work introduces a revolutionary stance to the role of the poet and poetry. The poet becomes a terrorist in defense of his poetry, language, and metapoetic concerns.

Chapter 3 turns to the works of Aḥmad ʿAbd al-Muʿṭī Ḥijāzī. I argue that although Ḥijāzī resembles al-Bayātī in many ways, particularly in his commitment to Nasser, Ḥijāzī's poetry displays a transition different from al-Bayātī's.

In his first three collections, *City without a Heart* (1959), *Aurès* (1959), and *Nothing Remains but Confession* (1965), Ḥijāzī tackled various topics such as his nostalgia for the Egyptian countryside, his support of Nasser, and the question of Palestine. After the fall of Nasserism and the 1967 defeat, Ḥijāzī attempted to move beyond this stage. Leaving Cairo and settling in Paris in 1974, Ḥijāzī continued to write poetry that was critical of Anwar Sadat's regime (*Creatures of the Night Kingdom*, 1978) and later of Hosni Mubarak's (*Cement Trees*, 1989). Then, after years of trying to incite his people to rise against their dictators and seeing no sign of resistance against Mubarak's regime, Ḥijāzī published no poetry collections for the next twenty-two years.

However, after the eruption of the January revolution in Egypt in 2011, Ḥijāzī made a comeback that year with *The Standing Ruins of Time*, a response to great literary figures of the earlier twentieth century, such as ʿAbbās Maḥmūd al-ʿAqqād and Ṭāha Ḥusayn, as though coming to terms with them, and in support of the January revolution. This turn in Ḥijāzī's poetics is highly politicized and marks a turning point in the trajectory of his poetry. Ḥijāzī found in the revolution a perfect time to publish his collection, an attempt to contribute poetically to the people's revolution. Here we see an example of revolutions inspiring poets rather than poets inspiring revolutions.

Ḥijāzī represents many modern Arab poets who were disappointed by their defeated people, who refused to rise and revolt against oppressive regimes. The Arab Uprising inspired many of these poets to resume writing committed poetry. It has resulted in the rebirth of literary commitment in Arabic poetry. Ḥijāzī, like many other poets, had been waiting for such a revolution for decades. The revolution inspired poets, writers, and artists to support it in their works and renewed their faith in the people and their right to fight dictatorships. With the revolution spreading to many countries in the Arab world, we are witnessing a great rise of literary production.

Chapter 4 examines the impact of the ongoing Israeli–Palestinian conflict on the works of Maḥmūd Darwīsh, the national Palestinian "poet of resistance." Like al-Bayātī and Ḥijāzī, Darwīsh supported Nasser, Arab nationalism, and the Palestinian cause. However, Palestine was a personal issue for him because it was his homeland. This chapter investigates the shift in the representation of the Palestinian self and the Israeli other in early and late works by Darwīsh. I argue that, in the 2003 collection *Do Not Apologize for What You Did*, Darwīsh starts to move from his earlier, more extroverted political poetry to a poetry that closely interrogates identity, in which the distinction between self and other begins to collapse. I compare major confrontational poems of resistance published between the 1960s and 2002 to poems published since 2003 and examine the politics of Darwīsh's poetics. Darwīsh's treatment of the self and the other tells the story of a young poet who resists his enemy through his poetry for decades. However, this treatment witnesses a shift toward a humanist look at the conflict and the parties involved.

In the conclusion I reflect on the literary responses of these poets to major political changes and their unique contributions to Arabic poetry. This conclusion demonstrates and confirms the argument of the book:

that major political changes in the modern Arab world have prompted significant new directions and transitions in the poetry of three important Arab poets. Their individual responses suggest three representative models in modern Arabic poetry. In the first of these, the metapoetic, the poet deviates completely from direct engagement with politics to find inspiration in stable and artistic resources. In the second, the recommitted, major political revolutions inspire the poet to resume writing and publishing collections of poetry. The third is the model of poets of ongoing conflicts who are born and die before such conflicts reach a resolution. This poetry is that of coexistence: it moves from militant to humanist.

Although all three poets began writing in the twentieth century, the trajectories of their careers present us with varying notions of the vocation of the poet in the modern world. In the conclusion I comment on the impact of the Arab Uprising on the reception of poetry and on the role of the poet in society, particularly in the Arab world. I explore the newly evolving meanings and connotations of "committed" poetry of the Arab Uprising. Finally, I discuss the challenges posed by audience, society, and language to the modern Arab poet.

CHAPTER 1

The Politics and Poetics of the Modern Arab World

ARABIC POETRY THROUGH TIME

Poetry has played an essential role in Arab culture since pre-Islamic times. Dating back to the sixth century, the *Jāhiliyya*, poets were the political spokespersons of the tribe. Each tribe had its own poets to write its history, defend its stature, and be its representatives and voice. Poets held esteemed positions in society not only to document the ins and outs of their tribe and define its identity, but also to promote their tribe among the other tribes. Poets described in carefully crafted verse the political and cultural aspects of their Bedouin society and used poetry to praise the tribe or attack its rivals. Praise, boasting, satire, and elegy were among the major functions of the pre-Islamic *qaṣida* (ode). Pre-Islamic poetry was oral, and its performative nature demanded rhyme and meter to draw the attention of the audience through its musicality.

Tribes competed through the talents of their poets, who would gather every year to present their finest poems to the public. The stronger the tribe, the more powerful the voices of its poets became. By the same token, the more gifted a tribe's poets, the louder its voice among other tribes. Poets moved men to go to war and recounted their exploits after they returned from the battlefield. If the tribe won a battle, its poets wrote verses in its praise, which quickly traveled among other tribes, raising its status. If it lost, poets wrote elegies and incited the tribe to avenge its heroic, slaughtered kinsmen.

The significance and impact of Arab poets have naturally evolved throughout the centuries. Poets remain influential in the modern Arab world, and their voices continue to be instrumental, especially when major political events take place. Since the mid-twentieth century, many poets have paid a hefty price for taking political stands. Because of their strong impact on Arab society, dissident poets have been relentlessly attacked by Arab regimes. For attempting to mobilize crowds or criticizing the political status quo, poets are often exiled, imprisoned, or even assassinated. As a result, Arabic poetry has both documented and intervened in Arab politics, especially over the second half of the twentieth century. In its documentary function, it provides an interesting perspective that can differ significantly from mainstream historical accounts. Yet while poetry has profoundly influenced modern Arab politics, it has also been transformed and reshaped by it. It is thus hard to attempt an understanding of it by dropping historical and cultural context in favor of close-reading strategies alone. The genius of Arabic poetry lies not only in its beauty and artistic quality, but also in its nuanced and remarkable ability to transform harsh and often static political matters into one of the most revered art forms in Arabic literature. The translation of these mundane realities into powerful, poignant, and passionate poetic accounts is a fascinating process that merits critical investigation. For this reason, an examination of modern Arab politics is essential to understanding the broad, multifaceted, and often complex ways in which modern Arab poetry has evolved in form, content, and subject matter.

THE ARAB–ISRAELI CONFLICT AND THE RISE OF PAN-ARAB SENTIMENT

One of the most important conflicts to take place in the Middle East during the twentieth century was the 1948 war between Arabs and Jewish settlers in Palestine. When Britain pulled out its troops, a war erupted in the region, ending in Arab defeat and the declaration of the State of Israel. In Arabic, the 1948 defeat is referred to as the *nakba,* which means "catastrophe." By the summer of 1949, between 600,000 and 760,000 Palestinians had been forced out of their homes as refugees. The majority of them ended up in camps in the surrounding Arab countries, including Jordan, Lebanon, and Syria. This defeat and the establishment of Israel became major issues of Arab nationalism. After 1948, Arab intellectuals debated the future of the Arab nation and the potential for bringing the scattered and frustrated Arab countries together under the umbrella of nationalism. Modern Arab ideologies, such as Nasserism, promised reform and the achievement of Arab nationalism. Nasserism became one of the most important and influential modern political ideologies not only in Egypt, but also in the Arab world.

Gamal Abdel Nasser (Jamāl ʿAbd al-Nāṣir), who was born in 1918 in the village of Bakos, near Alexandria, was a young major among the Egyptian officers who fought against Israel in 1948. Four years after the defeat, he led the Free Officers Movement that seized power in Egypt and overthrew King Farouq I in 1952. The officers promised to restore democracy and end corruption. At first they referred to themselves as a "movement," and then they replaced *movement* with *revolution*. Nasser ruled through three successive, centralized parties: Liberation Rally (1952–1957), the National Union (1957–1962), and the Arab Socialist Union (1962–1978).

Nasser became the president of Egypt on June 23, 1956. After proving himself on the state level, he took responsibility at the regional level. He nationalized the Suez Canal Company and raised the Egyptian flag in Port Said on July 26, 1956. In a remarkable three-hour speech to the Egyptians on that day, he declared himself the most responsible Arab leader. He said, "Now, while I am speaking to you, Egyptian brothers of yours are taking over the administration and management of the Canal company. . . . the Egyptian Canal Company not the foreign Canal Company."[1]

In what is referred to as the Tripartite Aggression, Britain, France, and Israel then invaded Egypt and fought the Egyptian army to regain control over the canal. Nasser refused to surrender. International pressure, supported by a United Nations resolution, demanded that the British, French, and Israeli forces withdraw. By putting an end to the British occupation, Nasser became the beacon of Arab nationalism. By the mid-1960s, the Nasserist ideology of nationalizing foreign and private holdings in Egypt had boosted the economy, raised the employment rate, and allowed the Egyptian government to gain control over the Suez Canal and French and British investments.

Nationalizing the Suez Canal had a major impact on politics in many other countries in the Arab world. In Iraq, a military coup in 1958 overthrew the monarchy. The Baʿth (Resurrection) Party, founded in 1949, was among the major political groupings that believed that their power lay in land reform. Romantic Arab intellectuals who rallied for Arab unity supported Nasserism and demanded social and economic reform. The Baʿth Party controlled Iraq until 2003 and still controls the government of Syria at the time of publication. However, the 2010 revolution in Syria, led by the opposition, has demanded the end of the Baʿth regime.

In Syria, demands for unification with Egypt led to the establishment of the United Arab Republic of Syria and Egypt, which lasted only from 1958 to 1961. Commenting on this union, Nasser said, "I am confident in the inevitability of unity between peoples of the Arab nation just as I am confident however long the night, dawn follows."[2] Nasserism had a far-reaching influence on major Arab countries and made Nasser a hero among other Arab leaders and nationalists. Nasser's call for nationalism found support throughout the Arab world.

For Nasser, the basis of Arab nationalism was common language (Arabic), shared history, and common interests. The National Charter of 1962 focused on the unity of language, history, and hope. Nasser maintained that what brings Arabs together is the way they respond to events occurring in the Arab world. He added, "Arab peoples all respond similarly to events, this is, if an incident occurs in any part of the Arab homeland, Arabs elsewhere from the Atlantic Ocean to the Arabian Gulf feel it."[3] Nasser constructed Arab nationalism so that every Arab country had to follow the Egyptian example of placing faith and power in the unity of Arabs, without which no Arab country would be able to meet the challenges facing the region.

James L. Gelvin defines nationalism as an ideology that transforms people into machines working for the common good.[4] He maintains that the emergence of a nationalist movement requires devoted nationalists who are able to articulate its goals and principles for the people.[5] The Nasserist nationalists in Egypt articulated the ideology of Arab nationalism for the Arab world and encouraged Arabs to participate in this movement and support its agenda. According to Nasserism, language and history are the main pillars of Arab nationalism. Membership in the Arab nation meant speaking Arabic and sharing the same historical tradition, irrespective of religion. Many Arab intellectuals and thinkers supported Nasser's project of nationalism.

The Syrian Arab nationalist thinker Sāti' al-Ḥuṣrī (1879–1968) formulated the systematic theory of nationalism as a modern and secular ideology. Al-Ḥuṣrī believed that religion can inspire people, but that it should not intrude in the sphere of politics. Although the Muslim Brotherhood opposed Nasser's disavowal of religion in politics, intellectuals and scholars supported his nationalism, including poets from across the Arab world. Nasser was popular in Egypt and in the Arab world, which explains why poets from countries such as Iraq and Syria celebrated him in their poetry in the 1950s and 1960s. Literary scholars such as the Egyptian intellectual and writer Ṭāha Ḥusayn (1889–1973) supported Nasser's focus on Arabic as a main pillar in achieving nationalism.

Ḥusayn believed that nationalism should not be associated with religion. Unlike the Islamists who associated the Arabic language with religious awakening, Ḥusayn argued that the Arabic language is of equal importance and value for Copts and Muslims. However, some scholars argued that Arab nationalism failed because it was riddled with difficulties and challenges related to the nature, history, geography, demography, and politics of the Arab world, and that neither Islam nor language had succeeded in achieving Arab nationalism.[6] The Arab world is very complex and diverse, and although Arabs share the same language and history, the many local, regional, and national challenges made Arab nationalism hard to achieve. Speaking the same language and sharing the same history might support unity, but it could not solve the problems in Arab politics or reduce Western interference in Arab political life. Arab nationalism involves not only Arabs but also the West and its interests, which challenges any nationalist project in the area.

On June 5, 1967, Israel initiated an attack against Egypt and its Arab allies, who turned out to be no match for the Israeli army. The war ended in two days in favor of Israel, which then occupied Egypt's Gaza Strip and Sinai Peninsula, the Syrian Golan Heights, and the old city of Jerusalem. Michael Oren argues that "there does not seem to be another example in history of an event that was so short and so limited geographically that has had such profound, long-term regional, and indeed global, ramifications" and that this war "never really ended . . . it is only just beginning."[7] This war marked the beginning of a long conflict between Arabs and Israel. Humiliated after the defeat, Nasser and the Arabs knew that they had lost not only a major war, but also their dream of nationalism.

The 1967 war also ended the "Nasserist domination of inter-Arab politics" and led to a stronger focus on Egypt in the era of Sadat and Mubarak.[8] No Arab leader inspired Arab nationalism and identified the destiny of his country with Arab nationalism as Nasser had. After the 1967 defeat, all the national slogans and dreams faded and Arabs felt betrayed and disappointed. Although Nasser's position in the Arab world was weakened after the defeat, in Egypt his position remained strong.[9] On June 9, 1967, assuming full responsibility for the defeat, Nasser resigned. This act "aroused widespread protests in Egypt and some other Arab countries," and Nasser acceded to popular demand and returned to office.[10] Arabs who had been promised victory in this war were taken aback by the defeat, and the question of Palestine became more complex than ever. Palestinians and Arabs alike shared the feelings of humiliation, disappointment, and defeat.

Nasser had been the broker between the Palestinians and the other Arab countries. In 1964 the Arab League had created the Palestine Liberation Organization (PLO), led by Yāsir ʿArafāt (Yasser Arafat, 1929–2004), under the control of Egypt. The PLO's army was part of the armies of Egypt, Jordan, Iraq, and Syria. The PLO committed itself to "direct military confrontation with Israel."[11] After the 1967 war, it was understood that the Arab armies were no match for the Israeli army and therefore Palestine was lost forever. Consequently, the PLO held itself responsible for the Palestinian people and operated its own activities and guerrilla groups independently in countries such as Lebanon and Jordan. Nasser tried to restrain the PLO's actions in these countries while recognizing its legitimate representation of the Palestinians. In 1969 and 1970, Nasser mediated between the PLO and the Lebanese government to reach an agreement by which the PLO limited its operations in southern Lebanon. In 1970 Nasser also mediated between the PLO and the Jordanian government after a long fight (the Black September) between the two.[12] That same year, Nasser suffered a heart attack and died after attending the Arab League summit. Nasser's vice president, Anwar al-

Sadat (1918–1981), a member of the Free Officers Revolution who had fought beside Nasser in 1952, became Egypt's president in 1970. Sadat launched the *infitāḥ* (open-door policy) program of economic liberalization in 1973. He maintained that the government had to control the political sector in order to bring about social reform.

Sadat signed the Camp David Accords with Israel in 1978, becoming the first Arab leader to recognize the state of Israel. As a result, Israel withdrew its forces from the Sinai Peninsula, and Egypt guaranteed stable diplomatic relations with Israel. Sadat was assassinated by the Muslim Brotherhood in 1981, ending another era in the history of Egypt.

Israel invaded Lebanon in 1982 to destroy the PLO's military and political base there. After this invasion, the Arab countries that had been in a state of war with Israel since 1948 were no longer willing to fight for Palestine and the Palestinians. The Palestinians fought Israel alone in the First Intifada (1987) and the Second Intifada (2000).

The PLO signed the Oslo Accords with Israel in 1993, which resulted in Israel's retreat from parts of the Gaza Strip and the West Bank and its recognition of the PLO as the official Palestinian authority. In 1994 Jordan signed a peace treaty with Israel as well. Despite these treaties, the state of hostility between the Arabs and Israel never disappeared. Israel's 1982 invasion of Lebanon, only three years after the signing of the Camp David Accords, gave many Arabs the impression that peace with Israel was impossible. Although most Arab countries and the PLO established diplomatic relations with Israel, the majority of Palestinians, represented by Hamas, refuse to negotiate with Israel. Arabs in general feel that the decisions made and treaties signed by Arab governments do not necessarily reflect their own desires. Therefore, in the collective Arab consciousness, there are two main challenges or obstacles to attaining freedom: the internal enemy, meaning Arab leaders, regimes, or governments, and the external enemy, meaning Israel.

These military conflicts and the peace treaties that followed them created ongoing frustration and disappointment throughout the Arab world. Major ideologies and movements, such as socialism and communism, played a vital role in shaping the region's social, cultural, and political life. Against this backdrop, and given failing political regimes that do not represent the will of the people, Arab intellectuals and writers have been constantly searching for the ideology best suited to their society. For many Arabs, the question of Palestine became a question of Arab identity and nationality.

The Arab communist movement's position on Palestine and Arab unity differed from Nasser's. Before Egypt's 1958 unification with Syria, the communists viewed nationalism as a means to defeat imperialism, whereas Nasser considered nationalism an ultimate goal.[13] After the unification, Nasser repressed the communist hard-liners and drew a clear line between communism and nationalism.[14] In 1959, the communist challenge to the Nasserists in Egypt led to Nasser's socialist transformation of the state and its single ruling party.

The Arab communists were anti-Western, antireligious, and pro-Soviet in their thought. As Tareq Y. Ismael writes, "The Arab world first encountered Marxism, though only on an intellectual level, at the end of the nineteenth century."[15] Marx and Engels's model for social change did not address the complex conditions in the Middle East, for it was believed that the Arab territories "contained very little, if any, revolutionary potential."[16] Marx and Engels viewed Arabs as barbarians whose tribal life and traditions precluded any possibility of progress like that of Europe.[17]

Arab communists opposed Nasser because he focused mainly on Arab unity and not on the working class and its struggles and concerns. After the 1980s, Arab communists aspired to play a role in the political developments in the Arab world, but they largely failed because they could not adapt their ideologies to the conditions of Arab societies. However, the Arab communist movement did play a significant role in the politics of the twentieth century through its influence on political and social changes in the Arab world from the 1940s through the 1970s.[18]

Although Arab communism and socialism promised political reform in the Arab world, the 1967 defeat discredited the nationalist and secular Arab regimes and their promises of freedom, political reform, and social equity. The breakup of the United Arab Republic also highlighted the failure of Nasser's nationalist movement and his secular regime. Nor had communism or socialism managed to address the political, social, and economic challenges in the Arab world. Arab intellectuals "ranging from liberals and Marxists to nationalists and Islamists" sought new alternatives to the status quo.[19]

In the 1950s, Arab writers discussed and debated the role of literature and the Arab writer in forming and registering the attitudes of Arab intellectuals and the Arab public in politics. For example, the Egyptian socialist scholar Salāma Mūsā (1887–1958) advocated for the role of literature in society and demanded that the Egyptian writer share the fate and life of the public. Saʿdallah Wannūs (1941–1997), a leading Syrian playwright, wrote about social criticism and Arab political decline. He argued that the Arab writers who escape in their writings from the military and political defeats of their societies are themselves defeated as writers. Arab intellectuals criticized writers who denied or failed to acknowledge the notion of a defeated Arab nation, on the grounds that escaping from the bitter truth would postpone healing. Hence, the term *iltizām* (commitment) started to appear in Arab literary circles, and a serious debate between Arab writers and critics over the role of literature in society took place, especially after 1950. Critics such as Mūsā, Luwīs ʿAwaḍ (1915–1990), and Ra'īf Khūrī (1913–1967), whose Marxist discussions and arguments on the political role of literature dominated the literary circles in the 1950s and 1960s, believed that literature should be socially and politically engaged and that any artistic activity should be associated with the society in which it was written.[20] They held the writer responsible for participating "in the liberation, modernization and democratization of the nation" and attacked those who wrote from their ivory towers (al-burj al-ʿājī).[21] In poetry, these discussions called for a major change in content and form. Poets demanded a new form that was more fitting for the new themes and subjects relevant to the newly independent states in the Arab world. Therefore, Arab poets looked to Western literature for new forms, and especially to T. S. Eliot's free verse movement.

THE FREE VERSE MOVEMENT AND THE PROSE POEM

During the political unrest of the late 1940s and early 1950s, Arab poets felt the urge to direct their attention toward the political and social scenes and to look for a new form of poetry, one that enabled them to express their society's prevalent emotions of despair and hope. T. S. Eliot provided them with such a form, free verse, which was better suited to the issues they faced than the meters and rhymes of classical and romantic poetry. Rashād Rushdī's Arabic translation of Eliot's "Tradition and the Individual Talent," which appeared in 1951, was very influential in Arab poetic circles, directing the poets' attention toward "a non-Romantic stance, an objectification of experience that suited the pose of the poet as a public intellectual."[22]

The resulting rigorous change reflects the Arab poet's constant desire to adapt his or her poetry to the social and political conditions of his time. Change and progress are key in Arabic poetry because poetry reflects the state of its people and society, and both are subject to change. Therefore, the introduction of and experimentation with free verse in the late 1940s and early 1950s went hand in hand with the poets' desire to move beyond classical and romantic rhymes and subject matter in order to express and give shape to the attitudes of the age. For the first time in the history of Arabic poetry, the poet was free to write about relevant new topics, in verse free from the meticulous rules of classical Arabic poetry. Al-Bayātī was among the first pioneers to experiment with free verse, along with his fellow Iraqis Nāzik al-Malā'ika and Badr Shākir al-Sayyāb.

In the 1940s, modern Arab poets had witnessed the independence of their countries from the imperialist powers, and they felt the need for a form that would enable them to freely express and shape the public's feelings and aspirations. The modern Arab poet was frustrated with the classical form and diction that continued to govern neoclassical and romantic poetry. The late-romantic poets of the late 1940s and early 1950s, such as al-Malā'ika, al-Sayyāb, and al-Bayātī, found Eliot's poetry and style very appealing. Eliot called for an escape from emotions and personality at a time when they were looking for a poetry that could break their emotional attachment to the past. Arab poets were looking for new forms and styles to reflect their bitter feelings and disappointments, especially after the establishment of the state of Israel in 1948 and the rise of Arab nationalism.

The translations of Eliot's works, especially "Tradition and the Individual Talent" and his poem "The Waste Land," encouraged Arab poets to experiment with free verse, using flexible meters and relying on the internal music of the words and the images instead of abiding by the strict rules of rhyme and meter. The free verse poem also dropped the classical two hemistiches, and its lines were shorter and of varying lengths, in accordance with the flow of emotion or the theme being treated. Masks were employed to escape from emotions and personality and to give the poet new voices. Realizing the significance in Eliot's writings of the poet's originality and grounding in tradition, Arab poets returned to the resources of Arab culture, religion, and literature for inspiration and influence. Poets such as al-Bayātī and al-Sayyāb "appropriated modernist poetic traditions and Western narratives, transforming them into a poetic dynamics to articulate domestic issues integral to the Arab world in the era of decolonization."[23] To treat issues of regional and national significance, the modern Arab poet adopted such Western forms and techniques as the prelude, the interior monologue, and the objective correlative.

Among the major techniques copied from modern Western poetry in general and from T. S. Eliot in particular is the reiteration of one word or more. Such repetition, mainly of the rhyme word, was used to emphasize a certain theme or to enrich the rhythm of the poem. In "Unshudat al-Maṭar" (Hymn of Rain), by al-Sayyāb, for instance, the word *maṭar* (rain) is often repeated to invoke fertility and hope in Iraq. Eliot's parenthetical sentence, which was borrowed from prose and employed in poetry, was also employed in modern Arabic poetry to emphasize the contrast between the poet's thoughts and emotions. Among the most influential techniques that Arab poets adopted from Eliot was the objective correlative, which helped express and give shape to emotions indirectly, adding to the aesthetics of poetry. Socialist realist poets such as Muḥammad al-Faytūrī (b. 1930), Ḥijāzī, and al-Bayātī experimented in free verse and contributed to its development in Arabic poetry. The first two free verse poems in Arabic appeared in 1947: al-Sayyāb's "Hal Kāna Ḥubban?" (Was It Love?) and al-Malā'ika's "Al-Kūlirā" (Cholera).

Arab poets adopted free verse because it enabled them to treat pressing issues in a more flexible and innovative form. The free verse movement also introduced a new content, a new diction, and a new language. For example, the use of myths, such as that of Tammūz, such legends as Sinbad, and religious symbols such as Christ and the Prophet Muhammad enriched the content of modern poetry and gave poets more flexibility to reflect on such myths and legends in treating social and political issues facing modern Arab society. Although Arab poets were no longer bound by strict prosodic rules, they maintained the foot in each line, with some flexibility. Thus, these poets kept part of the poetic tradition, but made it flexible so they could innovate and experiment with language and style. Given this freedom, poets could carry a theme or a series of emotions, and even the foot, to another line. This change was revolutionary because it not only broke from Al-Khalīl's prosodic rules but also made the poet an innovator in language. In their rebellion against the blind imitation of the past, modern Arab poets reflected the urgent importance of questioning the political and social norms of the second half of the twentieth century. They realized the need to express and give shape to the people's anguish and frustration, especially during and after major political events such as the 1948 and 1967 defeats. They experimented with the prose poem as well in an attempt to find the perfect form for the most fragmented content in the history of Arabic poetry.

The use of the prose poem as a poetic medium enriched modern Arabic poetry in breaking from the traditional diction of *iltizām* and employing deep visions of the human condition, anguish, and conflict in an age of repression and disorder.[24] The prose form had acquired its rightful place in contemporary Arabic poetry by the mid-1960s. Influential pioneers of prose poetry, such as Jibrān Khalīl Jibrān (1883–1931) and Amīn al-Rīḥānī (1876–1940), proved that original and powerful poetry does not need to be written in meter and rhyme.[25] Unsī al-Ḥājj (b. 1937), Yūsuf al-Khāl (1917–1987), and ʿAlī Aḥmad Saʿīd, known as Adūnīs (b. 1929), were among the first Arab poets to write prose poems. Prose poems contributed to the development of form, diction, and subject matter in modern Arabic poetry. Jibrān says, in his poem "Al-Shāʿir" (The Poet), "I am a poet. I versify life's prose; I render in prose what life has versified."[26] In this poem, Jibrān emphasizes that the poet should be able to write poetry in verse and prose.

As the free verse movement was a revolution in modern Arabic poetry, so was the prose poem. Suzanne Bernard asserts that the prose poem is "the fruit of rebellion against all kinds of form-oppression, which deny the poet the freedom to create a personal language for himself, and force him to mold his expressions in ready forms."[27] After the 1967 war and the death of Arab nationalism, many poets felt the need to break away from the traditional diction, images, and symbols of the Arab commitment of the 1950s.

The Syrian poet Adūnīs was a major advocate for the prose poem and called for breaking away from rhyme and meter altogether. He maintained that the poet's role in the twentieth century should be that of an innovator who, although grounded in tradition, is not limited by the constraints of prosody. Rather, poets should choose their topics and let the topic determine the form in which the poem should be written. For Adūnīs, the poet is a rebel who does not abide by any law and therefore makes his own rules and laws; this is what makes him unique and his poetry exceptional. He believed that modern poets should not write only the prose poem; rather, they should be able to write in any form they find appropriate. Unlike the other two poets, however, Adūnīs insisted on writing for the elite because they were the only ones who could bring about change for their societies. Although the prose poem could be written in the form of connected lines, like a paragraph in a short story, Adūnīs maintains that its poetic language, imagery, and diction make it poetry rather than prose.

Although many poets resisted the prose poem when it was first introduced in literary circles, and many critics rejected it completely, many poets experimented with it. The renowned Syrian poet Nizār Qabbānī (1923–1998) agreed with Adūnīs and maintained that the poet should not be imprisoned in one form of poetry; instead, poets should experiment and write in all forms. Darwīsh also experimented with free verse and the prose poem, but Ḥijāzī rejected the prose poem and has not yet experimented with it as of this writing.

SARTRE AND *ILTIZĀM*

Just as the free verse poem was a revolution in form, *iltizām*, a concept appropriated from Jean-Paul Sartre's idea of literary engagement, was thought to be a revolution in content. Sartre had a major impact on Arab intellectual life in the 1950s, especially in Beirut's *Al-Ādāb.* Arab writers were preoccupied with Sartre's philosophical, committed writings, particularly his call for literature to be engaged with sociopolitical concerns. The "Palestine tragedy of 1948" and "the 1952 Egyptian Revolution" contributed to the spread of *iltizām* in the Arab world.[28] Many Arab writers demanded that literature be committed to Arab causes and engaged with the changing demands of society instead of being romantic. In his series of articles, "Qu'est-ce que la literature?" (What Is Literature?), Sartre discussed "the relationship between writer and reader" and "emphasized the significance of freedom as a basis and message of committed literature."[29] In these articles, Sartre maintained that when the writer "causes the commitment of immediate spontaneity to advance, for himself and others, to the reflective," he becomes his people's model in commitment.[30] Sartre's form of commitment entails a great deal of meditation and responsibility from the writer. Arab literary circles adapted Sartre's commitment into the writer's responsibility, *iltizām*, toward his nation mainly through supporting Arab nationalism and the question of Palestine in the 1950s. However, this sort of literary commitment did not advance from immediate spontaneity to the reflective. Therefore, most modern Arabic literature of the 1950s and early 1960s became a tendentious promotion of Nasserism and shouting of its slogans that shared the language of *iltizām* and reflected the poets' faith in and excitement about the project of nationalism. Most of the poets' writings of the 1950s were romantic before the poets turned to social and socialist realism. Addressing the social ills of their societies, poets such as al-Bayātī, Egyptian poet and playwright Ṣalāḥ ʿAbd al-Ṣabūr (1931–1981), Qabbānī, and Ḥijāzī found their calling in *iltizām* in the 1950s.

Mohammad Mustafa Badawi argues that ʿAbd al-Ṣabūr's poetry turned from commitment to humanist and social ideals, which started to develop in his poetry after the 1967 defeat.[31] ʿAbd al-Ṣabūr believed poetry should not directly promote political positions; rather, it should be indirectly committed through serving language instead of using it.[32] ʿAbd al-Ṣabūr's repudiation of his Marxist tendencies in literature and *iltizām* resulted in some of his best tragedies, which were mystical and existential in nature.

Adūnīs, too, wrote extensively on the plight of the Arab citizen. However, he criticized the committed poets for failing to promote social change in their societies.[33] Adūnīs accused the poetry of *iltizām* of betraying "the spirit and meaning of freedom and the revolution" because it aspired "to nothing more than serving the revolution and describing its aims and achievements in an optimistic spirit, at times to the point of naïveté."[34] Therefore, Adūnīs rejected *iltizām* and the poets of commitment in the 1950s and 1960s. His poetry is metaphysical and abstract rather than committed to a specific revolution or cause.

Qabbānī's focus changed from romantic and erotic poetry to committed socialist realism. He was among the first Arab poets to respond to the 1967 defeat by writing one of the best poems about "the serious shortcomings of Arabs that resulted in their shattering defeat: 'Alā Hamish Daftar al-Naksa' (On the Margin of the Book of Defeat)."[35]

Although they recoiled from *iltizām*, these poets and many others continued to write about the plight of the Arab citizen as a victim of social and economic ills. However, *iltizām* indoctrinated the majority of writers into accepting Nasser as a symbol for Arab unity and dignity instead of questioning the practices of his authoritarian regime and demanding democracy for their nations. Perhaps this is the major flaw of *iltizām*, and one that explains why the committed literature of the poets of resistance in the Occupied Territories is "the most valuable and interesting recent development of Arabic literature."[36] Like their peers, poets such as Darwīsh and Samīḥ al-Qāsim (1939–2014) were committed to Arab nationalism and the question of Palestine. Nonetheless, their committed literature continued to flourish and reach the masses even after the 1967 defeat because, for them, *iltizām* was not a stage in their development. They were committed to defying the occupation in their poetry whether Arabs attained nationhood or not. Although he was a Nasserist, al-Qāsim's *iltizām* was different from that of other modern Arab poets. The message of his "directly inspired poetry by the June war is never one of despair, but often of sober realization of the grim facts and heroically continuing the struggle."[37]

In the 1950s and 1960s, *iltizām* determined the worth of any literary work, especially poetry. Sartre exempted poetry, music, and painting from literary commitment, but Marxist and socialist realist Arab writers and critics altered the idea somewhat when they adopted it. Anwar al-Maʿaddāwī, a member of the editorial board of *Al-Ādāb*, disagreed with Sartre's exemption of poetry from commitment and maintained that "Sartre is not committed enough."[38] Hence, the modern Arab poet was expected to write solely about Nasserism, Arab nationalism, and the question of Palestine.

Poetry is the poet's dynamite because it shapes the suffering and wrath of the nation, crystallizes political positions, and stiffens popular resistance by providing slogans to rally around and "unforgettable poems that no guns could suppress."[39] This applies to most of the Arabic poetry of resistance in the Israeli–Palestinian conflict, but not to the pro-Nasserist poetry. Sartre's ideal of the freedom and responsibility of the writer was translated into the writer's "artistic commitment in the service of Arab society and Arab nationalism."[40] However, the poetry of the 1950s failed at "stiffening popular resistance" because it blindly supported the Nasserist regime and its agenda rather than reflecting the people's demands and rights.

Baffled by the military defeat of 1948 and the loss of Palestine, Arab writers of the 1950s adopted Sartre's message of engagement because speaking meant acting.[41] Sartre assured frustrated writers that their words were action, and that the socially engaged writer plays an important role in bringing about change by revealing the status quo.[42] Therefore, Mūsā advocated a socialist realist model in committed literature in 1956, demanding that writers reach readers by identifying with them and writing about their social ills.[43] In doing so, Mūsā severely attacked the "traditional literature of the rulers" and its advocates ʿAbbās Maḥmūd al-ʿAqqād and Ṭāha Ḥusayn; he considered it hollow and belonging to the dark centuries.[44] He encouraged Arab writers to be socially committed by delivering a message that changes readers and educates them.

In writing engaged literature, frustrated Arab writers found an escape from the state of paralysis and humiliation that stamped the Arab psyche after the *nakba*. They believed that if they could write and engage the public in the politics of the time, they would be able to educate it and change its self-image as a defeated nation, a nation good for nothing. Only then would poets be able to move the public to restore the people's dignity, liberate Palestine, and bring the nationalism project to fruition.

However, some writers and critics viewed commitment in literature from a different angle. The main competing model of Arab commitment in the postcolonial Mashriq, which comprises Egypt, Lebanon, Palestine, Jordan, and Syria, is the pan-Arab Marxist model. Socialist realists understood *iltizām* as "a commitment in accordance with the social and political concern of an Arab world," which "was not bound to any aesthetic bounds or prescriptions."[45] The pan-Arab Marxists were accused "of connecting very strictly certain political and social objectives and writing styles with *iltizām*—so that it might be better be called *ilzām* (compulsion)."[46] Although there were minor differences between these models, both advocated the engagement of literature in the social and political life of the Arab world in an attempt to educate the Arab reader and serve Arab nationalism.

However, after the 1967 defeat the attitude toward commitment changed. The Arab writers initially responded with shock and confusion, and their works reflected themes of frustration, horror, despair, confusion, chaos, and loss of identity. Before and during the 1967 defeat, the term *iltizām* "became increasingly militant and anti-Israeli in tone" and sometimes turned into "radical *iltizām*," advocating the propagation of revolutionary literature.[47] This explains why Ghassān Kanafānī and other critics celebrated the poets of resistance in the Occupied Territories and considered them the shining example of true *iltizām* that everyone should follow.[48] Hence, the evolving meaning of *iltizām* before 1967 imposed limitations on the writer's freedom: the worth of any work of art was determined by how committed it was, and "commitment, whether moderate or extreme, seems to have been the rule rather than the exception."[49] Therefore, the majority of writers, and poets in particular, wrote on the question of Palestine, Nasserism, and Arab nationalism, and poets served the Nasserist regime and its propaganda under the umbrella of commitment and the dream of Arab nationalism.

Disappointed by Nasser and the 1967 defeat, poets across the Arab world were, like their nations, disillusioned; they realized that the utopia they had created in their poetry had fallen apart. Many realized that their words had lost their power in politics and came to see *iltizām* as a stage in their development, meaning that they now had to be realistic rather than idealistic.[50] Therefore, "many writers outgrew the limits of literary commitment as it was propagated by political literary circles and looked for new and individual solutions to the problem, asking themselves how literary writing could be significant in the present world."[51] While al-Ṣabūr found his calling in writing mystical poetry and drama, other Arab poets and writers were drawn to existentialism, surrealism, and symbolism.[52]

The career trajectories of al-Bayātī, Ḥijāzī, and Darwīsh each represent a unique transformation from *iltizām*. The following chapters will examine how these major modern Arab poets treated *iltizām* in their works and the solutions each came up with, representing new directions and transitions in modern Arabic poetry. I argue that the three poetic oeuvres under discussion demonstrate three distinct transformations from their early stages of development to their current form. Al-Bayātī moves from committed to metapoetic, Ḥijāzī from committed to Nasser to committed to people, and Darwīsh from militant to humanist. After *iltizām*, the two theoretical concepts that remain to be discussed are metapoetry and coexistence in the Israeli–Palestinian conflict in literature.

METAPOETRY

The Arab poet in the twentieth century was concerned with poetry itself. Although writing poetry is an active process of addressing poetic concerns and subject matter, some modern Arab poets found in metapoetry an escape from being overtly engaged with *iltizām* and its culture, especially in the late 1960s. In writing a metapoetic poem, the poet makes poetry his main subject, becoming critic and poet at the same time. Among the pioneers of metapoetry in modern Arabic poetry are Adūnīs, al-Bayātī, and Darwīsh.

Dorothy Baker maintains that metapoetry becomes "self-reflexive" when the poet questions his own role and status as a poet in the modern world.[53] Modern poets search for self-definition and question their craft and its role by becoming critics of their own work. Rene Wellek notes that "this meta-poetry is largely concerned with the self-definition of the poet and with his mission and function. It must be associated with the modern question of his status as seer/priest or sage. . . . We might even think of meta-poetry as the evocation of other poets in verse."[54] Therefore, modern poets turn to metapoetry in their search for identity and status as poets, and for the function of their poetry. In their quest for self-definition, they try to situate themselves within this tradition by evoking other poets and entering into dialogue or a conversation with present or long-dead poets.

Thus, to qualify as a metapoetic poem, the poem might take as one or more of its main themes or subjects poetry and the process in which it is produced, language, and the poet and his or her role or status. The poet becomes a critic of poetry and its function. Although metapoetry flourished in the West "during the second decade of the twentieth century, it made its advent in the Arab world much later."[55] The fall of Nasserism and Arab nationalism and the ultimate failure of *iltizām* after 1967 led some modern Arab poets to question their mission and the function of their poetry, and to ask how they could reinvent themselves and find inspiration far from *iltizām* and its jargon. This anxiety over poetic creativity became apparent in the poetry of some pioneers of modern Arabic poetry who had experimented earlier with metapoetry, such as al-Bayātī and Darwīsh.

In her discussion of the common issues modern Western poets deal with, Aida Azouqa states, "Among their distinct themes are the anxiety over poetic creativity, their concern for achieving immortality through art, the alienation of the poet in an age of crass materialism, and the role of a poet as *vates*, that is, as a visionary, and above all, the belief in the power of the imagination in transforming reality and of imposing order on what they perceive to be a chaotic world."[56] Repudiating *iltizām*, some modern Arab poets sought new voices and directions in Western modernism, answering Verena Klemm's question of how their "literary writing could be significant in the present world."[57] The 1960s generation also struggled with the failure of poetry to inspire or evoke change in society. Therefore, metapoetry freed poets and empowered them as visionaries whose imagination and descent to the underworld provided them with the necessary tools to transform their distorted reality. The poet's failure to associate with the surrounding chaotic world or find a purpose or function for poetry made the realm of the poem the poet's utopia. Metapoetic concerns make up the body of the poem, and the poet turns into a creator in an imaginative kingdom, able to reach immortality through art.

The metapoet relies on various tools to address and treat metapoetic concerns. Azouqa maintains that there are three representative groups of metapoets in the West: "one group resorted to dance imagery, based on ritualistic dancing," a second group "relied on Ancient and Classical fertility myths," and a third group abstracted its poetics through the "evocation of nature . . . and more importantly by alluding to the work of Avant-Garde artists."[58] The motif of descent to the underworld is also present in metapoetic poetry because the realm of the underworld is that of "the intellect, that is, of the imagination."[59] These representations found their application in modern Arabic poetry. In the chapter discussing the poetry of al-Bayātī, we shall see how the poet becomes a metapoet par excellence and how he finds in metapoetry a new realm for reinventing the poetic self. Metapoetic subjects are found in the work of all three poets, but the shift from commitment to metapoetry is more pronounced in the works of al-Bayātī than in the works of Ḥijāzī and Darwīsh, although Darwīsh himself is a master of metapoetry. Ḥijāzī engages with the evolving meaning of commitment during decades of active writing, and then writes and publishes about the Arab Uprising after more than two decades of no poetic publication. Darwīsh's later poetry negotiates coexistence with the other, with whose soldiers and government he fought viciously and called on to leave his country.

COEXISTENCE IN THE ISRAELI–PALESTINIAN CONFLICT

The majority of what we call resistance poetry by Palestinian poets, such as Darwīsh and al-Qāsim, has been stamped with a militant and anti-Israeli tone. Such works were considered the most committed in the 1950s, and such poets were shining examples of *iltizām*. Because Palestine and the plight of Palestinians are personal matters for poets of the Occupied Territories, their responses to the 1967 defeat and fall of Nasserism are different than those of other Arab poets; Palestine is the homeland. Because Israelis and Palestinians are enemies, coexistence is a constant struggle for both of them. Issues of fear and lack of trust are at the core of the Israeli–Palestinian conflict. Decades of Palestinian poetry assert the denial by the Israeli other of the Palestinians' right to exist and return to the homeland. Thus, to coexist with the other, from both contradictory perspectives, is to recognize the other and its relation to the self and its future. The problem on both sides is one of identity.

In literature, images of Palestinians and Jews remain mainly stereotypical, "reflecting a lack of will or perhaps desire to change this in any substantial way."[60] Recent Hebrew literary writings by prominent Israeli writers, such as Amos Oz (b. 1939), outline the Israeli identity by using the Palestinian other as a background and a contrast: the Palestinian is an extremist and a murderer.[61] Hence, distancing the identity of the self from that of the other in a racist manner means that "no political settlement can either take place or have any serious chance of success, as it would by definition mean the loss of hard-earned identity."[62] And because "there is no way for Israelis to get rid of the Palestinians or for Palestinians to wish Israelis away," as Edward Said noted in 1999, both nations will have to find a way to coexist on the same land and under the same sky.[63]

When we speak of each nation's denial of recognition of the other's identity, we do not necessarily speak of the moderate voices from each side of the conflict. These moderate voices calling for peace are unheard and uninfluential, and do not represent the public. Therefore, we speak here of representative voices that call for the removal of the Palestinians so the Israelis may live in peace in their state, and by the same token, the removal of the Israelis from Palestine so the Palestinians can live in peace in their country. To coexist with the other is to begin the accommodation process "with acceptance of the enemy as human, similar to oneself, and the state of conflict as a temporary aberration in the order of things."[64] This stage is an advanced phase of recognition and acceptance of the other, which cannot take place if both sides of the conflict are at war and denying each other's identity. For example, "removing Arabs" from greater Israel by creating "'negative magnets' that will induce Palestinians to pack their bags and leave" reflects one way to solve the conflict from an Israeli/Zionist perspective in the 1980s.[65] This mirrors a similar outlook on the conflict in Palestinian poetry of the 1980s, in which the Israelis in the Occupied Territories were advised to "pack their bags and return to the Diaspora."[66] The manner in which the Israelis and the Palestinians treat the conflict shows no potential for peace or coexistence in the near future, as it did not in the past.

However, a transition from militant and anti-Israeli to humanist can be traced in the poetry of the Palestinian poet of resistance, Darwīsh. "Humanist" suggests that the poet sees the other as a human, like himself, more than as an enemy or entity with whom he is constantly in a state of conflict. Recognition of the humanity of both sides of the conflict extends an invitation to each to begin a conversation and ultimately to engage in peace or coexistence talks. When poetry goes looking for the essence of humanity despite the open wounds that have festered for decades, the poet becomes a universal humanist.

Darwīsh's various poetic attempts to engage with the highly charged and unresolved political conflict of his nation with the Israeli other reflect a great responsibility he carried for decades. Political and personal factors influenced such poetic engagement and led to a transformation in the ways in which the Israeli other is treated in Darwīsh's poetry, and in the poet's insight into the conflict and its resolution. Such transition is key, at least from a literary perspective, because of the significant impact poets such as Darwīsh have on the youth: the mobilizing power in society. The chapter on the trajectory of Darwīsh's poetry will investigate the parameters of his earlier and late anti-Israeli poetry and its development into a humanizing of the other, despite what the poet sees as its heinous acts. Without dropping "the mask of otherness" and reaching a "total transformation of the self" in the Israeli–Palestinian conflict, "no real change is possible."[67] In his later poetry, Darwīsh has reached this stage and, more importantly, has invited the other to do the same. Doing so brings the whole conflict to a new level in literature, especially when a poet such as Darwīsh is doing it. Further discussion of issues of identity, the self, and otherness will enrich the examination of Darwīsh's poetry in chapter 4.

Al-Bayātī, Ḥijāzī, and Darwīsh are products of their age. Their poetry is the product of political dogma, social ideology, personal perspective, and unique poetic talent. In the following chapters, I examine how these three poets respond to and treat major political and social events and movements, and, more importantly, how they develop their unique poetic voices and break from their own poetic trajectories.

Al-Bayātī, Ḥijāzī, and Darwīsh were pioneers of the free verse movement in the Arab world. They belong to the same 1960s generation, and they witnessed the birth of *iltizām* in Arab literary circles and took part in shaping it as it evolved. They are major poets who continued to write Arabic poetry for decades. Al-Bayātī "is the most committed Arab poet and the leader of the socialist realist movement in modern Arabic poetry."[68] Ḥijāzī's body of work covers the history of Egyptian sociopolitics from before the Free Officers revolution to the present. Darwīsh, who is "naturally committed in the full sense of the term," is the celebrated poet of Palestinian resistance and a shining example of poetic creativity.[69] Each of the three has written extensively on Arab socialist realism and *iltizām*. However, each poet's poetry has witnessed a transformation from its early stages to its current form. They represent a generation of modern Arab poets whose poetry stood against the current and has continued to shine through the years. Despite their differences, each of them contributes to the development of modern Arab poetry in a unique way. Whether in form or content, they experimented and innovated in their poetry and remained committed to their role as saviors of their land, their people, and their language.

CHAPTER 2

From *Iltizām* to Metapoetry

ʿAbd al-Wahhāb al-Bayātī

ʿAbd al-Wahhāb al-Bayātī, one of the twentieth century's most prominent Arab poets, was a socialist realist who believed in the role of literature in society. He was among the first Arab poets to experiment with Western literary forms and techniques, especially the free verse form. Radical political changes in the Arab world inspired a transition in al-Bayātī's poetry from *iltizām* to metapoetry. Al-Bayātī, being one of the greatest supporters of Nasser and Arab nationalism, succeeded in moving beyond the initial stages of *iltizām* after the 1967 defeat. This transition took place gradually after his writing on the defeat of Arabs and poetry in the late 1960s. In mid-1970s, al-Bayātī started experimenting with a new kind of poetry, signaling a transition in content and language. Instead of waiting for political events or social changes to inspire him, al-Bayātī found his true vocation in writing poetry about language, the art of poetry, and the alienation of the poet in the twentieth century, among other subjects. Al-Bayātī's metapoetic poetry introduces a revolutionary stance to the role of poet and poetry in the Arab world in the twentieth century.

Al-Bayātī was born in Baghdad on December 19, 1926, and died in Damascus in 1999. He enrolled at the Higher Teachers' Training College in Baghdad in 1946 and received his BA in Arabic language and literature in 1950. Al-Sayyāb, Buland al-Ḥaydarī, al-Malā'ika, and Nihād al-Takarlī were among the Iraqi poets and artists who studied there with al-Bayātī.

Al-Bayātī read writers such as Lord Byron (1788–1824), Percy Shelley (1792–1822), John Keats (1795–1821), Anton Chekhov (1860–1904), Fyodor Dostoevsky (1821–1881), and W. H. Auden (1907–1973). These writers, among others, influenced him as a romantic poet in the early stages of his career, while others, such as Albert Camus (1913–1960) and Jean-Paul Sartre (1905–1980), shaped his "realist existential stand."[1] Among the classical Arab poets who made the greatest impact on al-Bayātī's poetry were Ṭarafa ibn al-ʿAbd (538–569), Abū Nuwās (756–813), Abū al-ʿAlā' al-Maʿarrī (973–1057), and al-Mutanabbī (915–65). Other poets, such as Jalāl al-Dīn al-Rūmī (d. 1273), Farīd al-Dīn al-ʿAṭṭār (d. 1229), ʿUmar al-Khayyām (d. 1123), and Rabindranath Tagore (1861–1941), influenced al-Bayātī's poetry through their mystical experience, their "piercing poetic vision," and their attempts to understand the universe and "uncover its totality."[2] Among the other poets whom al-Bayātī read were Pablo Neruda (1904–1973), Vladimir Mayakovsky (1893–1930), Paul Éluard (1895–1952), the Turkish poet in exile Nāẓim Ḥikmat (1902–1963), Federico García Lorca (1898–1936), and T. S. Eliot (1888–1965).

After graduating, al-Bayātī began his teaching career as a teacher of Arabic in the Iraqi city of al-Ramādī. For opposing the Iraqi ruler, al-Bayātī was dismissed from his teaching position in 1954. His contributions to the leftist journal *Al-Thaqāfa al-Jadīda* (New Culture), which was first published in 1954, were considered Marxist and against the Iraqi regime. As a result, the journal was banned in the year of its first publication and al-Bayātī was arrested and compelled by the end of 1955 to leave Iraq for Syria. He stayed in Syria for one year and then moved to Cairo for two years before returning to Iraq after the revolution of July 14, 1958, when he was appointed director of translation and publication at the Ministry of Education. In 1959 he was appointed cultural advisor to the Iraqi embassy in Moscow. He resigned from this post in 1961 and taught at the University of Moscow. The Iraqi government withdrew his passport in 1963 because of his political activism. He left for Cairo in 1964 and stayed there until returning to Baghdad in 1972. He was appointed the Iraqi cultural attaché in Madrid in 1979. He moved to Amman in 1992 and lived there until he moved to Damascus in 1998, one year before his death.

Al-Bayātī wrote more than twenty-five volumes of poetry, as well as other books and translations. He spent most of his life in exile because of his communist beliefs and writings that expressed his opposition to the Iraq government.[3] It is worth noting that although he was exiled by the Iraqi government for some time, most of al-Bayātī's exile was self-imposed, and he was on and off the Iraqi payroll. Like his socialist realist peers, Al-Bayātī wrote on *iltizām* and used his poetry as a platform to address and call attention to the plight of his poor fellow citizens.

Despite Eliot's rejection of social realism in poetry, al-Bayātī found in his free verse movement an escape from the traditional forms of Arabic poetry. Believing that the poet should be active in his society, al-Bayātī moved past his romantic stage and wrote poetry to express his political stances in support of his people, to rally behind Nasser's project of nationalism, to describe the daily struggles of the Arab peasant, and, more significantly, to treat and critique the 1967 defeat. He followed political and social movements in the Arab world, whether in Egypt, Iraq, Syria, or Palestine, and used his poetry as a political and social tool to engage in these movements and shape his social and political positions.

Shocked and confused after the 1967 defeat, al-Bayātī began experimenting with new artistic devices and subject matter. His poetry underwent a transformation from *iltizām* to metapoetry. This is not to say that he withdrew completely from writing about Arab citizens and their challenges, nor it is to say that he did not write metapoetic poetry before 1967. Rather, his poetics shift in form and content from mainly committed to metapoetic. This chapter investigates his answer to Klemm's question about how "literary writing could be significant in the present world" and his contribution to modern Arabic poetry beyond his committed phase.[4] To do so, I examine his poetry before and after the 1967 defeat, a turning point in Arab history and literature.

To investigate this transformation, I examine representative poems from the following collections: *Al-Majd lil-Aṭfāl wa-al-Zaytūn* (Glory to Children and Olive Trees, 1956), *Sifr al-Faqr wa-al-Thawra* (The Book of Poverty and Revolution, 1965), *Alladhī Ya'tī wa-lā Ya'tī* (What Comes and Does Not Come, 1966), *ʿUyūn al-Kilāb al-Mayyita* (The Eyes of the Dead Dogs, 1969), *Kitāb al-Baḥr* (The Book of the Sea, 1973), and *Mamlakat al-Sunbula* (Kingdom of Grain, 1979). This chapter will not explore al-Bayātī the romanticist because other works, such as Khalīl Shukrallāh Rizk's, have done so by studying the poet's first two collections, *Malā'ika wa-Shayāṭīn* (Angels and Devils, 1950) and *Abārīq Muhashshama* (Broken Pitchers, 1954).

Some recurring themes and topics in *Al-Majd lil-Aṭfāl wa-al-Zaytūn* are the urgency of Arab unification under Nasser's leadership, the poet's faith in his people's support of their fellow Palestinians against Israel, and the feelings of loss and despair dominant in the Arab world in the 1950s. Other themes include the poet's call for other poets to write socialist realist poetry, the challenging role of the poet in society, and the Palestinian children's constant struggle, as evident in the title of the collection and the poems mentioned below. These themes and topics are treated in poems such as "Ughniya min al-ʿIrāq ilā Nāṣir" (A Song from Iraq to Nasser), "Qaṣā'id ilā Yāfā" (Odes to Jaffa), "Ilā Ikhwatī al-Shuʿarā'" (To My Brother Poets), "Ughniya ilā Shaʿbī" (A Song to My Nation), and "Rabīʿunā lan Yamūt" (Our Spring Will Not Die). Poems that treat similar topics include "Khiyāna" (Betrayal), "Al-Majd lil-Aṭfāl wa-al-Zaytūn" (Glory to Children and Olive Trees), "Al-ʿAwda" (The Return), "Amal" (Hope), and "Al-Shiʿr wa-al-Mawt" (Poetry and Death). Poems addressed to specific Arab countries and their people include "Ughniya Khaḍrā' ilā Sūriyā" (A Green Song to Syria), "Kalimāt Mujannaḥa ilā al-Kuttāb al-Miṣriyyn" (Words with Wings to the Egyptian Writers), "Ughniyat Entiṣār ilā al-Maghrib wa-Tūnis wa-al-Jazā'ir" (A Victorious Song to Morocco, Tunisia, and Algeria), "Fī al-Maʿraka" (In the Battlefield), and "Ughniya Zarqā' ilā Fayrūz" (A Blue Song to Fayruz).

NASSER, REVOLUTION, AND NATIONALISM

"Al-ʿAwda" (The Return), "Khiyāna" (Betrayal), and "Al-Shiʿr wa-al-Mawt" (Poetry and Death) are among the key poems in *Al-Majd lil-Aṭfāl wa-al-Zaytūn*. Here al-Bayātī addresses his concerns about Palestinians in particular and Arabs in general, and his perspective on the role of poetry in Arab society in the 1950s. Many poems in this collection are about Palestine, Syria, Tunisia, Morocco, Algeria, and Egypt, with most dedicated to the Palestinian cause and Arab nationalism. Thus this collection is as committed as the poet himself. As Badawi explains, "Bayātī's *Glory*

Be to Children and the Olive Branch opens with a series of poems entitled 'Diary of an Arab in Israel' in which the poet, committed to the Arab cause, sounds more hopeful than in his previous collection *Abārīq Muhashshama* (Broken Pitchers, 1954)."[5] *Abārīq Muhashshama* belongs to the poet's romantic phase, in which he treats topics such as death, exile, and loneliness from a personal perspective. In *Al-Majd lil-Aṭfāl wa-al-Zaytūn* al-Bayātī finds peace and hope in nationalism, which promised to bring Arabs together under Nasser's leadership and to defend Palestine and the Palestinians. Boullata maintains that "al-Bayātī's voice occasionally becomes strident as he celebrates the rise of Nasser and Arab nationalism, the struggle of workers everywhere, and the national aspirations of the Iraqis and other Arabs."[6]

"Qaṣā'id ilā Yāfā" (Odes to Jaffa), a long poem comprising five shorter poems, treats the question of Palestine and encourages Palestinians and Arabs to resist and fight the enemy to achieve glory. In one of these short poems, "Al-ʿAwda" (The Return), the poet assures the Palestinians that they will all eventually return to Galilee with Christ:

العودة

الليل تطرده قناديل العيون
عيونكم، يا إخوتي المتناثرين الجائعين
تحت النجوم.
وكأن حلمت بأنني بالورد أفرش و الدموع
وكأن يسوع
معكم يعود إلى (الجليل)
بلا صليب.[7]

The Return

The lanterns of the eyes banished the night
Your eyes, O my hungry, scattered brethren
Beneath the stars.
It is as if I dreamt that I paved your road
With flowers and tears
And as if Jesus

Were returning with you to Galilee
Without a cross.

As its title makes evident, this poem reflects the poet's sympathy with the displaced, hungry Palestinians and conveys his "vision of the ultimate triumph of the Palestinian cause."[8] His dream to return with them and Christ to Galilee is suggested by two images: the covering of the earth with tears and flowers and the return with Christ, but this time without the cross. The speaker's dream expresses his vision of the ideal return to Palestine: a return preceded by pain and tears and followed by peace and happiness in which there is no longer a cross, a symbol of suffering and torture. Almost every Arab poet wrote about the Palestinian question in the 1950s, and al-Bayātī was no exception. In this poem, every displaced Palestinian becomes a Christ and pain becomes inevitable if Palestinians want to return to Palestine.

As employed by poets of the Tammūzī movement, Christ is a symbol for revival and rebirth. Modern Arab poets in the late 1940s and early 1950s were influenced by the use of ancient myths, including those of Tammūz, Baal, and Adūnīs, in Western poetry, especially that of Eliot. The Iraqi al-Sayyāb and other Tammūzī Arab poets employed these symbols and myths, as well as others from Arab and Muslim folklore and history, to enrich the content of their poetry because "in doing so they believe that they can 'recruit its failing energies and even raise it from the dead.'"[9] In "Al-Masīḥ baʿd al-Ṣalb" (Christ after Crucifixion), al-Sayyāb appropriates Christian themes and symbols to address social and economic ills in Iraq, where Christ becomes the hero and savior of his people from drought and hunger.[10] Likewise, al-Bayātī employs the symbol of Christ to treat the question of Palestine, albeit from a different perspective. Al-Bayātī envisions himself and the Palestinians returning to Palestine with Christ, the heroic savior. Using the symbol of Christ in this poem, al-Bayātī wants Arabs and Palestinians to believe that their return is predestined despite the great pain they endure. He wants the Palestinians to believe in the power of resistance and their right to return to Palestine after the 1948 *nakba.* What is significant about "Al-ʿAwda" is that al-Bayātī claims a role as a poet whose dream, whose poetic vision, assures the Palestinians that they will return by comparing their return to the resurrection of Christ. Christ is believed to have risen again by divine decree; thus al-Bayātī adds a religious dimension to the Palestinians' return.

Another comparison is drawn between night and light to suggest occupation versus freedom for Palestine. The use of *layl* (night) as a metaphor for the Israeli occupation of Palestine and of its opposite—"the lanterns of the eyes" of the poet's "hungry, scattered brethren"—is interesting. In al-Bayātī's vision, these hungry, displaced people succeed in expelling the enemy just as the light of the lantern expels the night. Although the diction in this poem is simple, it creates an image that invokes pain and hope at the same time. The poet juxtaposes two groups of verbs, adjectives, and nouns to create two images that represent the status quo in the Arab world and the vision of the poet. Juxtaposing the words *night*, *hungry*, *scattered*, *dreamt*, and *tears* with *lanterns*, *eyes*, *stars*, *flowers*, *banished*, *paved*, *road*, and *return*, the poet places great emphasis on his vision of the status of his brethren, the Palestinians, and contrasts their dark, painful present with a brighter future marked by their return to Palestine. The night is a source of darkness, while the stars and eyes are sources of light. Also, the dream in the dark night translates into paving the road with flowers and tears for the expelled Palestinians to return to Galilee.

In "Al-Shiʿr wa-al-Mawt" (Poetry and Death), al-Bayātī elaborates on his commitment to a new kind of love: nationalism.

الشعر و الموت

الشعر في صمت المصحّ بلا دموع
وبلا شموع
يموت في عيني كقديس شهيد
وعلى غطاء فراشي الدامي، شعاع
من شمس أيلول، تلالأ كالشراع
في عين بحّار:
أيا أبواب ليل المستحيل
لا تنزعيني آه من حبي الجديد
فالطين في رئتي و في فمي الصديد
وعلى الوسادة مضغة سوداء من جسدي القتيل.[11]

Poetry and Death

Poetry is without tears in the silence of the hospital
And without candles
Poetry dies in my eyes like a martyred saint
And on my bloodstained bedsheet: a ray of September's sun
Radiant as the sail
In the eye of the sailor:
O doors of the impossible night
Do not pull me from my new love
For there is mud in my lungs and pus in my mouth,
And on the pillow, there is a black piece of my slain body.

In this poem, the poet personifies poetry as a man dying in the hospital without tears or candles, and also as a martyred saint who dies in front of the poet. Seeing poetry dying, hopeless and unmourned, the poet sees a dark part of his own body die on his pillow. Poetry is a living part of the poet's body, and when this part dies on the bloodstained hospital bedsheet, a bright ray of sun shines in the eyes of a sailor, the poet, and calls for hope and resurrection. Suffering in the middle of the night and struggling between life and death, the poet sees light at the end of the tunnel and clenches the rays that become his sail, giving him hope for a new life and journey. Al-Bayātī employs the Christlike symbol of a martyred saint to treat the topic of poetry and its death, and of the poet's commitment to writing poetry as means of resistance.

This poem expresses the poet's sacrifice and faith in poetry as one kind of commitment and resistance. The poet sacrifices some part of his body and watches it die so that he can see light and come to life again. Although poetry dies in the poem, it rises again and gives life to the poet in a new fashion. The death that the poet experiences in this poem is necessary for him to rise again and return to life with "new love" and new voice. Here, al-Bayātī treats poetry from the perspective of someone who sacrifices himself for the sake of his cause, like Christ. The poet after this experience is different from the poet before it. Thus, it is as if the poet demands that one experience death to achieve a different level or quality of life, just as he encouraged his fellow Palestinians, in "Al-

ʿAwda," to resist and die so that their cause would resurrect again, without the cross. This life takes its meaning and value from its willingness to sacrifice itself. Also, al-Bayātī's new love comes to his rescue after mud fills his lungs and pus his mouth, a reflection on the status quo of Arabs after 1948. Nationalism seems to be the solution to the disease of his body and soul. Commitment to this much-needed new love brings life to him and his words. It is as if he is encouraging other poets to write committed poetry, which becomes a saint martyred in defense of its people and their causes.

The theme of death and rebirth is key in this collection. Most poems employ either the symbols of Christ and the cross or the Tammūzī theme of resurrection after death. Examining the Arab world's social and economic decline in the late 1940s and early 1950s, al-Bayātī employs the Tammūzī myth of resurrection to inspire hope in his fellow Arabs. Believing that the role of poetry lies in serving people, al-Bayātī wishes to continue writing socialist realist poetry that inspires his people and supports them. This poetry, according to al-Bayātī, is "a martyred saint" who bleeds and dies with the poet to shine and empower him to fight for his "new love."

In this melodramatic, romantic poem, the poet uses nearly the same diction he employed in his romantic phase, yet with a different aim. In his romantic phase he uses and juxtaposes words such as *dumūʿ* (tears), *shumūʿ* (candles), *shuʿāʿ* (sun ray), *shirāʿ* (sail), and *baḥḥār* (sailor) to express his love for nature and passion for life and youth, whereas in this collection, he uses this diction to treat his commitment to and engagement with the sociopolitical scene in the Arab world. This collection proclaims al-Bayātī as a socialist realist poet who writes on *iltizām*, as on Nasser, Arab nationalism, and the question of Palestine.

In *Al-Majd lil-Aṭfāl wa-al-Zaytūn*, Al-Bayātī uses poetry as a social and political tool to express his position on the social, economic, and political status quo of the Arab world in the 1950s. He invites all individuals in Arab society to play an active role in fighting social and economic decline in general, and the occupation of Palestine in particular. Al-Bayātī addresses men, women, children, soldiers, artists, singers, writers, and poets from various Arab nationalities and urges them to unite and put an end to their bitter reality.

Two years before the 1967 Arab–Israeli war, al-Bayātī published *Sifr al-Faqr wa-al-Thawra* (The Book of Poverty and Revolution) and *Alladhī Ya'tī wa-lā Ya'tī* (What Comes and Does Not Come). In the former collection, the first poem is "Ilā Nāṣir, al-Insān" (To Nasser, the Human Being). In this poem, the poet urges his people to believe in Nasser and his revolution and demands that they support him. Here al-Bayātī foresees the victory and redemption of Arabs under the leadership of Nasser:

إلى عبد الناصر الإنسان

أيا جيل الهزيمة .. هذه الثورة
ستمحو عاركم و تزحزح الصخرة
[. . .]
فهذا البرق لا يكذب
وهذا النهر لا ينضب
وهذا الثائر الإنسان عبر سنابل القمح
يهز سلاسل الريح
مع المطر
مع التاريخ و القدر
ويفتح للربيع الباب
فيا شعراء فجر الثورة المنجاب
قصائدكم له ، لتكن بلا حجّاب
فهذا المارد الثائر إنسان
يزحزح صخرة التاريخ ، يوقد شمعة في الليل للإنسان.[12]

To Nasser, the Human Being

O generation of defeat! This revolution
Will erase your shame and budge the rock
[. . .]
This lightning does not lie
This river is inexhaustible
This rebel across the spikes of wheat
Shakes the chains of the wind
With the rain

With history and fate
And opens the door for the spring
So, poets of the dawn of the revolution,
Let your poems to him be without a veil
This giant rebel is a man
Who removes the rock of history and lights a candle
in the night for [all] mankind.

In this pro-Nasserist poem, the poet focuses on three main elements: the emotional state of the audience, the poet's prophecy, and the charismatic leader of the people. Al-Bayātī addresses his people with "O generation of defeat" to remind Arabs of their humiliation and disgrace. He sees the revolution as inevitable and already underway. In the first and second lines he promises his people and his readers that if they follow Nasser, "This [Arab] revolution / will erase your shame." Al-Bayātī celebrates Nasser as the revolutionary who will liberate Arabs and take them from darkness to light, from poverty to abundance, and from defeat to victory. Furthermore, the poet encourages his fellow poets to believe in Nasser and write poetry for him. This poem serves not only to educate and awaken the Arab audience, but also to call for a committed poetry and literature.

Al-Bayātī wants his people to believe in Nasser and be part of his revolution; people should fight next to Nasser, and poets should write committed poetry like his. Thus, he determines everybody's responsibility in this revolution and demands that they all support it because otherwise they will be humiliated and defeated. The title of the poem highlights Nasser's humanity and guardianship of his people, in contrast to the self-serving and oppressive regimes of other Arab leaders. It is interesting how al-Bayātī uses images of natural forces in a poem that claims to be about Nasser the human being: shifting a rock to pave the way for his people (line 2), the lightning of the revolution does not lie (line 16), and the river of the revolution is inexhaustible (line 17). In these images, the success of Nasser and the revolution appears as inevitable as natural forces. In addition, in line 22, Nasser opens the door to spring, an image that links the revolution to resurrection and freedom. Nasser, the revolution, and rebirth are combined into one. Al-Bayātī links following Nasser's leadership to solving the problems of Arab society. Nasser becomes the hero of his socialist realist poetry.

In the collection's titular poem, "Sifr al-Faqr wa-al-Thawra" (The Book of Poverty and Revolution), al-Bayātī argues that revolution is the only way to end poverty and other economic and social ills in Arab society. This poem consists of six sections and is seven pages long, so I will focus on the parts that carry its main themes.

سفر الفقر و الثورة

(1)
[. . .]
أهذا انت يا فقري
بلا وجه ، بلا وطن
أهذا انت يا زمني
يخدش وجهك المرآه
ضميرك تحت أحذية البغايا مات
وباعك أهلك الفقراء
إلى الموتى من الأحياء
فمن سيبيع للموتى؟
ومن سيبدّد الصمتا؟
ومن منّا
شجاع زمانه ليعيد ما قلنا
ومن سيبوح للريح بما يوحي
بأنا لم نزل أحياء
[. . .]
لو أن الفقر انسان
إذن لقتلته وشربت من دمه
لو أن الفقر إنسان

(2)
ناديت بالبواخر المسافرة
[. . .]
بكل ما كان و ما يكو
[. . .]
أن نحترق

لتنطلق
منّا شرارات تضيء صرخة الثوار
و توقظ الديك الذي مات على الجدار

(3)
[. . .]
كأن شوارع المدن
خيوط منك يا كفني
تطاردني
تعلقّني
على شباك مستشفى
ومن منفى إلى منفى
تسدّ عليّ بالظلمة
شوارع هذه المدن التي نامت بلا نجمة
أما في قلبك الحجري من رحمة

(4)
غريبا كنت في وطني وفي المنفى
جراحاتي التي تشفى
ستفتح في غد فاها
لتسألني
لتصلبني
على شباك مستشفى
بعيد أنت ياوطني
[. . .]

(5)
أتسمع صيحة الديك؟
هي الثورة؟
[. . .]

(6)
[. . .]
وكانت القصيدة
أسلحتي الوحيدة
في مدن العالم ، في منازلي الشريدة

[. . .]
فليس للعالم من بديل 150
و ليس للثورة من سبيل
إلا بأن تدكَّ هذا الجبل الثقيل.[13]

The Book of Poverty and Revolution

(1)
Is that you, O my poverty?
Without a face, without a homeland
Is that you, O my time?
The mirror scratches your face 15
Your conscience dies under the prostitutes' shoes
Your poor people sell you
To the dead among the living
So, who is going to sell to the dead?
And who is going to break the silence? 20
And who among us
Is brave [enough] to repeat what we said
And who is going to reveal to the wind a sign
That we are still alive?
[. . .]
If poverty were a man, 31
I would have killed him and drunk his blood
If poverty were a man.

(2)
I called out to the traveling steamboats 34
[. . .]
I called all that was and will be 38
[. . .]
That we should burn
So that sparks would fly from us 50
To light up the rebels' screaming
And awaken the rooster that died upon the wall

(3)
[. . .]
As if the cities' streets
Are the threads of you, my shroud
They haunt me
They hang me
On a hospital's window
And from one exile to another
They choke me with darkness
O streets of this city, which slept without a star,
Is not there any mercy in your stone heart?

(4)
I was a stranger in my homeland and in exile
My healing wounds
Will open their mouths tomorrow
To ask me,
To crucify me
On a hospital window
Far away from you, my homeland
[. . .]

(5)
Do you hear the rooster's cry?
It is the revolution
[. . .]

(6)
[. . .]
The poem
Used to be my only weapon
In the cities of the world, in my stray dwellings
[. . .]
The world has no choice
The revolution has no way but
To demolish this heavy mountain.

This poem addresses three main themes. The first theme, lines 1–33 (section 1), is poverty. The second, lines 53–96 (sections 3 and 4), is the struggle of al-Bayātī and his people. The third, lines 34–52 and 97–163 (sections 2, 5, and 6), is the revolution. As in the first poem in this collection, "Ilā Nāṣir, al-Insān," al-Bayātī establishes his people's suffering and expresses his discontent and anger about the current situation, then calls for a revolution as the only solution. In his depiction of poverty, al-Bayātī blames it for the humiliation and death-in-life of his people and encourages Arabs to denounce the fear and submission dictated by their regimes.[14] Al-Bayātī takes the problem of poverty to another moral level when he says that because of poverty, families sell their children to those who are morally dead. This idea of moral or spiritual death in life is inspired by Eliot's "The Waste Land" and is appropriated in al-Bayātī's poem. In so doing, al-Bayātī attempts to remind his people of their misery and its consequences, which not only take away their dignity and consciousness, but also reduce human beings to goods and chattel that are bought and sold.

After confronting the Arab audience with its current situation, al-Bayātī raises some questions of commitment. He asks his people if there is anyone among them who is willing to repeat what the poet has said. In this context, repetition suggests supporting the poet's position and rejecting the status quo. When al-Bayātī encourages his people to reveal to the wind that "we are still alive," he is looking for someone who is able to break the silence and reject life as it is. He follows up with "If poverty were a man, I would have killed him and drunk his blood" to show his Arab reader his desire to defeat his and the reader's enemy: poverty. Also, "If poverty were a man, I would have killed him" is an Arab Islamic saying by ʿUmar bin al-Khaṭṭāb (586–644), the second Muslim caliph after the Prophet Muhammad's death. Employing this proverb twice in this poem stresses al-Bayātī's point and reminds his audience of the hard times Arabs and Muslims went through in the past. In so doing, al-Bayātī also compares what the caliph said in response to poverty in the past with what modern Arab leaders say. The caliph admits that there is poverty in the Arab world and that he wishes he could abolish it, while contemporary Arab leaders are precisely the reason why their people suffer from poverty. Saying that poetry is his only weapon, al-Bayātī stresses the role of poetry in inciting a revolution in the Arab world. The spread of poverty necessitates a revolution to break the silence and "demolish this heavy mountain." When "conscience dies under the prostitutes' shoes," the poet demands that his people "burn" to illuminate the scream of the rebels. In causing their people to starve, the Arab regimes are the prostitutes whose consciences are dead.

The last part of the poem introduces al-Bayātī's solution to his people: revolution. Like the first part, it follows a specific order to educate the audience and remind them of their responsibility. Al-Bayātī calls upon his people and asks them to burn with him so the path of revolution might be lit and those who are dead might be resurrected. Al-Bayātī asks his people whether they hear the rooster crowing, which is a sign of dawn, rebirth, and resurrection. This rooster, which was dead on the wall, is the Arab people; its crowing announces their awakening and resurrection to lead the revolution. The rooster's crow at daybreak is a symbol of new life after the darkness and death of night. Here, darkness suggests oppression and "new life" suggests revolution. Also, the poet emphasizes that it is not the world that should or will change; it is the people who should take the lead and change the world through revolution. Thus, the poem ends in an optimistic tone, asserting that as long as people believe in the revolution and its will to "demolish this heavy mountain," victory is certain.

Treating the topic of poverty in the first section of this poem indicates its significance for the poet and his readers. The two main images in this section are poverty personified as a man and a family selling its children because of poverty. The poet draws on the proverb, "If poverty were a man, I would have killed him" but adds "and drunk his blood," which indicates how angry the poet is and how desperate the situation. The poet uses this violent image only after he employs the image of a desperate family selling its children. Influenced by "The Waste Land," al-Bayātī employs Eliot's exact image to reflect the status quo in the Arab world. He maintains that in this time, the conscience is dead and people fail to reject the immoral practices or dare to "break the silence." At the end of this section, the poet questions his people's dignity and asks if there is anyone among them who is willing to speak out. This question takes us to the second section, where revolution is the only remaining solution.

The second, fifth, and sixth sections in this poem treat the issue of revolution on multiple levels. The second section represents the ultimate solution for the poverty and social ills from which Arab societies suffer, as mentioned in the first section. The poet calls upon his people to unite and burn together in the name of the revolution. He calls upon everyone from the past, present, and future to revolt with him in order for them to be resurrected. The image of sparks flying from burning people in lines 49–52 emphasizes the urgency of his call for Arabs to unite and revolt, to resurrect the dead rooster on the wall. Its death on the wall indicates not only that the Arabs and their revolution are dead, but also that this death was witnessed by all. It is a public death that people witness every day, and yet they continue their lives as if nothing is wrong. That is why the poet calls his people the living dead. Even so, the poet is optimistic and can see the rooster resurrected by means of the revolution.

The poem's third and fourth sections treat social ills and themes other than poverty and moral decline. After stating that revolution is the last choice remaining to Arabs, the poet depicts himself in sections 2 and 3 as carrying his burial shroud through the dark streets of the Arab cities. The poet and his people are dead, haunted from one city to another and from one exile to another. The poet employs the image of himself wandering in the dark, a stranger both in his homeland and in exile, to express how disoriented, lonely, and lost he is. Al-Bayātī himself was a stranger wandering the earth, traveling from one exile to another. Here, he sees his people as strangers, too, because one cannot call a place home if it lacks the basic necessities of a dignified life. The poet ends these two sections by saying that his wounds crucify him in a hospital far away from his home.

This image of a sick, lonely man being treated for a disease in a country that is not his homeland is a clear reference to al-Sayyāb's poetry of the early 1960s, when he was being treated in London, far away from his town of Jaykūr. Al-Sayyāb's "Sifr Ayyūb" (The Book of Job) appeared as a key poem in his 1962 collection *Al-Maʿbad al-Gharīq* (The Drowned Temple). Most of the poems in this collection treat topics such as exile, sickness, loneliness, and dying far away from home. Three years later, al-Bayātī's collection *Sifr al-Faqr wa-al-Thawra* was published, and the themes and images that appear in the poem of the same name bear a great resemblance to al-Sayyāb's "Sifr Ayyūb."[15]

On one level, the titles of these two poems are very similar. Both of them start with the word *sifr*, which means "book" (especially of the Bible) in Arabic. The man Ayyūb (Job) of al-Sayyāb's poem is a symbol of patience and suffering in Islam as he is in Judaism and Christianity. Likewise, the title of al-Bayātī's poem and collection encompasses the stories of the poet's and his people's suffering. Al-Bayātī added "and Revolution" to "The Book of Poverty" because his collection treats poverty and revolution as opposites. He indicates that it is only through revolution that poverty can be overcome.

On another level, al-Sayyāb's twenty-page poem, which is in ten sections, depicts in detail al-Sayyāb's experiences in a London hospital. Poor, hungry, and sick, al-Sayyāb feels loneliness and alienation in every aspect of his life. The poet employs images of dying flowers and stone-like birds in the windows of the hospital. The hurried people in the streets are unable to hear the singing of these birds. Other images of the poet suffering the pains of his wounds, which cut his body like knives continuously day and night, are employed in this poem and contrasted to other images. According to the poem, the same wounds that cut his body are as gifts from God to the poet, who embraces these gifts and thanks God for them. In this context, the poet's choice of the word *gifts* to describe his wounds is mystical because gifts are supposed to bring happiness, not pain. As discussed above, al-Bayātī employs some of the same images that al-Sayyāb uses, but the two poems end differently. Although al-Sayyāb's tone is pessimistic, he ends his poem by asking God to answer his prayer and let him return strong and healthy to his children, wife, and town. Al-Bayātī's poem ends with the call for revolution. When al-Sayyāb wrote his poem, he was dying; he knew it was unlikely that he would return to his town and live the life he dreamed of. He had lost his position and been exiled from Iraq because of his communist beliefs, and he died in 1964, two years after his arrival in London for medical treatment.

In contrast, al-Bayātī was neither poor nor sick. Most of his exile was self-imposed, and he did not receive medical treatment in exile, where he could not have afforded to pay his hospital bills. "Sifr Ayyūb" treats the struggle and profound pain of humankind in a universal language that evokes the deepest emotions and feelings. I believe al-Bayātī found in "Sifr Ayyūb" a sincere portrayal of al-Sayyāb's pains and aspirations and borrowed from it images and diction to evoke emotion in readers of his own poem in the same way "Sifr Ayyūb" had evoked his.

The diction in "Sifr al-Faqr wa-al-Thawra" is similar to that in "Sifr Ayyūb." Words that recur in both poems include *snow, night, cold, darkness, mercy, my wounds, cities, exile, hospital window, stranger, the dead, the tomb, heart, stone, the poet, age, claws,* and *rain.* The word choice in "Sifr Ayyūb" is mainly melodramatic, religious, and pessimistic in tone. Although al-Bayātī uses some of the same words, his tone changes from pessimistic to optimistic when he writes about revolution. In addition to using similar diction, al-Bayātī employs the exact Eliotian images of al-Sayyāb's poem, such as birds without nests; the lonely, sick man with no food, money, or home; the crucifixion of man and resurrection after death; and the alienation and dilemma of man in the modern time. Al-Bayātī also uses rhetorical questions in the same way al-Sayyāb does in his poem. One more similarity between the two poems, among many, lies in al-Bayātī's two lines: "And the poem / was my only weapon." In al-Bayātī's poem, these two lines occur twice at the beginning of section 6, in lines 135–36, and at the end of the same section in lines 161–62. True, al-Sayyāb does not claim that his poem is his weapon or anything close to that. The whole poem carries the spirit of a dying man who finds in writing poetry his last resort or haven from surrendering to death and defeat. Thus, "Sifr Ayyūb" was the poet's last weapon to fight death and pain during the long nights. In the context of "Sifr al-Faqr wa-al-Thawra," however, these two lines suggest that for al-Bayātī, the poem is a weapon—his only weapon—because it is his way of breaking the silence to awaken his people.

Al-Bayātī perceives his role in society as that of a poet who speaks out against the injustices in the Arab world. He sees only one way to achieve liberation from humiliation and poverty. Only a revolution, led by someone such as Nasser, will bring about Arab nationalism and liberation. Thus al-Bayātī's two poems, published before the 1967 war, see revolt against the economic, social, and political status quo as inescapable. This collection presents al-Bayātī as a committed poet who makes inspiring the reader and supporting the Arab national cause his duty. Furthermore, in these two poems, and in others as well, the poet addresses not only the Arab public and the Arab poet or artist, but also

Nasser as the leader of the Arab nation, the one in whom Arabs have placed their hopes and trust to set their nation free.

WAITING FOR THE WAR

In *Alladhī Ya'tī wa-lā Ya'tī*, published only one year before the 1967 war, the poet treats themes of life, death, and resurrection, as well as the role of the committed poet and the inevitability of revolution and war. The title of this collection, translated as *What Comes and Does Not Come*, echoes that of Samuel Beckett's *Waiting for Godot*.[16] Al-Bayātī devotes the title poem to the nexus of writing poetry and politics. The title poem, "Alladhī Ya'tī wa-lā Ya'tī," reflects the uncertainties that govern the state of the poet and the Arabs before the war. Al-Bayātī describes this poem as a recreation of the 1960s generation's experience of wandering aimlessly in a maze.[17] The poem reads as follows:

الذي يأتي ولايأتي

عائشة ماتت ، ولكني أراها تذرع الظلام
تنتظر الفارس يأتي من بلاد الشام
أيتها الذبابة العمياء
لا تحجبي الضياء
عني، و عن عائشة، ايتها الشمطاء
مغشوشة خمرة تلك الحان
سكرتَ بالمجان
وزحف الدود على جبينك الممتقع الاسيان
وجفّت العينان
مولاي، لا يبقى سوى الواحد القيّوم
وهذه النجوم
الكل باطل و قبض الريح
عائشة ماتت ، و لكني أراها مثلما أراك
قالت ، و مدت يدها أهواك
وابتسم الملاك
فلتمطري أيتها السحابة
أيان شئت ، فغدا تخضّر نيسابور

تعود لي من قبرها المنثور
تمسح خدي و تروّي الصخر و العظام
يأتي و لا يأتي ، أراه مقبلا نحوي ، ولا أراه
تشير لي يداه
من شاطئ الموت الذي يبدأ حيث تبدأ الحياة
من كان يبكي تحت هذا السور؟
كلاب رؤيا ساحر مسحور
تنبح في الديجور
أم ميّت الجذور
في باطن الأرض التي تنتظر النشور
من كان يبكي تحت هذا السور؟
لعلها الريح التي تسبق من يأتي و لا يأتي
لعل شاعرا يولد أو يموت. [18]

What Comes and Does Not Come

ʿĀ'isha died, but I see her measuring the darkness
Waiting for the knight, coming from Bilād al-Shām [the Levant]
O blind fly
Do not block the light
From me and from ʿĀ'isha, you hag
The wine of that bar is watered down
You got drunk for free
And the worms crawled on your gloomy, pale forehead
And the eyes dried
No one remains but the one eternal God, O my lord,
And these stars
Everything will die and vanish
ʿĀ'isha died, but I see her just as I see you
She extended her hand and said: I love you
And the angel smiled
Rain, O cloud
Whenever you want, tomorrow Nishapur will be green
She will return to me from her shattered tomb
To wipe my cheek and water the stones and bones
He comes and does not come, I see him coming toward me
and I don't

His hands point at me
From the shore of death, which begins where life begins
Who was crying from under this wall?
The dogs of a vision of an enchanted magician
Barking at dawn
Or is it he whose roots are dead
In the core of the earth, which is waiting for resurrection
Who was crying from under this wall?
Perhaps it is the wind that precedes that which comes
    and does not come
Perhaps a poet is born or dies.

This poem deals with revolution and the unavoidability of death. Al-Bayātī considers death the ultimate fate of humanity and says to the Arabs, since everyone will vanish and die, except for God and the stars, one should not worry much about death. Death is the ultimate fate of everyone, including 'Ā'isha, whose name means "the living woman," though she dies only to be reborn again. 'Ā'isha is the poet's beloved, muse, and inspiration, and a symbol of love, life, and the goddess of fertility (Ishtār), who changes forms and thus never really dies. Assuming "a fresh identity in each poem," 'Ā'isha, "the main heroine in al-Bayātī's works," becomes the lens through which al-Bayātī sees himself and the world."[19] The poet sees life in the ultimate death of everyone, as 'Ā'isha returns from her grave to bring poetry back to him, and rain and resurrection to his nation, only to disappear again. Al-Bayātī sees death as the medium of life; without it, no one would be resurrected and Nishapur would not be green again. Nishapur is the perfect city in which the poet dreams of living with his people. But unless one sacrifices one's life and welcomes death, 'Ā'isha will not return, nor will Nishapur be green again. Nishapur is burned alive so it may emerge pure, an act of liberation from its stained past.[20]

Putting the poem in its chronological context helps us understand the poet's doubts and uncertainties. Published one year before the 1967 Arab–Israeli war, this multivoiced poem treats the idea of revolution as well as that of poetic inspiration. In his previous poems about revolution in the Arab world, the poet puts his hope and trust in Nasser to solve the Arab world's socioeconomic ills. In *Alladhī Ya'tī wa-lā Ya'tī*, the poet addresses the Arab world in its entirety instead. The poet sounds optimistic yet uncertain. The title "What Comes and Does Not Come" suggests that the poet has been waiting for a very long time, but he is no longer certain that this thing will arrive.

In "Alladhī Ya'tī wa-lā Ya'tī," al-Bayātī employs Tammūzī images of death and resurrection to reflect on the spiritual death of Arabs and their potential resurrection. The poem can be thematically divided into three sections: the first section is lines 1–9, the second is lines 10–19, and the third is lines 20–30. In the first section, al-Bayātī presents to us the image of his beloved, 'Ā'isha, dead and yet waiting in the darkness for a knight coming from Bilād al-Shām, "the Levant," to bring her back to life. Whether 'Ā'isha suggests poetic inspiration or revolution in the Arab world, her resurrection is not certain.

The poet's choice of the Levant signifies the region's significance as the cradle of monotheistic religions. 'Ā'isha is waiting in the dark for this knight (probably representing Nasser) to resurrect her, and the speaker is waiting for the resurrection of 'Ā'isha, his poetic muse or inspiration, to inspire him to write provocative poetry. Thus, the poet identifies revolution with poetic inspiration, as two forces affecting one another. For a revolution to take place, the poet must be inspired to write poetry that calls for and supports it, and revolution is needed to sustain poetic inspiration. Likewise, Arabs need committed poets such as al-Bayātī to reflect the status of the Arab world, shape Arab national feelings, and incite change in the form of a revolution against oppression in the Arab world, and the poet is further inspired by their actions. Furthermore, since most of al-Bayātī's poetry before 1967 is committed to the Arab cause, it is not surprising to see the poet's uncertainty after 1967 about his ability to write or to continue to write poetry. The uncertainty in the 1960s about Arab nationalism and fate left the poet wondering whether his earlier poetry had failed him, and whether there was anything left to inspire him to write poetry. This is very significant because the poet links his poetics to sociopolitics. In fact, he makes of his poetry a political tool, whose success or failure is measured solely by its effectiveness in inciting people and bringing change. At this point, al-Bayātī is inspired by the potential of a people's revolution. Unsure of the effectiveness of his poetry, al-Bayātī is also uncertain of his legacy as a poet. He struggles with what is yet to come because he has dedicated his poetry and committed himself to his people and to Arab nationalism, yet Arabs have neither attained nationalism nor challenged their status quo. By inciting sociopolitical change, he believes, his poetry would reach its ultimate goal. Patriotism led to his engagement with the affairs of his fellow citizens; likewise, love of freedom and dignity should urge him to fight for such values. It is worth noting that in addressing the Arab dictators, the terrifying force behind people's submission, he challenges them and invites his people to do so as well: "No one remains but the one eternal God, O my lord / and these stars / Everything will die and vanish." This challenge is based on welcoming death, which the authoritarian Arab regimes use as a tool to silence dissident voices like that of the poet. In this regard, death for a noble reason, such as resistance to and rejection of oppression, is more worthy than an undignified life. Such a noble death brings about life.

The second section of the poem deals with the consequences of the resurrection of ʿĀ'isha. The poet maintains in lines 10–12 that no one is immortal except for God and the stars. Then, in lines 13–14, ʿĀ'isha rises from the dead, extending her hands to the speaker and saying, "I love you." In line 15, the consequences of ʿĀ'isha's resurrection are revealed: the angel smiles, the cloud rains, and the dead Nishapur comes back to life and becomes greener. In lines 18–19 ʿĀ'isha rises from her shattered tomb, wipes the poet's cheek, and waters the stones and bones of the dead. ʿĀ'isha resurrects the poet, the voice of the nation; Nishapur, the ideal city; and the dead people, the Arabs. In this section, the poet hopes to evoke the emotions of his fellow Arabs and convince them to take decisive action by revolting against the status quo. The optimistic tone in this section takes additional significance from its placement in the middle of the poem. In the first section, although ʿĀ'isha waits for a long time in the dark, she rejects death in its entirety and waits for something to happen. In the second section, ʿĀ'isha is resurrected and brings everything back to life with her.

The third section, lines 20–30, is marked by a state of uncertainty and suspense and ends the poem with a tone that is neither optimistic nor pessimistic. The poet projects the status quo of the Arab world and his own poetics. He presents to those who might or might not understand his words their own case and emphasizes their remaining two choices: to reject the status quo and follow the example of ʿĀ'isha or to accept humiliation and defeat and continue living in darkness.

The first line in this section reads "He comes and does not come, I see him coming toward me and I don't," and the last line reads "Perhaps a poet is born or dies." Thus, its beginning is as uncertain and indefinite as its end. Furthermore, the poet presents the image of a person or a thing whom the speaker sees and does not see coming "from the shore of death, which begins where life begins," walking toward the speaker and pointing at him with his hands. The place from which the poet is called is not any place; it is the shore of death where life begins. The speaker sees death as a precondition for life and wonders whether the sounds he hears belong to the barking dogs or to him "whose roots are dead." One possible way of reading the symbol of the barking dogs is by contrasting it to the symbol of "he whose roots are dead / in the core of the earth, which is waiting for resurrection." The latter could be a metaphor for the generations of dead Arabs whose rise and awakening will result in the resurrection of the earth. The barking dogs might then be a metaphor for the deluded Arab leaders. This man/nation who has been dead for so long is buried inside a land that is waiting for the right moment to be resurrected/revolt. The poem ends with the uncertain destiny of the poet whose life and death are contingent upon poetic inspiration. The poet's uncertainty about an Arab revolution and about his people's will to change and understand his poetry determines not only the legacy of his poetry, but also the destiny of his profession as a poet committed to his people and society.

In the majority of the poems in this collection, al-Bayātī sees life as death in darkness, Ishtār as a woman who died long ago, and Babylon as a city sinking in darkness, death, and an impossible dream of resurrection. However, life and death remain contradictory forces, and despite the poet's pronounced uncertainty about rebirth, he sees a glimpse of hope, as we see in "Al-ʿAwda min Bābil" (The Return from Babylon). In this poem, the poet links death to dignity and rebirth:

العودة من بابل

معجزة الإنسان أن يموت واقفاً، و عيناه إلى النجوم
و أنفه مرفوع
إن مات أو أودت به حرائق الأعداء
و أن يضيء الليل وهو يتلقّى ضربات القدر الغشوم
و أن يكون سيّد المصير
[. . .]
تموز لن يعود للحياة.[21]

The Return from Babylon

If man dies or if the fire of the enemy kills him
Then it is a miracle to die standing up, with his eyes
watching the stars
And his head held high
And to light up the night while receiving the blows
of the brutal fate
And to be the master of destiny
[. . .]
Tammuz will not return to life.

Here, the poet draws an image of death with dignity. The fighter dies on the battlefield with his head held high while receiving the blows of the enemy with courage and determination. Here, death on the battlefield is better than life in misery. What is interesting about this poem is not the poet's view of death on the battlefield as a restoration of dignity, but rather his pessimism and gradual loss of hope. According to this poem, death in battle is no longer the solution for Arabs' problems; it is instead the only remaining means of acquiring dignity. Life is meaningless, and therefore it is better to die than to continue living. The poet is so pessimistic that he employs three images of Tammūz, Ishtār, and Babylon differently than he did in his previous collections. Here, these three symbols represent not rebirth and resurrection but decay, death, and meaningless waiting. Babylon is a dead city, Ishtār is a dead woman who does not hear the calls of Babylon, and Tammūz "will not return to life." Thus, although al-Bayātī may still be waiting for "what comes and does not come," he seems less optimistic than he used to be. Nevertheless, and despite the obvious pessimism in the poem, its end is optimistic: "and rain falls." This is not to say that the poet is optimistic; rather, it confirms the overwhelming state of uncertainty in the poem and the collection. Such a state precedes major incidents or events, and war is not only a major event, but also a defining one.

THE DEFEAT

In 1967, Arabs went to war against Israel and that which "comes and does not come" came, though not exactly according to the poet's wish.

The Arabs were defeated and humiliated again, and the poet started to lose interest in writing solely for Arabs. *ʿUyūn al-Kilāb al-Mayyita* (The Eyes of the Dead Dogs), published two years after the defeat, gives shape to the poet's utter political disappointment. This collection reflects the loss and betrayal Arabs felt after the defeat, as well as the poet's criticism of Arab society, people, and regimes. One of the key poems in this collection, and in all of al-Bayātī's poetry, is "Bukā'iyya ʿalā Shams Ḥuzayrān," (Lament for the June Sun), which reads as follows:

بكائية على شمس حزيران

طحنتنا في مقاهي الشرق
حرب الكلمات
والسيوف الخشبية
والأكاذيب
وفرسان الهواء
نحن لم نقتل بعيراً
أو قطاه
لم نجرب لعبة الموت
ولم نلعب مع الفرسان
أو نرهن إلى الموت جواد
نحن لم نجعل من الجرح دواة
ومن الحبر دماً
فوق حصاه
شغلتنا الترهات
فقتلنا بعضنا بعضاً
وها نحن فتات
في مقاهي الشرق
نصطاد الذباب
نرتدي اقنعة الأحياء
في مزبلة التاريخ
اشباه رجال
لم نعلق جرساً
في ذيل هر أو حمار
أو نقل للأعور الدجالِ
لم لذت

بأذيال الفرار؟
نحن جيل الموت بالمجان
جيل الصدقات
هزمتنا في مقاهي الشرق
حرب الكلمات
والطواويس التي تختال
في ساحاتِ
موت الكبرياء
ومقالات الذيول الادعياء
آه لطخْ هذه الصفحة
هذا الخبر الكاذب
يا سارق قوت الفقراء
وحذاء الأمراء
بدم الصدق
ومت مثل فقاعات الهواء
لم نعد نقوى على لعق الأكاذيب
ونجيد الهُراء
واجترار الترهات
نحن جيل الموت بالمجان ،
جيل الصدقات
لم نمت يوماً
ولم نولد
ولم نعرف عذاب الشهداء
فلماذا تركونا في العراء ؟
يا الهي
للطيور الجارحات
نرتدي اسمال موتانا ،
ونبكي في حياء
آه لم تترك على عورتنا
شمس حزيران رداء
ولماذا تركونا للكلاب
جيفاً دون صلاه
حاملين الوطن المصلوب في كفٍ
وفي الأخرى التراب
آه لا تطرد عن الجرح الذباب
فجراحي فم (أيوب)

وآلامي انتظار
ودم يطلب ثار
يا إله الكادحين الفقراء
نحن لم نهزم
ولكن الطواويس الكبار
هـُزموا هم وحدهم
من قبل أن ينفخ ديّار بنار
آه يا قبر حكيم نام بين الفقراء
صامتاً يشعل نار
صامتاً يلبس أكفان الحداد
قم تحدث:
نحن موتى
نحن جيل الموت بالمجان
جيل الصدقات.[22]

Lament for the June Sun

We were ground in the coffeehouses of the East by
The war of words
The wooden swords
The lies
And the fake knights
We did not kill a camel
Or a grouse
We did not play the game of death
We did not play with knights
Or give up even one horse for death
We did not make an inkwell from the wound
And blood from ink
Upon a single pebble
Trivia preoccupied us
So, we killed each other
And here we are: crumbs
In the coffeehouses of the East
We swat at flies
We wear the masks of the living

In the garbage dump of history
We are ghosts
We did not hang a bell
On the tail of a cat or a donkey
Or tell the Antichrist:
Why did you flee
As a coward?
We are the generation of meaningless death
The recipients of alms
In the coffeehouses of the East we were defeated by
The war of words
And the peacocks who strut
In the halls
Where pride is dead
And the speeches of the obedient hacks
O stain this page
This false news
You, thief of the poor men's food
And the princes' shoes,
With the blood of honesty
Then die like bubbles in the air
We no longer can swallow lies
And master trivia
And engage in idle talk
We are the generation of meaningless death
The recipients of alms
We neither died one day
Nor were [re]born
Nor knew the anguish of martyrs
Why did they leave us naked,
O my God,
For the predatory birds
Wearing the tatters of our dead
And crying in shame?
Ah, the sun of June
Left our genitals naked

And why did they leave us for the dogs
Corpses without a prayer
Carrying the crucified nation in one hand
And dust in the other?
Oh, don't brush the flies from the wound
My wounds are the mouth of Job
And my pains are patience waiting
And blood seeking revenge
O Lord of the poor workers
We were not defeated
But only the giant peacocks
Were defeated
Quicker than the flicker of a flame
O grave of the wise man, who slept among the poor,
Silent, sparking a fire
Silent, wearing the shroud of mourning
Rise up and speak:
We are dead
We are the generation of meaningless death
We are the recipients of alms.[23]

Al-Bayātī composed this poem to give shape to the feelings of disappointment and defeat sparked by the events of 1967 and to provide the reader with an analysis of the war and its consequences. It represents the poet's literary position on the war and contributes to the understanding of the overall situation at the time. In a time of utter defeat and crisis, al-Bayātī offers a poem that serves to resolve that crisis and interpret that defeat. The poem treats three main issues: the war and defeat, the responsibilities of the Arab leaders and their people, and the poet's position on the postwar era.

This poem marks a crucial transition in which the poet's call for vengeance suggests some commitment to the Arab cause or people. Although he expresses some doubts about the status quo of the Arab world in "Alladhī Ya'tī wa-lā Ya'tī," al-Bayātī, a pro-Nasserist poet before the defeat, does not seem to accept responsibility for or feel guilty about the defeat. Al-Bayātī calls the 1967 war a "war of words" and "lies and empty heroes" with "wooden swords," which explains why the Arabs were defeated. The June war is "the game of death" in which people died for nothing "in the halls where pride is dead." The defeat was masked "with the blood of truth," and "this false news" deceived people into thinking they could win or were winning the war—in other words, the war leaders lied to their people. Al-Bayātī does not consider it a war of equals. He considers it a game of death in which killing was easy and the Arab peoples' lives were of no value. Furthermore, he expresses his disappointment with the war, not because he did not believe Arabs should have gone to war against Israel, but because he believed there were so many lies that surrounded this war and made it a war of words.

This war of words resulted in defeat, both in the number of the people dead for nothing and in the psychological defeat that cannot be healed and the suicidal pride that can no longer be recovered. Al-Bayātī's account of the war represents the account of the Arab public and intellectuals who felt they had been betrayed. Al-Bayātī supported Nasser, seeing in his regime the end of stagnation and humiliation in the Arab world. However, the June 1967 war proved not to be the ideal solution al-Bayātī had waited for and dreamed of. The poet blames the Arab leaders, including Nasser, and their people for the defeat, the poet's disappointment, and decay in the Arab society.

Al-Bayātī blames Arabs before he even mentions the Arab leaders, whom he calls "the peacocks" for a reason. Although the leaders are responsible for the defeat, al-Bayātī holds the Arab public responsible for approving of their leaders' acts. Al-Bayātī analyzes the state of Arabs before and after the war and suggests what might have led to the defeat. In criticizing the Arab armies and the Arab public, the poet points out their major shortcomings. The poem begins by stating that the Arab armies lost this "war of words" thanks to the incompetence of their armies, which should not have been expected to win a war when they did not even "kill a camel or a grouse." Furthermore, not only did these armies with "wooden swords" lack sufficient war weapons, but they also "did not play the game of death" in which blood is made "from ink." Their swords are wooden and their experience worthless because they "neither died one day nor were born / nor knew the anguish of heroes." Al-Bayātī changes from a committed poet serving Nasser and his regime to one who writes to serve a broader Arab cause instead.

Furthermore, al-Bayātī considers the defeated Arabs "ghosts" who "wear masks of the living." Thus, for al-Bayātī, the Arabs are living a meaningless life that has left Arabs to the "garbage dump of history." Besides, as the poet puts it, Arabs can also be criticized for approving of their leaders without any intention of opposing their regimes. This last statement brings to mind the poet's role in politics and presents him as a committed Arab whose poem exemplifies his rejection of the status quo and criticism of the Arab leaders. In addition, the poet's criticism of the Arab leaders emphasizes this transition in his commitment to the Arab cause. Arabs are also called beggars, the "recipients of alms," and "the generation of meaningless death" because they accept the humiliating life they lead and live on the "alms" of their kings or leaders, which hinders their ability to speak out and oppose the corrupt governments or leaders.

Al-Bayātī's reaction to the defeat could be understood in the context of his committed poetry. He wrote poetry to Nasser, Arab nationalism, and Palestine and believed his poetry would move the crowds. However, after the defeat, he discovers he has nothing to look for or write about, other than his disappointment and frustration. "Lament for the June Sun" is the poet's way of expressing to himself and to others why Arabs left him nothing to write about. His is the generation of defeat, and he is a defeated poet writing helplessly to a deaf audience.

Al-Bayātī calls his generation the generation who died for nothing because their deaths are over meaningless trivia, pointless because in dying they neither protected the Arab land, as the poet wished, nor restored Arab dignity. On the contrary, this defeat intensified the humiliation of Arabs. Al-Bayātī holds the Arab public responsible for their own stagnation and inability to lead responsible lives that serve their nation instead of dragging it backward.

After the defeat, al-Bayātī rejected this pointless death and stressed that to understand it, one needs to rebel against it.[24] Thus, the poet calls his people to rebel not just against their defeat but their understanding of the defeat, and the life they are living. The poet expresses his utter disappointment with Arabs and their lives by presenting, in lines 14–20, an image of Arab men wearing the masks of the living, talking about trivia, fighting and killing one another for trivial reasons, and wasting their time swatting at flies and sitting in the coffeehouses of the East, which the poet calls "the garbage dump of history." Al-Bayātī, who "looked upon the whole 1967 scene as one of waste, failure, lies, and utter negligence," foresaw the defeat of his people in such coffeehouses.[25] Thus, he blames the Arabs who have not tasted the real death (lines 45–46).

The second responsible party in this defeat, according to al-Bayātī, was the Arab leaders, whom he calls "the peacocks who strut in the halls / where pride is dead," and who ordered their "obedient hacks" to write their speeches and make the promises. In this poem, al-Bayātī "highlighted the deficiencies of Arab society" and "bitterly criticized the Arabs and attacked the corruption of the Arab rulers who deceived their people with propaganda, cover-ups, and misleading news broadcasts about the reality of their situation."[26] The misleading news broadcasts refer to the Egyptian radio stations that broadcasted the victory of the Arab armies against Israel during the June War, when in fact they were being crushed and defeated by Israeli soldiers.

Al-Bayātī blames the Arab leaders and holds them responsible not only for the 1967 June defeat, but also for the decay in and deficiencies of Arab society. The poet divides Arab citizens into three main categories: the obedient hacks, the common people, and the opposition. The obedient hacks are the Arab leaders' servants, their means to deceive the public and facilitate bribes, corruption, and crime in society. These flunkies write speeches for their leaders and stain the page with false news intended to mislead the public. The second category consists of the common people, who live on the government's "alms" and lead lives beguiled by trivia. They form the majority in every Arab country, and in their silence and preoccupation, they encourage Arab governments to continue stealing the wealth of their countries and ruling by force. The third category is the minority: the opposition. It consists of people who reject the strategies of the government and oppose the regime.

There are also some people among the public who oppose the government but do not play a role in politics and do not express their opposition; this puts them between the opposition and the common people. Those who oppose silently, without criticizing the wrongdoings of their governments or leaders are as ineffective as those who lead trivial lives. In their silence they drag the country backward and support corrupt governments. The silent, neutral public does not help the opposition and hinders and delays attempted reform because it is a liability. Of particular interest here is the poet's own political maneuvering and soul searching. Although al-Bayātī does not seem to take responsibility for the defeat, his self-condemnation as an Arab surfaces more than once in this poem. He attacks the Arabs and their practices and implies that some Arab poets, as well, belong in the category of people who support their government and accept its alms. However, his criticism of Arab leaders and emphasis on the Arab public and cause mark him as one of the poets who changed their attitudes as a result of the 1967 war. The defeat altered his voice and political stance and made him question his own legacy as a poet of the Nasserist regime.

Al-Bayātī's interpretation of the reasons for the 1967 defeat gives voice to the Arab public. His criticism of the Arab armies and public before he attacks the Arab leaders and governments is purposeful and didactic. When al-Bayātī calls the Arab leadership the "thief of the poor's food," he sends an alarming, powerful message to his people. To depict these Arab leaders as stealing the food of their poor people and assassinating the truth in order to lie to their people "with the blood of honesty" is to portray them as liars and corrupt thieves. They rely on false news and fake speeches written by their obedient hacks to manipulate the Arab public for their personal benefit. Al-Bayātī blends corrupt politics with social ills in this poem by indicating that the roots of the political defeat are socioeconomic. In addition, blaming the Arab leaders for stealing their poor people's food and dreams focuses Arab citizens on the major cause of all of their social, economic, and political problems. By blaming the Arab public at the beginning of the poem for accepting this reality, without the slightest effort to change or oppose corrupt governments and leaders, the poet empowers citizens to act. Al-Bayātī wants the Arab public to realize that it has the power to change and throw these "peacocks" in the "garbage dump of history."

After this gradual introduction, al-Bayātī proposes his solution in the last part of the poem. Before he gets there, however, he depicts the Arab nation as living in continuous isolation, poverty, shame, violence, and pain. The entire Arab nation is in the same situation and shares the same internal enemy, whom it has to defeat before going to war against external enemies, such as Israel. Al-Bayātī draws an image of death and violence on the battlefield right before he presents his position on the situation. This image is not one that will pass peacefully through the minds of Arabs. It is an image of the corpses of Arab fighters left naked on the battlefield for the dogs and birds to feast up in a monstrous way. Not even the slightest respect was paid to the corpses of the martyrs, nor were prayers read or even their genitals covered. Having said this, the poet blames the Arab leaders and the enemy, Israel, for this humiliating defeat that tarnished Arab dignity and pride. The leaders are also blamed because they went to war against Israel with incompetent armies. They neither armed their people well nor knew when it was best to go to war. These leaders and their officers, the peacocks of society, used the poor soldiers in their lost battle.

This striking war image is drawn from pre-Islamic Arabic poetry in which the poet praises the slain kinsman and incites his tribe to avenge him through the image of a defiled corpse, unburied and unavenged.[27] The poet uses this method to stimulate his people's tribal values and *Jāhiliyya* traditions so that the survivors either live forever with the shame of their kinsman's death or else take revenge to regain respect and social status among the other tribes. Al-Bayātī likewise asks his people, "who slept among the poor / silent, wearing the shroud of mourning," to "Rise up and speak: / we are dead," realizing that the ugliness of the present reality and the uselessness of idle talk in the coffeehouses will not lead to revolution. The poet asks his people not to "brush the flies from the wound" because his "wounds are the mouth of Job" and his "pains are patience waiting" and "blood seeking revenge." The abandoned corpses of soldiers slain in war are waiting for blood vengeance. Thus, al-Bayātī rejects defeat and declares to his people that revenge is the only way to erase shame from their lives and regain dignity. The poet empowers his people at the end of the poem by asserting, "We were not defeated." Rather, he lays responsibility at the feet of the Arab leaders, whose defeat was "quicker than the flicker of a flame," and against whom the poor workers will take revenge. Therefore, poetry in this sense assumes its old function: writing elegies and provoking people to avenge the slaughtered kinsmen. In addition, al-Bayātī assumes the role of critic by laying out the deficiencies of Arab society, which are at the heart of its problems. He proposes a revolution unlike the revolution he called for previously: a revolution led by the people against Arab regimes and the stagnant Arab culture.

This revolution is characterized first by the people's vocal opposition to the dictatorial regimes and then by their revenge against these leaders and their governments, which will result in the people's sovereignty and social, economic, and political reform. Indeed, this poem is one of the most important and committed in modern Arabic literature. The poet believes in his people and their will to revolt and break their silence. Although this poem was published some fifty years ago, one can hear its echoes in the people's revolutions in the contemporary Arab world. Arabs in several countries, such as Tunisia, have taken off their masks, awoken from their long sleep, and thrown their dictators into the "garbage dump of history," as al-Bayātī wanted them to. Although the Tunisian example has since been successful in bringing change to the country and reexamining the status quo, revolutions in other countries, such as Egypt and Libya, have changed only the people in power. Furthermore, the Egyptian example affirms that the revolution has not yet achieved its potential because those in power at the time of writing are Hosni Mubarak's military cabinet. In this poem, al-Bayātī warned of such a result when he wrote, "Trivia preoccupied us / so, we killed each other." Syrians are killing each other because supporters of the current regime are in a state of war with those who oppose it; this is also the case in Egypt. Al-Bayātī realizes that in the end, the Arab individual is the victim because after people's revolutions resulted in the death of thousands of Arabs, the same kind of leader returned to power, so that the change was in names alone. Al-Bayātī wants his audience to wake up from its sleep and revolt against *itself.* Being defeated in war or by a dictator seems to end in similar results due to the lack of conscious society, which needs change from within.

This poem belongs to the credible literature discussed by Suhayl Idrīs. In 1953, Idrīs established the journal *Al-Ādāb* to call for a literature of commitment (*adab al-iltizām*).[28] Idris defined credible literature as literature that does not isolate itself from society. Committed Arab writers such as al-Bayātī reflected the demands and needs of their societies in their poetry. In this poem, al-Bayātī not only laments the Arab defeat but also believes in creating a conscious Arab reader who takes responsibility for his nation and its freedom.[29] It is true that this is a committed poem, but it does not call for supporting a leader such as Nasser or an ideology like Arab nationalism because change has to come from within the nation's citizenry.

There is no doubt that "Bukā'iyya ʿalā Shams Ḥuzayrān" is a committed poem par excellence. Badawi stresses that in this poem al-Bayātī "ruthlessly expressed the kind of bitter self-criticism and self-condemnation which was typical of the feverish soul-searching and breast-beating that Arab intellectuals went through soon after the Six-Day War."[30] Al-Bayātī's "Lament for the June Sun" is a committed transitional poem in which the poet questions the Arab public's ability to rise again and condemn their social deficiencies and blind obedience to their political leaders and their agendas. Al-Bayātī condemned the Arab leaders and their agendas although he had praised them, mainly Nasser, previously. The Arab people's failure to revolt against their governments and the deficiencies in their societies discouraged the poet from writing only poetry that treats issues related to the politics of Arab world. This poem represents a transitional stage and a turning point in al-Bayātī's poetics after the 1967 defeat. Beyond this point, he looks for inspiration elsewhere. The remaining poems in this collection are critical of Arab regimes, like "Mercenaries,"[31] and sad, like the poems dedicated to the martyrs of the 1967 war, such as "To Another Martyr"[32] and "Martyrs Will Not Die."[33]

Al-Bayātī continued to write and publish poetry collections after the 1967 defeat. However, his postwar poetry neither addresses Nasser and Arab nationalism nor calls for war or liberation of Palestine. Instead, after *What Comes and Does Not Come*, the poet calls for a world revolution led by the oppressed poor, thus moving from the local to the global. In assuming this new role he is forever the wandering, exiled poet whose voice is that of every oppressed and poor citizen of the world. The collections published in the late 1960s and early 1970s include *Al-Mawt fī al-Ḥayāh* (Death in Life, 1968), *Al-Kitāba ʿalā al-Ṭīn* (Writing on Clay, 1970), and *Qaṣā'id Ḥubb ʿalā Bawwābāt al-ʿĀlam al-Sabʿ* (Love

Poems on the Seven Gates of the World, 1971). These collections include elegies and treat themes of life and death in a melodramatic tone. The poems published in *Al-Mawt fī al-Ḥayāh* include "Death in Granada," "Death in Love," "Lorca's Elegies," "Elegy to 'Ā'isha," "Writing on 'Ā'isha's Tomb," and "On Birth and Death." *Al-Kitāba 'alā al-Ṭīn* includes poems such as "The Nightmare of Day and Night," "Elegy to the City That Has Not Been Born," and "Writing on the Tomb of al-Sayyab." *Qaṣā'id Ḥubb 'alā Bawwābāt al-Ālam al-Sab'* includes poems on love, death, exile, and Sufi themes, such as "'Ā'isha's Lover" and "Letters to Imam al-Shāfi'ī," as well as "On Waḍḍaḥ al-Yaman, and Love and Death," in which the poet writes, "I did not find salvation in love, but I found God."[34] And in the title poem, love is lost forever because "lovers are sentenced to death, the land is dead, language is a prostitute and history is an illusion."[35] In this collection, the poet is a wandering, lost soul in exile, whose failure to find love again pushes him to look for it in other, more stable sources such as Sufism. Despite its melodramatic tone, it places some hope in the rising of the poor of the world, who have been struggling in "the cities of poverty, in the age of torture and revolutions."[36] Here, al-Bayātī's poetry begins to make sophisticated use of Greek mythology. Because he is no longer bound only to *iltizām* or politics, al-Bayātī excels in his treatment of various subjects and in the use of masks and mythology. Now, the poet can wear different masks to distance himself from his causes; he is no longer writing for Nasser or Palestinians, and he is no longer content with the old diction and imagery that marked his 1950s and 1960s poetry.

Instead, al-Bayātī undertakes the journey to reinvent his voice by means of descending into the underworld to equip himself with a unique language. This journey begins after the 1967 defeat, a wake-up call for Arab poets, and continues after his death, for his poetry outlives him. After 1967, al-Bayātī traveled to and lived in Arab and European countries, enriching his experience as a poet by meeting remarkable critics and poets such as Nāẓim Ḥikmat, Khalīl Ḥāwī, and Iḥsān 'Abbās. After his 1969 collection, al-Bayātī gradually concerns himself with issues of metapoetry, in which the voice of the critic is louder than that of the poet we have been accustomed to in his previous collections. This gradual transition leads to a complete transformation in his poetics, in content and style. In content, his voice becomes that of a universal poet concerned with his craft, as well as the liberation of the crushed human being. In style, his poetry changes from direct and spontaneous to meditative and sophisticated through his extensive use of masks and mythology, including Greek, Near Eastern, and his own invented myths. Also, he encourages innovation regardless of form, thus announcing that no form or subject can imprison the poem. This transformation is gradual, and although examples of poems that embody it are many, lack of space limits the number that can be examined here. I will focus on poems from his 1973 collection, *Kitāb al-Baḥr.*

THE DEPARTURE

Al-Bayātī announces his departure from his past in *Kitāb al-Baḥr* (The Book of the Sea), in which he begins his exploration of new styles, themes, and subject matter. He innovates in his language to enhance the poetics of his free verse poetry. The poet's search for poetic inspiration and voice are better understood if *Kitāb al-Baḥr* is read in the context of al-Bayātī's other works. After writing in the 1950s and 1960s on commitment, inspired by his patriotism and communist beliefs, al-Bayātī needed new sources for inspiration. Thus, his poetry changes from mainly committed to mainly metapoetic. The period following 1967 also witnesses his experiments with new language and themes to break from the diction and imagery that marked his committed poetry. This is not to say that the poet did not write metapoetic poems before 1967, or that his post-Nasserist poetry does not deal with issues other than metapoetry. Metapoetic concerns, on various levels, appear in all stages of his work as the poet's reflection on his own poetry, but some of his post-commitment works are highly metapoetic. Al-Bayātī never loses touch with his fellow human beings—their struggle is his—but in these later works he invents a new language to give shape to their suffering and add a new, human value to his poetry.

In "Aḥmil Mawtī wa Arḥal" (I Pick Up My Death and Leave) the poet gives shape to the fears, challenges, and dreams of someone who is exiled and eternally tortured.

أحمل موتي و أرحل

[. . .]

(2)
يحمل العاشق في غربته
موته ، تاريخه، عنوانه
وعذابا كامنا في دمه
وحضورا أبديا كانه
[. . .]

(5)
[. . .]
وأنا حطمت حياتي
في كل منافي العالم
بحثا عن لارا و خزامى
وعبدت النار
مارست السحر الاسود في مدن ماتت
قبل التاريخ وقبل الطوفان
واستبدلت قناعي بقناع الشيطان
ظهرت لي لارا و خزامى في موسيقى الأشعار
في حرف السين و حرف الهاء و حرف التاء

(6)
برحيلي رحلت كل الاشياء.[37]

I Pick Up My Death and Leave

[. . .]

(2)
The lover carries in his exile
His death, his history and his address
And an internal torture in his blood
And an eternal real presence
[. . .]

(5)
[. . .]
And I destroyed my life
In all the exiles of the world
Looking for Lārā and Khuzāmā
I worshipped the fire
And practiced black magic in dead cities
Before history and before the flood
And I exchanged my mask with the mask of Satan.
Then, Lārā and Khuzāmā appeared to me in the music of poetry
In the letters S, H, and T

(6)
With my departure, everything departed.

Al-Bayātī announces his death and utter disappointment at being an exiled lover who is unable to accomplish his dreams. He has spent his life wandering from one exile to another, even worshipping fire and practicing black magic, and yet he could not find Lārā or Khuzāmā, figures who suggest poetic inspiration. Al-Bayātī searches for his dream in a nontraditional way: exchanging masks with Satan. This unconventional method leads the poet to his dream, and he realizes that he can find his satisfaction only in one place: poetry. Thus, the music of poetry and the sounds of letters in language become the medium through which Lārā and Khuzāmā appear to the poet, achieving what he fails to achieve in reality. Furthermore, the last line in this poem—"With my departure, everything departed"—reflects the poet's decision to move on. Poetry will be the world he departs to with faith. Thus, poetry, language, inspiration, and other metapoetic concerns become al-Bayātī's major concern in the poems and collections that follow.

At this stage, "to write or not to write" is the question, and "what comes and does not come" is the answer. If the poet receives his poetic inspiration and writes, a poet may be born; yet, if the poet is unable to write due to lack of inspiration, a poet may die. After the poet witnesses the 1967 defeat and the absence of a revolution in the Arab world, he calls for a different kind of revolution within his own poetry; his success as a poet is no longer measured in political terms, for he no longer depends on the occurrence, or potential occurrence, of political events to write poetry. Although the poet once awaited, in "What Comes and Does Not Come," war and poetic inspiration—two sides of the same coin—in this collection it is poetic inspiration alone for which the poet waits and searches. In "I Pick Up My Death and Leave," the loss and disappearance of the beloved, poetic inspiration, leaves the poet in utter anguish and sorrow.[38] However, he overcomes this despair and frustration by searching for his poetic voice in his own poetry. This beloved gives hope to the poet and challenges him to write the poetry through which he achieves immortality. These metapoetic concerns not only revive al-Bayātī's poetry and shift it from one phase to another, but also resurrect him and enable him to find his voice and reinvent his poetics. At this stage, the poet has announced his departure from his past and stated his intent to look for a new reality in his poetry by looking for inspiration in poetry itself. Only then is al-Bayātī able to continue writing poetry despite the political upheavals around him. To be able to move beyond commitment toward metapoetry suggests the poet's ability to perceive his poetry independent of politics.

METAPOETRY

In "Sa'anṣubu Lakī Khayma fī al-Ḥadā'iq al-Ṭāghūriyya" (I Will Pitch a Tent for You in the Tagore Gardens), al-Bayātī experiments with his poetry: he mixes monorhymed poetry with free verse poetry and lyrical poetry, which makes his poem a garden. This poem is influenced by "The Gardener," a long poem by the Bengali poet Rabindranath Tagore. Tagore translated his poem into English in 1915 and rendered it in free verse. "The Gardener" is a manifestation of Tagore's metapoetic concerns. In it Tagore expresses his faith in poetry and art as mediums through which the gardener, the poet, is able to send his "glad voice across an hundred years" to his anonymous reader, who reads "my poems an hundred years hence."[39] Moreover, Tagore contrasts the mortality of love, beauty, happiness, work, and life with the immortality of innovative poetry in stanza 68: "One sole poet has not to sing one aged song" because "there must come a full pause to weave perfection into music."[40] Only poetry, music, and art are perfect because of their exceptional ability to use imagery to make beauty immortal, as in stanza 59: "Poets are weaving for you [beautiful woman] a web with threads of golden imagery."[41] In stanza 85, Tagore incites his reader to "feel the living joy that sang one spring morning, sending its glad voice across an hundred years."[42] Tagore is the gardener whose mastery of his profession outlives him and takes the reader on journeys through his gardens even a century after the writing of his poem.

Al-Bayātī writes "Sa'anṣubu Lakī Khayma fī al-Ḥadā'iq al-Ṭāghūriyya" to make a place for himself and his beloved, poetry, in the "Tagore Gardens." Further, the poem is an attempt to give his beloved all that she wishes for through poetry. He gives her a house made of poetry: "the magician knelt in your house / which is made of poetry."[43] He tells his beloved that he excels other poets because their poetry is impersonal: "beneath the poets' pillows, I saw rivers of ready-made words that have neither souls nor feet / running in all directions / and sold in the slave market and traded in all ages,"[44] while his words, like Tagore's, are innovative and new. In another stanza, al-Bayātī says, "I will tell the words to be flowers and I will tell the poets to be honest."[45] Thus, after realizing that his satisfaction lies solely in poetry, al-Bayātī criticizes the other poets who write traditional and "aged" poetry, as Tagore maintained that the poet should not sing an aged song. Distinguishing his own work from that of others of his generation, al-Bayātī decries the stale works of the poets of his age as neither innovative nor credible.

Looking for a new kind of poetic language, al-Bayātī writes:

سأنصب لك خيمة في الحدائق الطاغورية

(1)
[. . .]
وكلمات لم نقلها و لم
تبح بها غزالة البحر
أغتصب العالم فيها و في
حروفها أموت في الأسر
مرتديا أكفان كينونتي.[46]

I Will Pitch a Tent for You in the Tagore Gardens

(1)
[. . .]
Words that we have not said and
The Sea Gazelle has not revealed
With which I rape the world
And in whose letters I die imprisoned
Wearing the shrouds of my existence.

This is a free verse poem in which al-Bayātī is capable of "raping" the world with words by using language in an unfamiliar manner. The innovative language al-Bayātī claims to use in his poetry enables him to exert his power on the world instead of being controlled by it. Such unconventional words are able to break the conventional world in which we live and create a revolution from within the self. "Wearing the shrouds of [his] existence," the speaker dies in the letters of these new, innovative words; he is imprisoned in language, and he is liberated because dying for the sake of his art makes him immortal. Thus, poetry becomes the challenge and the medium through which the poet overcomes this challenge, and liberates himself from a life he considers a punishment, as he says in the poem's last two lines: "I am awaiting my death sentence / and life is my punishment."[47] The notion of language as both the prison and the liberation of the poet is a metapoetic one. Only after the poet dies in the prison of his language is he resurrected and able to rape the world, asserting control over it with words and language unlike any other.

Language, its power over the poet, and the immortality of the poem are three key notions treated in this poem. To stress the immortality of poetry and the power of language, al-Bayātī here employs images of houses made of poems, fake poems and words dropping dead, and words becoming immortal flowers that become the tent of the beloved. His use of lyrical, monorhymed, and free verse makes this poem a garden, rich in a vitality of form and content. Only through poetry is the poet able to create a new reality, which he offers to his beloved. In doing so he also creates his own kingdom and becomes the master of everything, including language. Al-Bayātī finally feels capable of moving forward from the defeated tone that had recently imprisoned his poetry; at this critical point, he is ready to move on confidently. He finds that his freedom and his dreams come true in his poetic kingdom, where poetry itself becomes his inspiration. Only then can the poet assume control over his vocation and refuse to subject his poetry to the ups and downs of politics and society.

The collections published after *Kitāb al-Baḥr* are *Sīra Dhātiyya li-Sāriq al-Nār* (Autobiography of the Fire Thief, 1974), *Qamar Shīrāz* (The Moon of Shiraz, 1976), *Mamlakat al-Sunbula* (Kingdom of Grain, 1979), *Ṣawt al-Sanawāt al-Ḍaw'iyya* (The Sound of the Light Years, 1979), *Bustān ʿĀ'isha* (Aisha's Orchard, 1989), and *Al-Baḥr Baʿīd Asmaʿuh Yatanahhad* (The Sea Is Distant, I Hear It Sighing, 1998). In his late works, he better understands "the dialectic of life and death, and the tragic transformation of man, love and poetry into a myth, and vice versa."[48] In these works, al-Bayātī excels and becomes a mythmaker, especially when he breaks from allusions to myths.[49]

Mamlakat al-Sunbula consists of thirteen poems, including some of his best metapoetic poems. Key poems that treat exile and metapoetic concerns in this collection include "Al-Ḍaw' Ya'tī min Gharnāṭa" (The Light Comes from Granada),[50] "Ilā Silvādor Dālī" (To Salvador Dali),[51] "Maqāṭiʿ min ʿAdhābāt Farīd al-Dīn al-ʿAṭṭār" (Fragments on the Suffering of Farid al-Din al-Attar),[52] "Dam al-Shāʿir" (The Blood of the Poet),[53] "Ṣura lil-Suhrawardī fī Shabābih" (An Image of the Sahrurdi in His Youth),[54] and "Ḥajar al-Taḥawwul" (Stone of Transformation).[55] Other poems treat love, longing, loneliness, exile, and the poet as a Sufi and rebel, among them "Sīmfūniyat al-Buʿd al-Khāmis al-Ūlā" (The First Symphony of the Fifth Dimension),[56] "Sa'abūḥ bi-Ḥubbik lil-Rīḥ wa-lil-Ashjār" (I Shall Reveal My Love for You to the Wind and the Trees),[57] "Ru'yā fī Baḥr al-Balṭīq" (A Vision in the Baltic Sea),[58] "Al-ʿArā'" (Wilderness),[59] and "Ta'ammulāt fī al-Wajh al-Ākhar lil-Ḥubb" (Meditations on the Other Face of Love).[60]

In her discussion of the metapoetics in al-Bayātī's later works, Aida Azouqa writes, "Like his Western peers, he relied heavily on Ancient and Classical myths to become the Arab mythmaker par excellence. Accordingly, for a poet intent on change, it is neither surprising that metapoetic concerns should become a prominent element of al-Bayātī's oeuvre, nor that al-Bayātī, and to the best of my knowledge, should become one of the pioneers of metapoetry in the Arab world. His work also manifests that he used metapoetical strategies similar to those in the works of the Western composers of metapoetry."[61] It is not surprising that every poem in this collection treats metapoetic concerns in one way or another, by experimenting with language and making metapoetry its main subject matter. In some poems, the poet treats the challenges he encounters as an exiled poet who fails to return to his homeland or adapt to constant traveling. He becomes an innovative rebel in an age of literary corruption, resisting stagnation in literature and language; his role involves criticizing other poets and critics. He celebrates the new role of the Arab poet: the terrorist. This is best seen in three poems: "Al-Ḍaw' Ya'tī min Gharnāṭa" (The Light Comes from Granada), "Dam al-Shā'ir" (The Blood of the Poet), and "Ta'ammulāt fī al-Wajh al-Ākhar lil-Ḥubb" (Meditations on the Other Face of Love).

In "Al-Ḍaw' Ya'tī min Gharnāṭa,"[62] the poet uses ekphrasis, myth, and masks to express his "anxiety over poetic creativity." Ekphrasis is "the verbal representation of non-verbal texts."[63] In this poem, al-Bayātī uses the masks of a lonely orphaned child, the Prophet Muḥammad, and a blind musician, and references from Islamic mythology to give shape to his anxieties as a poet:

الضوء يأتي من غرناطة

(1)
أتكور طفلاً كي أولد في قطرات المطر المتساقط فوق
الصحراء العربية، لكن الريح الشرقية تلوي عنقي، فأعود
إلى غار (حِراء) يتيما، يخطفني نسر، يلقي بي تحت
سماء أخرى. أتكور ثانية، لكني لا أولد أيضًا ، أتخطى
الوضع البشري، أدور وحيدًا حول الله و حول منازله في
الأرض، يلاحقني صوت كمان يعزف في الليل عليه مئات
العشاق المسكونين بنار الميلاد، أحاول أن أتوقف عند الوتر
المرتجف المقطوع، ولكن الموسيقى تجرفني، أصرخ
عند الذروة، إيقاع مصحوب ببكاء إنسانيّ يندفع الآن
ويخبو، موسيقي أعمى ينزف فوق الأوتار دما، يرفع مثلي
يده في صمت فراغ الأشياء، ويبحث عن شيء ضاع
يدور وحيدًا حول الله، بصوت فمي أو فمه يصرخ، تحمله

الذروةُ نحو قرار الموجة، يبكي تحت سماء بلاد أخرى
لكن الاوتار تظل تلاحقني في صمت القاعة. من منا يولد
في هذي الصحراء الآنْ
[. . .]

(3)
ما يبقى هو هذي النار
وعذاب الشعراء.[64]

The Light Comes from Granada

(1)
I curl up like an infant to be born in the drops of rain
falling on the Arabian Desert,
but the wind of the East twists my neck. I return an orphan
to the cave of Hira'
and an eagle snatches me up, releases me under another sky.
I curl up once again,
but this time I am not reborn. I transcend the human condition.
I circle
alone around God and his dwellings on Earth. I am pursued
by the sound
of a violin made to tremble in the night by hundreds of lovers
haunted
by the flame of birth. I try to stop myself at the broken,
vibrating string,
but the music transports me. I cry out at the climax. A rhythm,
accompanied
by a human sob, bursts forth now and fades away.
The blood of a
blind musician flows over the strings. Like me,
he raises his hand in the silence of the void. He searches for
something lost. He circles alone around God. He cries out
with the voice of my
mouth or his own. The climax carries him to the trough
of the wave. He weeps

beneath the sky of another country. But the strings continue
to pursue me in the
silence of the hall. Which of us is now born in this desert.
[. . .]

(3)
What remains is this fire
And the suffering of the poets.[65]

In this free verse poem, the poet shapes his struggle and dilemma as a poet by using the mask of an orphaned child struggling to be born in the Arabian Desert. This alludes to the Prophet Muḥammad and the poet's use of prophecy to describe his poetry. However, the wind of the East twists the child's neck and forces him to return to the cave of Ḥira', a cave in Mecca where the Prophet Muḥammad used to meditate alone and receive the revelations of the Quran. Although the child circles around God and his dwellings on Earth, he continues to wander lonely—and so does the poet. Al-Bayātī uses masks to appear objective instead of didactic in expressing his feelings and passion for human dignity and freedom in relation to modern problems.[66] He uses the mask of the Prophet Muḥammad to express his feelings and thoughts about the anxieties of the modern poet. The use of masks is interesting in this regard because, in the fourth stanza, the poet uses the mask of a man-child to express his thoughts and feelings:

(4)
[. . .]
ويظل الرجل الطفل سنينا في سفر. ما يبقى يهدمه أو ينبيه الشعراء
ويقول لها من منّا الخاسر في لعبة هذا الحب الهدّام؟
ولماذا يسكنني هذان الضدان؟
"لن يبني بيتا من لا بيت له الان."[67]

(4)
[. . .]
For years the man-child continues his journeys. What remains is
destroyed or built by the poets. He says to her: Which one of us is
the loser in this destructive game of love?

And why am I possessed by these two contradictions?
"He who has no house will never be able to build one."[68]

Although the persona of the poet is a mature adult in age and appearance, inside he is a child who needs to continue his journey in order to fully achieve his quest. This man-child poet is challenged by two contradictions: the compelling desire to "build a house" and the destructive influence of his past. The poet believes poets can either build and contribute to poetry, literature, and language or destroy and ruin them. Thus, he is torn between his desire to contribute to literature and preserve language and his fear of failing, which causes anxiety over poetic creativity. Also, the poet explains his fears by questioning the ability of one who has no house to build one. Thus, the poet's loneliness poses a struggle for him yet inspires him to innovate in his poetry. The child hopes "to be reborn in the drops of rain falling on the Arabian Desert." Likewise, the poet hopes to be reborn by being able to use language in poetry innovatively in order to preserve language and build it, as we see in lines 30–32: "A traveling man totters as he crowns a woman with her braids and embraces her, saying: 'O light of love, O language through which, from which, and for which is born this child.'"[69] The Arabic language is the poet's love through which, from which, and for which he will be resurrected.

In his struggle to write poetry, the poet realizes that language is superior to man.[70] Al-Bayātī realizes the power of language and its superiority to him. He struggles in his attempts to experiment and innovate in poetry in order to preserve and build language and vice versa. He realizes that he needs to wear different masks and play certain games to capture the magical side of language. He falls in love with language, yet he knows how superior this kind of love is: it is the most rewarding and yet complicated kind of love. This love requires the poet to accept his inferiority to language and lose his soul while journeying within the soul. This love guarantees rebirth only when the poet gives up everything for his beloved language and fears no one and nothing. He liberates himself from the past and delves wholeheartedly into his adventure. According to this poem, the speaker goes on a journey through language in an attempt to write poetry that will enable him to be reborn. Accordingly, this poetry is written from language and for language; the poet uses his innovative language to write poetry to preserve and build language. In addition, he does so to resurrect his poetic voice and desire to continue writing poetry. Why would a poet such as al-Bayātī doubt his ability to build language when his legacy speaks volumes of his poetics? His decision to commit himself to language and metapoetry after a long history of commitment to *iltizām* is not arbitrary. Al-Bayātī knocks on the door of metapoetics as his final attempt to resurrect as a poet from within, proving to himself that poetry can be both his inexhaustible source of inspiration and his subject matter. However, he knows well that he will struggle to write this kind of poetry, an art that demands the artist to live up to the challenge.

In another stanza, al-Bayātī employs ekphrasis by using language to write poetry that describes the art of a blind musician. The poet hears an enchanting music that transports him until he cries at the climax. This music is the sound of a violin and "a rhythm, accompanied by a human sob," that "bursts forth now and fades away." This blind musician "raises his hand in the silence of the void" while his blood "flows over the strings." Then "he searches for something lost" and "circles alone around God."[71] The success of this poem depends on al-Bayātī's description of the musician's art and its effect on the poet who listens to this music. This music, "accompanied by a human sob," transports the poet and makes him "cry out at the climax." Thus, the poet expects his poetry to have a similar influence and evoke a similar reaction from his readers. Furthermore, the poet's and musician's voices overlap and become one when the musician cries out with the voice of the poet. As the poet, the man-child, is released under another sky, and the blind musician "weeps beneath the sky of another country." Like the musician's music, the poet's contribution to art and humanity has to be of a transformative nature. In this poem, the point of such ekphrasis is that it is metapoetic: the blind musician and his music are metaphors for the poet and his poetry. In his struggle to write poetry, al-Bayātī realizes that language is superior to him, as music is for the musician.

This poem succeeds in its aesthetics and poetic value and in its ability to use language to describe another work of art to reflect the poet's struggle as an orphaned child and a blind musician. The orphaned child needs a home to return to as much as the Arabian Desert needs rain to be born. Likewise, the poet is in need of a journey that enables him to write poetry that builds more than it destroys and gives more than it takes. In addition, the poet becomes a blind artist who bleeds for his art to see light. Although the musician is blind, his music is able to make the poet cry at the climax as a sign that it has transported him. Likewise, the poet might seem restless and unable to see his direction clearly, and yet he is able to write poetry that moves and transports those who read or listen to it. Thus, according to the poem, "what will continue to exist is this fire / and the torture of the poets."[72] This fire is the blaze of innovation whose flames inspire the poets who write, through their torture, their best pieces of art, like the blind musician whose bleeding is key in the making of his music.

This poem treats themes distinct to metapoetic poetry. Azouqa remarks, "Among the distinct themes [in metapoetic poetry] are the anxiety over poetic creativity, [the poet's] concern for achieving immortality through art, the alienation of the poet in an age of crass materialism, and the role of a poet as *vates*, that is, as a visionary, and above all, the belief in the power of the imagination in transforming reality and of imposing order on what they perceive it to be a chaotic world."[73] These five themes overlap in "Al-Ḍaw' Ya'tī min Gharnāṭa," but they are mainly treated in the first stanza. Here the key theme is the alienation of the poet. The poet employs images of a lonely wandering child and the desperate musician at the beginning and end of this stanza, with an emphasis on the speaker's failure to overcome this alienation. Despite his attempts to escape the silence of the void, the loneliness and the desert, the speaker "weeps beneath the sky of another country," a sign that he is destined to move from one exile to another. At the end of the poem the poet remains as lonely and "out of place" as he is at the beginning. In the third stanza, the poet maintains that nothing remains but "the sufferings of the poets." Thus, al-Bayātī, as a metapoetic poet, stresses the eternal suffering of poets.

Al-Bayātī's use of the mask of the Prophet Muḥammad alludes not only to "the alienation of the poet in an age of crass materialism" but also to the role of the poet as a visionary and prophet whose love for humanity and his art costs him his earthly life. The role of the Prophet Muḥammad was to restore order and bring moral and religious direction to a society that was governed by chaos. Likewise, according to al-Bayātī, the role of the poet is to bleed for his art, which will resurrect him and others, as in line 10, and to struggle for years because nothing remains except what the poets build, as in line 34. Another metapoetic theme in this poem is anxiety over poetic creativity. In lines 36–37, the poet says that he is "possessed" by two contradictions: the desire to create and his anxiety and fear of failure. Also, in lines 4, 11, and 14, the poet maintains that his attempts to be reborn are marked with failure. He is looking for something he lost, but he is unable to find it anywhere. The poet is looking for poetic inspiration to help him write the poem that will break the silence of the room.

In his struggle to find inspiration, the poet has two choices. The first is to realize the difficulty of shaping his feelings and translating them into poetry, which translates into his failure to write.[74] The second is to overcome this challenge by refusing "to surrender to the limitations of language . . . bearing in mind that such a limitation can never be wholly overcome but only diminished."[75] Al-Bayātī refuses to surrender to the "silence of the void" and continues searching for his poetic inspiration to overcome these anxieties. He realizes that his task is difficult, yet he welcomes the challenge. He is aware of the limitations of language, which he is partially able to overcome when his love, poetic inspiration, appears to him, only to disappear again. This state of living on the edge, waiting for what comes and does not come, or what comes only to disappear, strands the poet between life and death. Death is near when poetic inspiration is far, and life comes back when it returns. When poetic inspiration has disappeared, the poet is never certain whether it will appear again. Therefore, he is constantly looking and waiting for it. Poetic inspiration and language are superior to the poet, for his life relies on the "coming" of poetic inspiration.

The poet's realization of the superiority of language is another metapoetic theme treated in this poem. In lines 7, 8, and 14, the poet says that although he tries to stop himself "at the broken, vibrating string," music transports him. Music, a metaphor for poetry and language, is superior to the poet, and thus, even though the poet tries to control his language, he fails. Poetry and language control the poet and "pursue him in the silence of the hall" in lines 14–15. However, "even if the poet eventually writes, he cannot fully articulate the experience he undergoes, even if he strives to use all the languages of the world."[76] Thus, what remains after all these attempts is "this fire / and the suffering of the poets" in lines 28–29. This fire is a metaphor for poetic creativity, whose anxieties make the sufferings of the poets eternal. It also suggests the fire of the intellect, which will never be extinguished. The suffering of the poet fuels a fire that ignites a revolution.

Al-Bayātī perceives his poetry as a medium in which to express his metapoetic concerns. This poem expresses the challenges and anxieties of poets, the value of poetry as the medium through which art is immortal and language is preserved, and the relationship between the poet and language: "A traveling man totters as he crowns a woman with her braids and embraces her saying: 'O light of love, O language through which, from which, and for which is born this child.'" Language is the traveling, wandering poet's beloved, whom he embraces and lives for, and through whom and from whom he is born. The relationship between the poet and language is eternal, and the death of one results in the death of the other. For al-Bayātī, writing defies time when it never reaches a resolution because it is not an event that will be complete.[77] He struggles through his poetic challenges and anxieties to maintain his poetic voice. Writing, for al-Bayātī, never reaches a point of closure, because poetic inspiration constantly appears and disappears. The process of writing is an experience fraught with danger, in which the poet offers his blood for his art, by which both become immortal.

The bleeding of the artist/poet in order for the art to be successful is highlighted in "Dam al-Shā'ir" (The Blood of the Poet). This poem, which is in free verse, defines poetry and treats the poet's struggle with his poetic inspiration and the border between the poet and his peers.

دم الشاعر

(1)

صوت الشاعر فوق نحيب الكورس يعلو،
منفردًا، منحازًا ضد الموت وضد تعاسات البشر الفانين،
بنار سعادته السوداء يجوب العالم، منفيًّا يتطهر،
لا اسم له، وله كل الأسماء، بقانون أزلي يتحول،
يقتل هذي الوحشة يقضي بالشعر عليها،
كم هو شريرأن يسكنك الشعر: "إلهي بين يديك أنا قوس فاكسرني"، ومحب محبوب

فاهجرني، كم هو شرير هذا الحب القاسي ،لا اسم له، وله كل الأسماء،
فتيًّا كالريح على أبواب المدن المسحورة يأتي أو لا يأتي،
كرماد حريق يتوهج في قلب الشاعر منطفئًا أو مشتعلاً،
يولد مبتورًا أو مكتملاً ينمو في أدغال النفس الوحشية
طفلاً يحبو في أصقاع النور ليشعل نار الإبداع.
[. . .]

(7)
47 ما بين الشاعر والكومبارس
هذا الباب المغلق والمتراس.

(8)
بدم الشاعر، هذا الحب القاسي.[78]

The Blood of the Poet

(1)
The voice of the poet rises above the weeping of the bit players,
Lonely and biased against death and the miseries of the perishing
people.
With the fire of his dark happiness, he roams the world
and he is exiled to purify himself.
He is nameless and he has all the names. An eternal law
transforms him.
He kills this desolation with poetry. How evil it is to be
possessed by poetry.
"God, I am a bow between your hands, so break me,"
and I am the lover and the beloved
So, leave me. How evil this love is. It is nameless and
it has all the names.
Young, like the wind on the doors of the enchanted cities,
it comes and it does not come like the ashes of a fire
glowing in the burning or dying heart of the poet.
It is born complete or amputated, and it lives in the brutal
jungles of the self, like a child crawling in all the
directions of light, to spark the fire of innovation.
[. . .]

(7)
Between the poet and the chorus 47
Is this closed door and barricade.

(8)
With the blood of the poet
This cruel love writes the history of the soul.

In this poem, the poet compares two kinds of poetry: one that is like the weeping of the chorus and another that rises above this weeping and fights against "death and the miseries of the perishing people." Thus, the poet distinguishes between his poetic voice and the poetry of others. Although sad and exiled, he roams the world "with the fire of dark happiness" and writes about people's misery and death. Al-Bayātī becomes Prometheus by stealing the fire of innovation from the gods and writing a superior kind of poetry. In his committed poetry, al-Bayātī uses the symbol of fire as a metaphor for the revolution, under the leadership of Nasser; in his new context, he uses it as a metaphor for innovation and poetic creativity, a revolution within his poetry that ignites another revolution in people's lives. Despite the hefty price poets pay in society, in part for saying out loud what others do not or cannot, they are alienated and lonely.

Al-Bayātī gives shape to his feelings of loneliness and banishment in lines 1–5 by portraying the poet as a lonely exiled man who roams the world and resists the misery and death around him. The weapon the poet uses to kill this desolation, al-Bayātī continues, is poetry. This poetry possesses the poet and becomes a love that refuses to leave him. Thus, the poet is torn between his need for poetry and the torture and pains that come with it. The poet's anxieties over poetic creativity make him look for poetic inspiration everywhere. Poetic inspiration becomes the poet's beloved, who, just like love, is nameless and yet has all the names. The poet and his love for poetry and poetic inspiration become inseparable and unite in one entity: "I am the lover and the beloved" (line 6). This is a Sufi-like expression. Poetic inspiration is nameless because it is indescribable, and yet at the same time, it has all the names because all the names used by the poet for his beloved in his metapoetic poetry are metaphors for it. ʿĀ'isha, Lārā, Khuzāmā, and any other beloved, named or nameless, in al-Bayātī's late works suggest eternal love and poetic inspiration. This love is "based on an earthly, Sufi and mythical understanding . . . [It is] the essence of active existence . . . because it connects earthly love with that of that divine . . . Therefore, it never dies."[79] Uniting with this eternal love, al-Bayātī himself turns into an immortal myth whose secrets, like those of language, are not revealed to others. His poetry transcends him as well as those who are able to unveil his Sufi and mythical signs. Poetry is transcendent when it reaches its revolutionary potential, that is, transfiguration.[80]

ʿĀ'isha is "the symbol of femininity, revolution, myth and she is equal to mysticism. She is a new human vehicle, born of all things to become a new creature giving birth to new things."[81] Therefore, the myth of ʿĀ'isha allows for rebirth on the personal, national, and universal levels. She resurrects the poet's voice by constantly inspiring him and rescuing him from death after waiting for her; here death is not the earthly death. Likewise, she is the seed of the revolution of the oppressed, weak people of the world, whose human revolution is the miracle the poet waits for and is certain of.[82] This human revolution will liberate mankind and announce the triumph of love, freedom, and justice over hatred, oppression, and evil. Al-Bayātī's poetry becomes this powerful and revolutionary vehicle. Therefore, he realizes his language needs to be innovative and extraordinary. Speaking in the name of the oppressed, miserable people, he hopes their suffering and misery will lead to their revolution. When they stop fearing death, like the poet, they will see it as a passage to attaining freedom, justice, and infinite love.

Another metaphor for poetic inspiration is "the ashes of a fire glowing in the burning or dying heart of the poet" (line 9). This love, poetic inspiration, is like ashes in the burning or dying heart of the poet because the glow of these embers determines whether the poet lives or dies. Poetic inspiration also is a fire that "lives in the brutal jungles of the self / like a child crawling in all the directions of light" (lines 10–11). Poetic inspiration burns the poet and resides inside his heart, the brutal jungle of the self, intensifying his pains and making his struggle eternal. In "Dam al-Shāʿir," the death and bleeding of the poet suggests his rebirth, "for poetry assumes a regenerative power of its own."[83] If these embers spark the fire of innovation inside the poet, he receives his poetic inspiration and succeeds in writing an innovative poem (lines 9–11). Prometheus's stolen fire is a metaphor for poetic inspiration—a creative power stolen from the gods, a theft for which the thief is punished. Therefore, the poet bleeds so "this cruel love writes the history of the soul" (line 49). Finally, the theme of the immortality of poetry is emphasized in the last line, line 49, where the poet's suffering and sacrifice unite with poetic creativity, the cruel love, to write the history of the soul that will defy the passage of time.

For al-Bayātī, poetry is what distinguishes him from others; it is the weapon he uses to kill the desolation around him, it is the love he waits for, and the fire that glows in his heart to keep him alive. It is born inside him, complete or incomplete, helping him spark "the fire of innovation" (line 11). It is this kind of poetry that the poet aspires to write. Al-Bayātī mentions that it is evil to be possessed by this love, poetry, and poetic inspiration, because the poet has to overcome his challenges and cling to life while waiting for something that comes and does not come. In addition, the poet also knows well that these challenges—along with his determination to write this kind of poetry, as he defines it—and "this closed door and barricade" distinguish him from the bit players, the other poets whose poetry is weeping. What also distinguishes al-Bayātī's poetry is his willingness to write his poetry with his blood. In the last line of this poem, he emphasizes that this cruel love writes the history of the soul with the blood of the poet. As the musician in the previous poem bled, lonely, on his violin to produce a distinguished piece of art that speaks of a universal suffering and misery, so the poet in this poem writes his poetry with blood. Lonely, he writes poetry that tells the history of the soul: its sufferings, misery, and dark happiness. In these two poems, the poet writes about the misery of the soul and the role of the poet in transforming this misery into a work of art that becomes part of history and a tool of innovation.

Al-Bayātī defines great poetry by associating it with innovation in language; the composition of each poem is the creation of a new language.[84] Innovation is measured not in introducing new forms in poetry, such as the classical, free verse, or the prose poem, but rather based on how creative the content is, surpassing the poet's selfish concerns to address and treat the immortal essence of humanity: misery and death.[85] Treating the universal anguish of the human psyche in an innovative language that continues to recreate itself transforms poetry into "a space vehicle surpassing time and place."[86] Only then is poetry liberated from the cells of political movements or personal concerns; it belongs to humanity, as it is its voice. Looking forward, for al-Bayātī, the fire of innovation that resists the universal, social, or political humiliation of humanity is the savior of Arabic poetry, something that is missing from the current poetic scene in the Arab world.[87] By carrying the fire of poetry for decades, pursuing innovation, and paying for it with his blood, al-Bayātī sets an example of the ideal commitment to Arabic poetry.

In this poem, al-Bayātī maintains that although his love for poetry challenges him at times, it also empowers and inspires him to innovate. This love lives within the poet and "the brutal jungles of the self" and crawls like a child in its attempts to inspire the poet and burn him in the fire of innovation. This burning is a rite of passage whereby fire transforms the poet and ignites life in him. For the poet, poetry is the desired balance between death and life, and to write he must die and be reborn. It is interesting how this poem presents poetic inspiration through a group of contradictory images. It is the disease that might kill the poet and also the medicine he needs to be cured. It is the love that he waits for and the evil that burns his heart while he waits for something that might never come. It is nameless and it has all the names, it comes and it does not come, it is both complete and amputated.

Mamlakat al-Sunbula is indeed rich in poems treating metapoetry. For example, in "Maqāṭiʿ min ʿAdhābāt Farīd al-Dīn al-ʿAṭṭār" (Fragments on the Suffering of Farid al-Din al-Attar), poetry becomes the sole reason for the poet to survive: "I shall not be defeated until I write the last verse of poetry, so let us drink in the blue vault of this night until the eternal night reaches us, and we sleep in the belly of the earth."[88] According to al-Bayātī, his ability or inability to write innovative poetry determines whether he is defeated or not. In other words, failing to write poetry means the poet's defeat and therefore death. In "Ḥajar al-Taḥawwul" (The Stone of Transformation), the poet explains why writing poetry is not only a challenge in this time but also a revolutionary act: "Poetry is disobedience / and happiness that is destined to struggle in all times."[89] In "Ru'yā fī Baḥr al-Balṭīq" (A Vision in the Baltic Sea), although the poet might die while fighting against injustice in his society, he will remain alive through his words: "The dictator dies and the poet remains."[90] In "Ḥajar al-Taḥawwul" al-Bayātī says, "In the name of the defeated, a conflict has just begun now,"[91] and "the rebels' prophets came from the fire of poetry."[92] Writing unique, innovative, and revolutionary poetry, al-Bayātī, as a prophet, challenges the poets and poetry of his time. In "Al-ʿArā'" (Wilderness), he addresses his poetry, which is ahead of its time: "You are knocking on the doors of the coming century, with words."[93] His poetry enables him to rise above the horizon and enjoy the taste of success and victory, though alone: "you taste victory alone / you rise above the horizon with the fire of poetry and you summon the ancestors' spirits."[94] Thus, al-Bayātī's poetic creativity enables him to rise above the horizon of his time and summon the ancestors' spirits to challenge his present and look for a better future: "Between the present and the myth / man challenges his fate."[95]

Al-Bayātī believes in humans' responsibility to challenge their fate and reject life as it is. He believes in his responsibility as a poet to revolt against his time and make his own myth/destiny. This is to say that al-Bayātī's poetry becomes universal and timeless when it treats issues that pertain to the struggle and aspirations of humankind through the eye of an ambitious poet. In so doing, he implores his readers to accept the same responsibility, rejecting the status quo and walking against the current until justice is served. No matter how and in which form, humankind should burn to be free. Likewise, poets should burn and bleed to write universal poetry, regardless of the form in which it is written. Innovation is the new form: it is the new poetic language that poets should knock on all doors to summon. The prose poem is another challenge al-Bayātī is willing to take on, under two conditions: first, that content should not be compromised on behalf of form, and second, that readers and critics realize that the prose poem is more challenging than the classical one. To write the classical poem well, the poet must know language and the science of rhyme and meter. To write the prose poem well, gift and innovation are the poet's only means to success, not knowledge.[96]

POETRY AND TERRORISM

Writing free verse with a new language, al-Bayātī breaks through the barriers of the traditional form and content of the poetry of his time and the traditional heritage he challenges and attacks. The final poem I discuss in this chapter is "Ta'ammulāt fī al-Wajh al-Ākhar lil-Ḥubb" (Meditations on the Other Face of Love).[97] This is one of the most revolutionary and key metapoetic poems in modern Arabic poetry. It is worth noting that this poem has been neither translated nor studied before, despite its great significance in the development of metapoetry in modern Arabic poetry and in al-Bayātī's oeuvre. In this poem, al-Bayātī treats five main overlapping themes. In lines 1–7 he treats the role of the poet in the twentieth century. In lines 8–20 he defines poetic language. In lines 21–32 he criticizes plagiarist poets and expresses the revolutionary and "terrorizing" role of the poet in society and language. In lines 33–37 he encourages poetry to fight against his frustrated tradition and literature, and in lines 38–60 he criticizes Arab literature, leaders, thought, poets, and readers.

What is interesting in this collection in general and in this poem in particular is the shift in al-Bayātī's vision of himself and his poetry. In most of the collections written before 1973, the poet sees himself as the awakener of his people whose goal is to remind them that it is their responsibility to fight against their societies' tyrants and enemies. In addition, he sees poetry as the most influential tool for treating political and social issues in Arab societies, and he links his success as a poet to the success of his poetry in a sociopolitical context. However, what we might term his "post-committed" poetry—the poetry written after 1973, especially that collected in *Mamlakat al-Sunbula*—focuses mainly on the overlapping and authoritative role of poetry and language not only in literature, but also in thought, civilization, and humanity. Appealing to the Arab audience and treating social and political subject matter in the Arab world are no longer his one and only purpose. Instead, he aspires to write poetry that raises the intellectual level and value of Arab literature and the Arab reader, as well as the universal man. Al-Bayātī creates his own kingdom in poetry and becomes the master of invention; neither the traditional conventions of language nor the limiting conditions of his life and society can stop him from excelling among his peers as one of the most influential pioneers of contemporary Arabic poetry. Thus, poetry becomes an innovative tool that uses language to contribute to the development of literature and break into a new level of poetics. It also enables the poet to critique other poets who, according to al-Bayātī, drag the Arabic literary movement backward.

Lines 1 to 7 of this free verse poem describe the poetry of the twentieth century:

تأملات في الوجه الآخر للحبّ

(1)
لا أكتب شعرا من ذاكرتي أو ذاكرة الموروث المحبط لكني
في حرب عصابات الشعر على الأعراف المحشوة قشا
والموت المجاني ، وراء المتراس دماً أنزف، مسكونا بقوى
الثورة و الكون المتغير، أصنع ذاكرة لوجود الانسان الغائب
و الحاضر. روحي مركبة ترحل نحو الداخل و الخارج باحثة
عن جوهر هذا الحب الثابت والمتحول في قاع الإبداع
التاريخي وفي بهو مرايا القرن العشرين.[98]

Meditations on the Other Face of Love

(1)
I do not write poetry from my memory or from the collective
memory of the confused heritage. But I bleed behind the barricade
in the guerrilla war of poetry against traditions that are stuffed with
straw and meaningless death. I am haunted by the forces of revolu-
tion and the changing universe. I create a memory for the existence
of the absent and present man. My soul is a vehicle that travels
within and without, looking for the essence of this stable and
transforming love in the depth of historic creativity and in the hall of
mirrors of the twentieth century.

Al-Bayātī underlines in this section the role of the poet and poetry in the war against traditions that limit creativity and cause poets to bleed to protect their poetry and their right to have sources of inspiration other than the collective heritage. The image of the poet fighting in the guerrilla war of poetry against tradition, and bleeding behind the barricade, speaks of the challenges the poet must overcome to write poetry that rises above the norm. Haunted by the forces of revolution and the changing universe, al-Bayātī expresses his role in society: he creates a memory for the absent and present man. Being creative in his poetry and refusing to be restrained by tradition, al-Bayātī is determined to look for "the essence of this stable and transforming love." The poet's soul becomes a vehicle looking for the essence of his love for poetry—poetic inspiration—in the twentieth century. In it he journeys both within himself and around the globe to glean the experience and motifs necessary to write poetry that transcends him and becomes his love.

What makes this love special and genuine is not only its "stable and transforming" form, but also its ability to carry the poet into the unknown to bring back creation, innovation, and transformation: the role of the poet, as he describes it. Al-Bayātī rejects proclaiming a specific form as the most fitting for poetic expression. Experimenting with subject matter, language, and style in his free verse, he continues to innovate. Breaking from the monorhymed and romantic lyrical poetry in the late 1950s, he declared a revolution in form and content in his poetry. In experimenting with new themes and subjects in free verse, al-Bayātī again breaks from the poetry of commitment to treat metapoetic as well as universal issues.

Lines 8 through 20 treat al-Bayātī's poetic language and what distinguishes it from other languages:

(1)
لغتي تخرج من معطف أبطال البشر الفانين
تسكنها صيحات سكارى و مجانين
ولدوا من اوجاع العصر الذري و طوفان حروب التحرير
جنوا في أقبية التعذيب
ماتوا في حرب الطبقات الشعبية مجهولين
حلّت فيهم روح الشهداء القديسين
في بهو مرايا القرن العشرين
تتسكع حاملة قنبلة بيد و بأخرى أوراق الريح
تخطف جلادا أو ملكا ديناصورا
تعدمه باسم قوانين التحرير
تسقط أزمنة شاخت وتقيم على أنقاض الأزمان جسور
اللغة الفعل النار النور
تعلن ميلاد الإنسان الشاعر في كوكبنا المهجور.[99]

(1)
My language comes from the coat of the vanished human heroes
It is haunted by the screams of the drunk and the mad
Who were born from the pains of the atomic age and
the floods of the liberation wars
They lost their sanity in the torture chambers
And perished, unknown, in the war of popular classes
The spirit of the martyred saints has alighted in them
In the hall of mirrors of the twentieth century,
My language wanders while carrying a bomb in one hand
and pages of the wind in the other
Kidnapping an executioner or a dinosaur king
To execute him in the name of liberation-war laws
It topples aging times and constructs bridges on their ruins
Language, deed, fire, light
Declare the birth of the man-poet on our abandoned planet.

In this section, al-Bayātī employs various images to explain why his language is different from other poetic languages. The essence of his language combines heroism, drunkenness, and the madness of humanity. It "comes from the coat of the vanished human heroes" as a spirit "haunted by the screams of the drunk and the mad," and thus it brings back to life the stories and pains of those who "lost their sanity in the torture chambers" and "perished, unknown, in the war of popular classes." Haunted by the stories of these people in whom "the spirit of the martyred saints has alighted," the poet's language transforms into a bomb capable of igniting a revolution. Melting heroism, madness, and holiness in one pot, the poet's language is capable of "kidnapping an executioner or a dinosaur king" and executing those in power "in the name of liberation-war laws." This language destroys obstacles to building bridges on the ruins of "aging times" and fights the war that started a long time ago and has not ended yet. The poet fights this battle with his own weapon: language that acquires its power from the memories and past pains of mankind and the aspirations and hopes of the future.

Al-Bayātī sees his post-committed poetry as a weapon against stagnation in language and literature as well as against universal malaise and injustice. This is a major transition that proves al-Bayātī to be one of the most prominent modern Arab poets. He refused to jeopardize the potential of his poetry after the recurring defeats of Arabs. He realized that if his poetry was to leave a mark on history, it should not continue to associate itself with regimes or transitory causes. He realized that although he continued to be concerned about the status quo of his country and nation, his best bet would be in writing timeless poetry. For poetry to be timeless and universal, it should explore new topics, treat new issues, and go where he never imagined it—or himself—going. Such journeys within and without equip him with the tools necessary for the revolution he anticipates in his poetry. Only then can he create his own poetic kingdom in which language is superior to everyone, including the poet. This language determines its rules and innovates in ways that distinguish the poet from his peers. Al-Bayātī mixes verbs with fire so his poetry becomes a weapon capable of enlightening his deserted and barren planet, which he opposes, and announcing "the birth of the man-poet." Acquiring its legacy from infinite human pain, poetry calls for a future revolution, starting with language itself.

Al-Bayātī is no longer content with the poet's role he advocated in the past: a romantic and then a socialist realist who utilized his poetry to support a regime or incite his people to fight against their social ills, that is, a committed poet. His awareness of the role his poetry fulfilled in the past empowers him to lead a revolution in his language and poetry. Language is what defines the poet, and as a result, poetry is what distinguishes the poet from others. "Others," for al-Bayātī, are poets who do not change and so neither does their poetry. He believes that for poetry to be successful and influential, it should be innovative, creative, and explosive, as if it is "carrying a bomb in one hand and pages of the wind in the other." Al-Bayātī's poetry has reached a stage in which change is inevitable, and for this change to take place, it has to begin within. For a poet such as al-Bayātī, the shift from politically committed to metapoetically inspired poetry requires a great deal of transformation in language.

Lines 21 to 32 present the poet's perspective on poetry and the revolutionary role of the poet:

(2)
فليستيقظ صنّاع الكلمات
ومغنّو الثورات

(3)
الثورة شعر و الشاعر إرهابي ضد اللامعنى واللامعقول

(4)
قانون جدلي يتحكم بالكلمات، فيفرغها من معناها أو
يملؤها ويجسد فيها طاقات لا حصر لها، يصبح من فرط
غناها هو إياها، يتحكم بالإنسان الشاعر، بالأرض
المجنونة و هي تدور.

(5)
الشاعر إرهابي ضاق به التعبير
يسكن عقل الثورة، مسكوناً بقوى التغيير
وبآلات التدمير

(6)
يسكن أحيانا في فخ خديعة أهواء الليل ويصبح بوقا أو طبلا
أجوف في ركب السلطان.[100]

(2)
Let the word makers
And the revolution singers awake!

(3)
Revolution is poetry, and the poet is a terrorist against the meaningless
and the absurd

(4)
A dialectical law controls words and empties them of their meanings
Or fills them with infinite powers. It merges into the words
because of their richness.
The poet controls man and the mad Earth
While it revolves.

(5)
The poet is a speechless terrorist
He is the mastermind of the revolution
He is haunted by the forces of change and the weapons
of destruction

(6)
He sometimes falls in the trap of the deluding whims of night
    and it becomes a trumpet or
A hollow drum in the procession of the sultan.

In lines 21–32, al-Bayātī continues to treat the unorthodox role of the poet. The poet distinguishes himself from other poets who are "word makers" and "revolution singers" and asks them to awaken and recognize how poetry can be revolutionary. The poet criticizes other poets and does not approve of their meaningless poetry. In other words, the poet identifies himself only with a specific kind of poetry and condemns the rest. He compares two types of poets: the singers of revolution and the terrorist rebels. While other poets make up words, sing, and let their poetry become part of "the procession of the sultan," al-Bayātī defends the rebel poet who is in control not only of the revolution, but also of language and words. Poetry becomes the revolution the poet leads with "the forces of change and the weapons of destruction." Thus armed, al-Bayātī calls for a new kind of revolution, a revolution in poetry and language in which the poet is the terrorist rebel and his innovative poetry is his weapon. For a poet to be a rebel, "it is in the essence of his rebellion to be unique and unpredictable in thought and language."[101] This is why al-Bayātī, at some point in his poetic career, found it best for his poetry to shy away from the traditional and predictable and to claim a new voice in his poetry. Upon arrival at this point in the poetic journey, he looks back on his work and decides to have his own identity and voice, even if it means rebelling against the poetic conventions of the time, national and social taste, and his own poetic trajectory.

In this section and the sections to follow, al-Bayātī conveys anger and violence in his language. Poetry becomes the revolution and the poet a terrorist against the meaningless and the absurd. He embraces the new mission he creates for poets such as himself and aims to write new poetry that empowers rather than disappoints. He associates poetry with control and power of man and earth, and he emphasizes the role of the poet in igniting revolutions. For al-Bayātī, in identifying himself with poets who are the rebels and masterminds of revolutions, terrorism becomes an act of bravery, at least in poetry. Terrorism acquires a new meaning in this poem as it empowers poet-rebels and equips them with the forces of change and weapons of destruction. When the poet refuses to become one of the sultan's singers or drummers, his language and poetry become his weapons of destruction. Here, al-Bayātī rejects the poetry of his time and calls for a revolution in thought and literature, and in the vision of society's future. He welcomes terrorism in poetry because peace has made poets into puppets. He knows that for poetry to acquire a better status and for poets to be more influential and memorable, some great change must first take place in society. Poets become speechless terrorists who deploy their loyal soldiers, words, against the absurd. Al-Bayātī's goal at this stage of his career is to preserve the Arabic language and thought. Language is the vehicle or instrument through which thought is carried, so if language is not preserved from decay, thought is not either. In the Arab world, poetry is one of the most powerful means to preserve language and advance thought. Al-Bayātī assumes the role of the man-poet who welcomes the transformation into a terrorist to protect his nation's thought, language, and literature. For al-Bayātī, it is necessary in the twentieth century to turn oneself into a rebel who fights against the stagnation of society. What is left are the pains of the poets and their poetry. Therefore, their seeds of revolution are worth their lives, for the seeds will come back to life when it rains. Although he is not sure when this rain will come, al-Bayātī knows it will rain one day, and that is what matters most to him.

Lines 33–37 depict the poet's journey with his poetry:

(7)
سيدتي، لم تؤمن، حتى الآن بأن الأرض تدور
وبانّا ذرات لا تفنى، سابحة في النور
نتعانق تحت نجوم الليل و في ضوء الشمس نموت
نترك ما تتركه الثورات المغدورة من نار وبذور
في رحم الأرض المحروث.[102]

(7)
My lady still does not believe that Earth revolves
And that we are eternal atoms swimming in light
We embrace beneath the stars and die in the sunlight
We leave what the betrayed revolutions left behind of fire and seeds
In the womb of the plowed land.

In this section, al-Bayātī and his beloved choose to leave ("deposit" or "plant") in the fertile land the fire and seeds that the revolution abandoned. Al-Bayātī's poetry, like the poet himself, refuses to be indoctrinated, even when it comes to believing in facts. He revolts against the norm and the scientific. The poet's land is plowed and ready for revolution, but the revolution was betrayed by the sultan's singers and word makers, who abandoned its seeds. Al-Bayātī is very angry and disappointed, but, believing in the power of poetry and seeing hope where others see none, the poet and his poetry refuse to accept the death of the revolution and plant their seeds and fire in the womb of the land. For al-Bayātī, poetry is the last remaining partner in his long-awaited revolution.

In the last section of this poem, al-Bayātī's language becomes more angry and violent in response to the challenges he described earlier:

(8)

أطلق، من خلف المتراس، عليك النار

يا طاووس المجتمع المتسلق، يا قاذورة عار

(9)

أنسف ذاكرة الانسان العربي المستلب المأخوذ

أنسف ذاكرة العبد المملوك

والموروث المحبط والملك الصعلوك

أنسف ذاكرة الشعراء المأجورين وذاكرة القرّاء المخدوعين

أنسف ذاكرة الثوار المرتدين

والعملاء المذعورين

(10)

الشاعر إرهابي ضد الإرهاب

يخرج من معطف ثوار التاريخ ويخرج من معطفه الثوار

(11)

أرمي قنبلة في قاعات لصوص الشعر وأحشو أفواه جواري

السلطان رمادا، أنزف خلف المتراس دما، أتوقف بين

كنوزي و شباب الارض الخالد محروما، فاستيقظ يا ألم

الحب، مددت إليك يدا أستعطي فملأت دياجيري بالبرق

Line numbers in margin: 40, 45, 50

الخاطف. لن يغشاني بعد اليوم نعاس أو نوم أو ينزع عني
أحد هذا الإكليل الشوكي، صليبي و أنا: فوق لصوص
الشعر المأجورين وفوق شعارات المرتدين. صعودا! يا ألم
الحب مددت إليك يدا، أستعطي، فملأت سلالي بثمار
الليل الذهبية، ها أنذا اجثو تحت سماء الوطن العربي المنهوب
وأرمي قنبلة في وجه ملوك البترول البدو. صعودا! فالشاعر
إرهابي مجنون يسكن عقل الثورة، مسكونا بقوى التغيير

(12)
العالم ساحة إرهاب للشعر، ومنزل حب للشاعر
في القرن العشرين.[103]

(8)
I open fire on you from behind the barricade,
Mounting peacock of society, O defiling shame

(9)
I blow up the memory of the deceived exploited Arab
I blow up the memory of the owned slave
And the frustrated heritage and the vile king
I blow up the memory of poets-for-hire and deceived readers
I blow up the memory of retreating rebels
And terrified agents

(10)
The poet is a terrorist against terrorism
He comes from the coat of the rebels of history, and the rebels
come from his coat

(11)
I blast a bomb in the hallways of the thieves of poetry
and I fill the sultan's slave girls'
Mouths with ashes. I bleed behind the barricade.
I stand deprived between my treasure and the youth of earth.
So, O pain of love,
Wake up. I extended my hand to you and begged you,

But you filled my darkness with a flash of lightning. I will not
sleep after today, and no one can deprive me of this crown
of thorns. My cross and I will rise above the thieves of poetry
and the slogans of the apostates. Ascending! O pain of love,
I extended my hand to you and begged you, but you filled
my baskets with the golden fruits
of night. Here I am, lying under the sky of the exploited
Arab world and
Blasting a bomb at the faces of the Bedouin oil kings.
Ascending! Thus, the poet
Is a mad terrorist and a mastermind of the revolution,
who is haunted by the forces of change.

(12)
The world is an arena of terror for poetry and a loving home
for the poet
In the twentieth century.

Lines 38–60 boldly voice al-Bayātī's violent anger with Arab society, the Arab people, their heritage, and the current status of their literature. This section of the poem represents the poet's response to the challenges poets like him encounter in the Arab world. Al-Bayātī blasts his society, Arab kings, Arab heritage, plagiarist poets and thieves of poetry, deceived readers, retreating rebels, terrified agents, the sultan's slave girls, and the Bedouin oil kings. Interestingly, the emphasis on poetry is key in this section. The poet attacks the backwardness of the Arab world and its poetry in the second half of the twentieth century. Although he treats metapoetic concerns throughout the poem, he treats them best in this section. Here he no longer blames Arabs for not fighting against their regimes or against their enemies. He criticizes their backwardness, its negative impact on Arab intellectualism, and the stagnation of Arabic literature/poetry. In so doing he becomes a critic warning of a fall in literature and the failure of culture and civilization in the modern Arab world. The absence of a constructive, philosophical future vision—beyond seeing reform only as a small group of politicians fighting oppression—is the sole reason for the death of revolutions and of poetry.[104] Reform in poetry, he claims, should call for a universal revolution on all levels: social, economic, political, spiritual, literary, and so on. Only then can poetry become a means of living a noble life, rather than bringing about only short-lived change.

In this section, al-Bayātī draws a complete image of the state of poetry in the Arab world and treats the causes of its degradation. These causes fall into three categories: society and heritage; poets and readers; and kings, slave girls, agents, and rebels. The relationship between these three categories lies mainly in their shared responsibility for and negative impact on the development of poetry. Al-Bayātī "blows up" factors from the past, present, and future that have contributed to his poetic anxieties and challenges. All these factors terrorize the poet and prohibit him from being innovative, creative, original, and artistic. Thus "haunted by the forces of change," the poet opens fire on his society, bleeds, and becomes the mastermind of a revolution unlike other revolutions, a revolution for poetry in the twentieth century.

It is worth noting that combining tenses (paralyzing factors from past, present, and future) in this section adds another dimension to the metapoetic concerns and themes the poet treats in this poem. Claiming to blow up the memory of the frustrated Arab heritage, society, and man, al-Bayātī brings change to the way poetry is written and received in the Arab world. He rejects the past and its frustrated memories, which chained the Arab psyche and prohibited poets from being original and innovative in their poetry. In his fight against blind allegiance to the old tradition and heritage, al-Bayātī boldly presents us with his revolution.

In addition to blowing up Arab heritage and enslaved mentality, al-Bayātī blasts Arab poets and readers. He places great emphasis on the challenges plagiarist poets and deceived readers create for poets such as himself. In his struggle against the degradation and decline of the role, quality, and value of poetry in the Arab world, the poet confronts poets who are neither original nor honest. These plagiarists and paid-for-hire poets either steal other poets' poetry or write poetry to please their kings. Al-Bayātī insists on fighting them, blasting "a bomb in the hallways of the thieves of poetry." In addition, he attacks readers who cannot distinguish between original and plagiarized poetry due to their illiteracy and ignorance. Together, these poets and readers make the poet's mission to be original and innovative a difficult, if not impossible, one.

To further complicate the matter, al-Bayātī adds a third category to his metapoetic battle: the retreating rebels, the terrified agents, the vile kings, the sultan's slave girls, and the Bedouin oil kings. This category combines elements that overlap in the past, present, and future. The agents and rebels come from the Arab past to drag the poet down and challenge his ability to write beyond what has already been written in the history of Arab poetry. Blowing up this memory, the poet breaks the chains that bind him to writing about the past. The poet blows up the haunting memories of Arab kings and the slave girls they hired or owned to sing their praises in poetry. Filling the mouths of these slave girls with ashes, the poet announces the end of the poems, songs, and degrading practices that are still common in the Arab world. Al-Bayātī then blasts a bomb in the faces of the Bedouin oil kings for exploiting the Arab world, indicating his present and future worries and concerns. He accuses the kings of the Arabian Gulf, too, of exploiting poets to write poetry and slave girls to sing their praises. Al-Bayātī despises this practice and calls for a revolution against tradition. He bombs these people and becomes the mad terrorist and the mastermind of the revolution. His revolution promises terror for everything and everyone contributing to the death of civilization. Al-Bayātī maintains that "the Arab world today is plagued with polluted culture and environment, which results in defected art prohibiting it from cultural innovation."[105] He asserts that "this applies to innovation in poetry because when poetry loses its cultural dimension, it becomes inhumane," leading to the creation of individuals "who lack responsibility or commitment towards anything and everything."[106] This is the problem of our time, al-Bayātī affirms, because instead of creating a conscious, intellectual generation, poetry today is creating a generation of consumers and rebels with "no cause," "no mission," and "nothing to give back to society."[107] Therefore, to contribute to the literary canon, and to rescue Arab civilization, culture, poetry, and people, we need a Christlike poet, who understands the complexity of his mission and is willing to risk his life for it.

Ascending, the poet announces himself the Christ of Arab poetry and insists that he and his cross "will rise above the thieves of poetry and the slogans of the apostates." Thus, he welcomes the pains of his cross (love, poetry), as Christ welcomed his pains. It is worth noting that this

Tammūzī element appeared, al-Sayyāb–like, in some of al-Bayātī's earlier poems, but only here does it appear in this very angry and violent context. Al-Bayātī concludes the poem with a sense of the contradictory life of Arab poets in the twentieth century: the world becomes "an arena of terror for poetry" and at the same time "a loving home for the poet." Thus, welcoming the pains of poetry and haunted by the forces of change, the poet finds some sense of direction and purpose and makes himself a loving home in an arena of terror in the world. This home is not a traditional home, one that keeps the poet safe and warm. On the contrary, this home is in the middle of an arena of terror that does not welcome the poet or even recognize his existence. Al-Bayātī welcomes this challenge and makes himself a home amid chaos and danger. He is a rebel who does not accept life as is: he sees change as an inevitable force in life. It is worth noting that in this poem, al-Bayātī praises the poet who stands against the current and fights for his pursuit, even if his world turns into "an arena of terror for poetry." Only this kind of poet will succeed in building a loving home in this arena of terror. Only then will the poet defeat the revolution singers and word makers and rise with his poetry above all. In so doing, al-Bayātī hopes, the fire of his poetry and the seeds he and it planted in the womb of the plowed land will revolt, with the help of the Arab reader.

This poem presents to us the transformation in the works of al-Bayātī from commitment to metapoetry at its best. Instead of following the established tradition of writing poetry on politics or *iltizām*, using the language and diction of that era, al-Bayātī leads his own revolution in poetry and literature. He calls for a new kind of poetry that is written neither to imitate nor to entertain. He treats themes concerned with the status of Arabic poetry, culture, and future, stressing the impact of readers on the development of Arabic poetry and holding the reader responsible for the level Arabic language and poetry have reached. Poets cannot improve their poetry alone because they need readers and critics to play a constructive role in this process. This transformation in his own perception of his poetic voice and role as a poet paves the way for new experiments in language and an opportunity for the poet to highlight the ongoing challenges and anxieties modern Arab poets must overcome. Finally, calling for change and innovation, al-Bayātī welcomes and invites the next generation of poets to explore other venues in poetry. Al-Bayātī experiments with poetry, themes, and styles and calls for a revolution in which other Arab poets will explore, innovate, and contribute to their poetic heritage, even if it means becoming rebels and terrorists against the meaningless and the absurd.

A great poet's mission and profession are meant to be neither easy nor conventional. Al-Bayātī carries inside his chest a reckless adventurous heart that wants to go the extra mile, knowing that the rewards are limitless and timeless. In this collection, al-Bayātī succeeds in his attempts "to resist death and defeat it by adding a new human value to poetry and its role, and to man and his role in history."[108] Such attempts are al-Bayātī's answer to Klemm's earlier question of how "literary writing could be significant in the present world." Al-Bayātī states that it is through artistic creativity that we are able to defeat death and time, guaranteeing the artist immortality.[109] Therefore, al-Bayātī's vision of writing significant poetry involves adding a new human value to his work, highlighting the human value in humankind and its role in history, bringing about justice and love for all. Although al-Bayātī does not claim to have realized such a vision, his constant creative search for "the secret of language" and the ways in which humans find salvation and advance their cause do indeed grant him immortality.

In the previous three representative poems and in his late works, al-Bayātī's poetics witness a transformation: man is present in language, which becomes "a living creature, having what the human, river and nature has of life, full of people, happiness, sadness, rebellion and exile."[110] Al-Bayātī's literary liberation from *iltizām* in its traditional sense sets him and his poetry free. Furthermore, it distinguishes him from other poets who failed to reinvent their art and come back with new voices after the disappointment of the 1967 defeat, which was a wake-up call for all Arabs.

Love and death are forever present in al-Bayātī's poetry. He succeeds as a poet when he invokes salvation and immortality in people through love. When earthly love is connected to that of the divine, it becomes the essence of existence, and it neither dies nor changes.[111] Therefore, humans are able to rebel against the status quo and blind tradition, fearing nothing and no one because "death is a tunnel or a cave to reach farther lands, not an end."[112] In becoming an unconventional Sufi mystic who seeks the kingdom of God and humankind on Earth rather than in the hereafter, al-Bayātī announces he has found salvation in "forgoing all kinds of malaise and evil and uniting with the spirit of the world and the music of the universe, which is present in the poem, and which makes the poem a creature swimming by the name of truth, freedom, justice, and the greatest love."[113] To resist malaise and evil, humankind should revolt and welcome death: the tunnel to truth, freedom, justice, and love. This is not to say that al-Bayātī stops writing poetry committed to his people; rather, he continues to be conscious of his duty as a poet to his people and culture. However, he focuses on writing poetry about poetry and the challenges poets face in the twentieth century. His voice becomes that of a universal rebel who writes not only to express reality or reflect it, as we see in his commitment stage, but to treat reality as he would want it to be. He becomes a visionary whose voice carries the pains and aspirations of his fellow humans, and poets. He becomes more concerned with innovation and creativity in language, which takes on a new role in his later works. Language becomes the poet's means to rejuvenate culture, history, literature, and thought.

Among the many other poems in *Mamlakat al-Sunbula* that treat metapoetic concerns are "Nār al-Shiʿr" (The Fire of Poetry), "Al-Nuqqād al-Adʿiyā'" (Dishonest Critics), "Al-Mughannī al-Aʿmā" (The Blind Singer), "Al-Shahīd" (The Martyr), "Ilā Buthaynā Aliksāndrā" (To Buthaynā Aliksandra), "Al-Shāʿir" (The Poet), "Al-Qaṣīdā" (The Poem), "Ilā Bashshār Kamāl" (To Bashshar Kamal), and "Bukā'iyya ilā Shāhīn" (Lament to Chahin). Other metapoetic elements can be explored in al-Bayātī's last two collections as well, *Bustān ʿĀ'isha* (Aisha's Orchard) and *Al-Baḥr Baʿīd Asmaʿuh Yatanahhad* (The Sea Is Distant, I Hear It Sighing). As we have seen in this collection, al-Bayātī successfully and skillfully shifts his poetics from *iltizām* to metapoetry. Influenced by the commitment of the 1950s, like most Arab poets, he was inspired by key political events in the Arab world in the 1950s to late 1960s. During this period, he wrote poems and collections dedicated to Arab leaders such as Nasser, notions such as the project of Arab nationalism, Arab wars such as the 1967 war, and major issues including the question of Palestine. However, after the 1967 defeat, al-Bayātī began questioning his allegiance to the Nasserist regime, his faith in his Arab audience, and his poetic legacy. He then started experimenting with new topics and issues and looking for sources of inspiration other than political changes and events. After a period of self-doubt and questioning, al-Bayātī announced a new trend in his poetry. This turning point in his poetics inspired him to regain his powerful poetic voice and recreate his poetic kingdom.

Like a phoenix, al-Bayātī resurrects himself from the ashes of the past and excels among his peers through his innovative use of language and employment of myths and masks. In so doing, he preserves language and poetry and inspires his audience, becoming concerned mainly with metapoetry and the struggle of humankind. He moves from the personal to the universal, and his poetry shifts from simple, direct, and spontaneous to objective, meditated, and sophisticated. He announces the new role of the modern Arab poet as a terrorist who fears nothing and no one. This terrorist's mission is to terrorize those who terrorize him and the oppressed human being. Therefore, he uses his forever evolving poetic creativity to rebel against the meaningless and the absurd in all aspects of human life. His poetry becomes a universal vehicle that derives its power and regenerative energy from love against malaise and evil. His poetry treats the national as well as the universal. It transforms from the echoes of the crushed individuals' voices of rejection and rebellion. This rebellion is an ideology in itself; he is looking for the seeds of rejection and rebellion in the human psyche. Whether it is rejecting oppression and rebelling against it, or rejecting the culture of defeated poets and poetry, he is advocating for a revolution and innovation in language. Language is the vehicle of history, civilization, culture, thought, literature, and humanity. It constructs or destroys.

Al-Bayātī understands well the value and role of language not only in literature, but also in civilization and thought. Therefore, he revolutionizes his poetic language, which creates a loving home for himself in an arena of terror for poetry and humanity. He is at home and in love when his poetic language refuses to submit to terrorism. He reverts the acts of terrorism against humanity and poets by becoming himself a terrorist. He is not afraid of being called a terrorist because such a term empowers him: in calling himself a terrorist it is as if he is saying that people, including poets, should not accept being enslaved, and if it is necessary to do so, they should turn into terrorists. Terrorizing those in power, or those who corrupt and pollute societies, cultures, thought, and literature and destroy nations is a noble cause for which to die. Al-Bayātī does not claim to be a reformist, but his poetry thrives to resurrect the creative, rebellious spirit in people, to see their anguish and decades of misery as an inspiration to contribute to civilization instead of being passive-aggressive citizens. Likewise, he sets an example to poets to contribute to the literary canon by being innovative, nonconventional writers who guard the legacy of their language and write poetry that fears none.

Every poem in al-Bayātī's later works, especially in *Mamlakat al-Sunbula* and *Bustān ʿĀ'isha*, has its unique language and realm. Al-Bayātī exemplifies the poets in the modern Arab world of the twentieth century who refused to be defeated after political defeats on the ground. Another poet who belongs to this group is Qāsim Ḥaddād (b. 1948), a Bahraini poet whose poetic transformation from commitment to metapoetry is similar to that of al-Bayātī. They rise after such defeats and look for victory in unique places such as poetry itself. We shall see in the next chapter how the poetry of other poets, such as Ḥijāzī, witnesses a different transformation despite belonging to the same 1960s generation.

CHAPTER 3

From *Iltizām* to the Arab Uprising

Aḥmad ʿAbd al-Muʿṭī Ḥijāzī

Aḥmad ʿAbd al-Muʿṭī Ḥijāzī was born in the village of Ṭala in al-Manūfiya, Egypt, in 1935. His family was one of the middle-class peasant families in the Egyptian countryside, where he was educated and brought up. When he was eighteen years old, in 1953, he wrote his first poem, "Bukāʾ al-Abad" (Weeping of Eternity), which was published in *Al-Risāla al-Jadīda* (The New Message) in 1955.[1] He graduated with a diploma from the Teachers College in Cairo in 1955 and moved in the same year to France. The next year, he returned to Egypt to edit the magazine *Ṣabaḥ el-Khayr* (Good Morning). In 1965 he became the editorial director of the political magazine *Rose al-Yūsuf* in Cairo. His first collection, *Madīna bilā Qalb* (A City without a Heart, 1959), was published in Beirut, and his second collection, *Awrās* (Aurès, 1959), was published in Damascus. These two collections reflect his experience in Cairo and what it meant for him to live in a big city.

In 1965, two years before the 1967 Arab–Israeli war, his third collection, *Lam Yabqā illā al-Iʿtirāf* (Nothing Remains but Confession), was published in Beirut. In 1972 Ḥijāzī published his fourth collection, *Marthiyat al-ʿUmr al-Jamīl* (Elegy of the Beautiful Life), also in Beirut. In late September 1973, two weeks before the October Arab–Israeli war, Ḥijāzī, along with other intellectuals who opposed the government of Anwar al-Sadat, was fired from his job as a journalist for *Rose al-Yūsuf*, and he left Cairo for Paris in 1974. He taught Arabic literature at the University of Vincennes in Saint-Denis and obtained a degree in anthropology from the Université de la Sorbonne Nouvelle in 1978. He also published his fifth and sixth collections, *Kā'ināt Mamlakat al-Layl* (Creatures of the Night Kingdom, 1978) in Beirut and *Ashjār al-Ismint* (Cement Trees, 1989) in Cairo, before leaving France in 1990.

Ḥijāzī wrote and published only a few poems after the publication of *Ashjār al-Ismint*. After his return to Cairo, he was appointed to *Al-Ahrām Weekly* and then to *Al-Maṣrī Al-Yawm* (The Egyptian Today), where he continues to write a weekly column. Ḥijāzī did not publish any poetry collections in the next twenty-two years; his next and most recent collection, *Ṭalal al-Waqt* (The Standing Ruins of Time), was published in Cairo in 2011. Ḥijāzī has written twenty-five books in prose as well, and his poetry has been translated into many languages, including English, Spanish, Russian, and French. He has received many awards, among them the African Poetry Award in 1995, the Egyptian State Incentive Award in 1996, and the ʿUwais Award in 1997. Ḥijāzī is a permanent member of the Egyptian High Council for Culture and director of the House of Poetry.

In this chapter, I examine the impact of key political events and ideologies on Ḥijāzī's poetry, from his early works to his latest collection. Although Ḥijāzī's poetry, like that of al-Bayātī, is highly involved with *iltizām* in the 1950s and 1960s, it undergoes a gradual transformation, mainly in content, becoming the voice of the people against tyrannical regimes. His voice becomes critical rather than emotional, especially after it is resurrected by the Arab Uprising in 2011, after over twenty years of absence, announcing a new kind of *iltizām*.

THE NASSERIST

In his first collection, *Madīna bilā Qalb* (A City without a Heart), Ḥijāzī expresses his feelings of loss and alienation in Cairo and his experiences as an individual longing for his village after he moved to the city for work and education. The migration from the countryside to the city was one of the greatest social phenomena in Egypt and most of the world in the twentieth century. Ḥijāzī's account of his life in the countryside, in his second collection, *Awrās*, as well as in *Madīna bilā Qalb*, is romantic. Although in these two collections Ḥijāzī focuses on personal experiences and notions of alienation and disconnect between him and the city, he treats topics of political and national interest as well. Published in *Madīna bilā Qalb*, "ʿAbd al-Nāṣir" (Nasser) and "Suriyā wa-al-Riyāḥ" (Syria and the Winds) are examples of the poet's involvement with *iltizām*. "Al-Majd lil-Kalima" (Glory to the Word) is an example of committed poetry in *Awrās.* On one level, while he was writing and publishing these two collections, Ḥijāzī was familiarizing himself with modern urban life in Cairo. On another level, he was witnessing the rise of a national political symbol, Nasser, and the political union between Syria and Egypt, the United Arab Republic (UAR). These two collections represent Ḥijāzī's poetry in the 1950s and reflect "his strong tendencies for socialist change and justice."[2]

Ḥijāzī voiced his support for Nasser in the 1950s in free verse poems such as "ʿAbd al-Nāṣir."[3] This poem is an example of Ḥijāzī's involvement with *iltizām* and Nasser as the embodiment of Arab nationalism. Its tone is not short of hero worship:

عبد الناصر

[. . .]
فلتكتبوا يا شعراء أنني هنا
أشاهد الزعيم يجمع العرب
ويهتف "الحرية .. العدالة .. السلام"
فلتلمع الدموع في مقاطع الكلام
وتختفي وراءه الحوائط الحجر
[. . .]
لِيظهر الإنسان فوق قمة المكان
ويَفتح الكوى لصبحنا
يا شعراء يا مؤرخي الزمان
فلتكتبوا عن شاعر كان هنا
في عهد عبد الناصر العظيم.[4]

Nasser

[. . .]
Poets, write that I am here
Watching the leader gather the Arabs
And calling out "Freedom, Justice, Peace"
And let tears sparkle in the syllables of speech
While the stone walls disappear behind them
[. . .]
So that mankind becomes his priority
And he opens the windows for our morning.
O poets, historians of the time,
Write about a poet who was here
In the era of Nasser, the great.

In this poem, Ḥijāzī focuses on two main ideas: his support for Nasser and the relationship between politics and poetry. Ḥijāzī has admitted that he used "to be enthusiastic about Nasser despite being aware of the injustice and corruption in his time."[5] This is indeed one of the problems of the 1960s generation: they wrote *iltizām* poetry, which was spontaneous and emotional instead of critical. This poem is ardently and uncritically pro-Nasserist. As leader of the UAR (1958–1961), Nasser becomes the nationalist leader who leaves his mark on history. Ḥijāzī not only sees Nasser as a hero, but also links his own success as a poet to him, like al-Bayātī in his committed phase. The significance of his poetry stems from its relation to Nasser. In the last section of this poem, Ḥijāzī asks his fellow poets, whom he calls the historians of time, to write that he is here watching Nasser unite the Arabs, calling out "Freedom, Justice, Peace." In addition, he asks them to write about a poet, himself, who lived in the era of the great Nasser. Ḥijāzī here maintains that when Nasser, the embodiment of revolution, succeeds, poetry succeeds, and when Nasser or the revolution fails, poetry is broken, alienated, and lost.[6] It is as if Ḥijāzī's legacy as a poet relies on that of Nasser. In this collection in general and this poem in particular, Ḥijāzī praises Nasser and gives value to his poetry by identifying it with Nasser and his accomplishments. Highlighting Nasser's role in bringing change to the nation, Ḥijāzī uses poetry as a political tool to infuse his ideal image of Nasser into the public opinion.

In the free verse poem “Sūriyā wa-al-Riyāḥ” (Syria and the Winds), Ḥijāzī celebrates Nasser and Egypt’s union with Syria:

سوريا و الرياح

[. . .]
ما أروع الإصرار!
ما أروع النزال حينما يفر الآخرون
ولا يظل غير الفارس وحيد
من خلفه الأطفال ، والأحلام ، والبيوت
تلوح من بعيد
تموت لو. . ...يموت!
ووقتها كل الحياة تنتفض
[. . .]
يا فارس الشمال
يا قلب سورية
أنت الذي بقيت في المجال
فاسبح عليه إن اتسع
املأ مكان من وقع
واسبح على كل الجهات
إن العروبة انتقتك ، عمدتك فارسا لها
فاحرس شطوطها الطوال
من غزوة الريح البدائية.[7]

Syria and the Winds

[. . .]
How wonderful determination is!
How wonderful fighting is when others flee
And no one remains but the lone knight
Behind whom are children, dreams, and homes
Waving from afar
They die if he dies!
And then, all of life upraises
[. . .]
O knight of the north
O Syria’s heart
You are the one who remained on the battlefield

So, swim to it, if there is enough space
Fill the space of him who fell
And swim in all directions
Arabism chose you and baptized you its knight
So, guard its long shores
From the attack of the primitive wind.

In lines 18–24, Ḥijāzī treats Nasser as the national leader upon whose shoulders rests the responsibility for guarding Egypt, Syria, and all the shores of the Arab world. Ḥijāzī portrays Nasser as standing alone on the battlefield, determined to fight when others—the other Arab leaders—flee the scene. Nasser fills the empty places they have left and fights like a lone knight to protect children, dreams, and homes. The entire nation places its trust and faith in the knight of the north, whose death means the nation's death, and whose revolution means the nation's revolution and uprising. In lines 38–46, Ḥijāzī calls Nasser the heart of Syria and the last remaining hope on the battlefield. Thus, he asks Nasser to swim across the battlefield, as if it has become a sea, and fill the spaces of those who fell, a reference to Nasser's ability to lead the Arabs and fix the mistakes of their failing leaders. Ḥijāzī asks Nasser to swim in all directions, for Arabism has chosen and baptized him as its knight, in whom Arabs see their salvation. Thus, he is responsible for guarding their shores from any attacks.

In this poem Ḥijāzī places his ultimate faith in Nasser. As Ḥijāzī himself puts it, "Nasser, as a revolution and a man, was an ideal subject for the new poetry. An ideal subject but not a traditional one. . . . The new poetry treated Nasser as a dream and a companion."[8] In this poem, Nasser becomes the dream of a nation waiting for salvation and change. In a time of political crisis and formation of national identity, Arab poets and people needed an ideal leader to lead them to a better future, uniting and guarding them from the assaults of outsiders. Thus, according to Ḥijāzī, Nasser became not only the dream but also the companion of every Arab citizen. Ḥijāzī idealizes Nasser and does not criticize him or his regime in any way. Although he treats political themes in this collection, his voice remains direct, emotional, and wholeheartedly supportive of all that Nasser stands for.

Published in the same year as *Madīna bilā Qalb* was *Awrās*, a short collection of nine poems.[9] It is named after the Aurès, an Algerian mountain range, which becomes Ḥijāzī's muse and poetic inspiration in his poem "Awrās."[10] This collection is an extension of *Madīna bilā Qalb* in its themes and subject matter, treating themes of alienation in the city and longing for the countryside, and the role of creative writing in politics. This collection emphasizes the urgent need for a revolution, led by Nasser, in the Arab world. The choice of title is not arbitrary. The Algerian revolution for independence from France in 1954 began in the Aurès Mountains. This title poem is about revolution and freedom.

In "Al-Majd lil-Kalima" (Glory to the Word),[11] one of the key poems in the collection, Ḥijāzī treats the role of language, writing, and poetry in politics and society:

المجد للكلمة

[. . .]
شكراً للمطبعة الصماء
يدها البكماء
تكتب الفاظاً تتكلم
تصرخ ، تتنهد ، تتألم
تبقى
لا تطمسها الظلمه
تجمعنا نسجد للكلمه
الكلمة طير
عصفور حر
و الكلمة سحر
أربعة حروف صادقة النبرة
حاء
راء
ياء
هاء
تشعل ثوره
[. . .]
يا شعراء!
يا كتّاب!

يا حراس الكلمه
قولوا: المجد لها
حارسة الوحدة.[12]

Glory to the Word

[. . .]
Thanks to the deaf printing press
Its mute hand
Writes words that speak
Scream, sigh, and feel pain
They remain
Unerased by darkness
It makes us bow down to the word
The word is a bird
A free bird
And the word is magic
Four letters ring true:
Ḥ
R
Y
H
They ignite a revolution
[. . .]
O poets!
O writers!
O guards of the word
Say: "Glory to her"
The guardian of unity.

In this poem, Ḥijāzī celebrates the power of the written word and the role of the printing press in politics. He praises the printing press and maintains that although the printing press is deaf and its machines are mute, it writes words. Here Ḥijāzī highlights the role of literature in politics and society and employs images that express his faith in the power of the written word. In lines 6–7 the written word becomes a human being that speaks, screams, sighs, and feels pain. In lines 8–9 it becomes an eternal force that cannot be demolished or destroyed by darkness. In lines 10–11 the written word becomes a god to whom the poet and his people bow down. In lines 12–13 the written word becomes a free bird and magic. The personification of the word at the beginning of the poem and the attribution of divine power and magic to it in the middle make it a creature of supernatural power that can be a human, a bird, or a god. In lines 14–19 Ḥijāzī explains the magical power of the word by listing the letters of the word *Ḥurriyya* (freedom). These four letters ring true and ignite a revolution. Thus, for Ḥijāzī, writing, especially poetry, is what will ignite a revolution leading to freedom.

In the last six lines of this poem, Ḥijāzī asks his fellow poets and writers, whom he calls the guards of the word, to realize the power of the written word as the guardian of Arab nationalism and the uniting force of Arabs. In "Nasser," discussed above, Ḥijāzī calls poets the historians of time, which attests to his stance on the role of poetry in politics and society. As the historians of time, Arab poets are capable of directing history and, more importantly, of making history by inciting revolutions. In this poem, Ḥijāzī refers to the writers' and poets' political influence and to their ability to "strike a chord" in the hearts of the people, thereby inciting revolutions and promoting the cause of *al-adab al-multazim* (committed literature).

Despite the poet's experimentation with free verse form in this collection, Ḥijāzī's tone remains direct and his diction simple.[13] Only one poem is written in the classical form: "Ilā al-Ustādh al-ʿAqqād" (To al-Aqqad).[14] The poet's choice to write this poem in the classical form is quite deliberate. ʿAbbās Mahmūd al-ʿAqqād (1889–1964) wrote prose and poetry and was a major critic and thinker in Egypt. He considered poetry written in the free verse form to be prose.[15] Al-ʿAqqād's opposition to the free verse movement was not new. He had also opposed the participation of free verse poets in the poetry festival held in Damascus in 1961. Ḥijāzī wrote "Ilā al-Ustādh al-ʿAqqād" to criticize al-ʿAqqād for failing to understand and appreciate the employment of free verse in modern Arabic poetry. Ḥijāzī wrote this poem in the classical form to prove to al-ʿAqqād and his supporters that he writes in free verse not because he is incapable of writing in the classical form, but by choice. Ḥijāzī believed this new poetry freed the poets of the 1950s from the limitations in both form and content of classical Arabic poetry. The free verse school celebrated language as a means of creation, and so did Ḥijāzī.[16]

Ḥijāzī also mentioned, in his essay collection *Al-Shiʿr Rafīqī*, that the new poetry, free verse poetry, "rebelled against the institutions of our old society, which created misery in our spiritual and material life."[17] He joined the new poetry school, wrote free verse poetry, and defended its flexible form as suitable for issues of modern life and society. He departed further from tradition by writing about politics, nationalism, and Nasser. Ḥijāzī said in 1959, "I have found in the idea of Arab nationalism an embodiment of the spirit of the people, as well as my own personal salvation from a violent intellectual crisis which nearly drove me to a psychological breakdown."[18] Ḥijāzī needed Arab nationalism to inspire him to write poetry, and poets such as Ḥijāzī tried to shape Arab nationalism and guard a much-needed revolution in the Arab world by writing committed poetry. The new form and new content in his poetry went hand in hand.

In 1965 Ḥijāzī published his collection *Lam Yabqā illā al-Iʿtirāf* (Nothing Remains but Confession) to confess to his fellow Arab citizens that they had been defeated and humiliated on many occasions and their only remaining haven lay in following Nasser and supporting his project of Arab nationalism. In this collection Ḥijāzī praises Nasser and the Arab Socialist Party, in which he "hoped to find the answer to problems of urban life," as well as political and national problems, and weeps for the collapse of the United Arab Republic.[19] The title of one poem in this collection, "Al-Baṭal" (The Hero), is followed by a dedication to Nasser. In "ʿAbd al-Nāṣir 2" (Nasser 2) Ḥijāzī again praises Nasser's nationalism, modesty, and heroism.[20] (It is also a sequel to "ʿAbd al-Nāṣir" in the previous collection, *Madīna bilā Qalb*.)[21] In "The Sad October," Ḥijāzī reminds the Egyptians of the 1956 Tripartite Aggression against Egypt over the Suez Canal and demands that they follow Nasser to redeem themselves because he is "the only one who has not forgotten that attack."[22] Other poems, such as "Ughniya li-Ḥizb Siyāsī" (Song for a Political Party), "Tammūz" (Tammuz/July), and "Rithā' ilā al-Mālkī" (Elegy to al-Malki), are committed to Nasser and Arab nationalism. In this collection Ḥijāzī also treats issues of a romantic nature in such poems as "Hadiyyat ʿĪd al-Mīlād" (The Birthday Present), "Nughannī fī al-Ṭarīq" (We

Sing along the Way), "Romantīkiyya" (Romanticism), "Al-Mawt Faj'ah" (Sudden Death), and "Lā Aḥad" (No One).

In "Ughniya li-Ḥizb Siyāsī" (A Song to a Political Party) Ḥijāzī addresses the Arab Socialist Union.[23] Ḥijāzī delivers it as a political address, which makes it hard to distinguish between the voice of the "poet" and his "speaker." In the first and second stanzas, Ḥijāzī addresses the party: "O refuge, O poor peasants," and "O country of the alienated workers."[24] He asks the socialist party to be his family because he does not have one. He also asks it to be his capital city because since he left the green country—the Egyptian countryside of his childhood—he has no homeland. Thus, according to Ḥijāzī, he finds his lost homeland by joining the Socialist Union. In the third stanza, Ḥijāzī asks the Socialist Union to become the epic poem that he narrates to the modest people, so he may do heroic things with them such as riding horses, liberating cities of love, and setting prisoners free. In the fourth stanza, Ḥijāzī asks the party to become his sword, horse, and song, promising that he will ride the horse, defend himself with the sword, and sing for freedom if "they" appeared at night, calling the names of these opposing the union to be punished and carrying poets to death. This "they" refers to those opposing the Arab Socialist Union and the poets who sing the union's songs of revolution. Ḥijāzī asks the union to be his savior and refuge. In the last stanza, he calls upon the country's nationalists to hold their heads high because "the flag of the country is handed to them now." In this poem, Ḥijāzī supports the Arab Socialist Union, which he sees as a refuge for the poor, a homeland for the alienated, and a savior for the poets.

Unlike the rest of the poems in *Lam Yabqā illā al-I'tirāf*, "Tammūz" (Tammuz) and "Rithā' ilā al-Mālkī" (Elegy to al-Malki) are not written exclusively in free verse form. "Tammūz" is written in classical monorhyme and meter, applying the rules of the classical form, and "Rithā' ilā al-Mālkī" employs both classical and free verse forms. "Tammūz" treats the poet's love for his beloved, his longing for life in the countryside, and his faith in the UAR.[25] The poem was written in September 1961, the same month that the union between Syria and Egypt collapsed.[26] In this poem, Ḥijāzī draws on the ancient Near Eastern myth of Tammūz, a symbol of rebirth and resurrection in modern Arabic poetry, which is also the name of the month of July in the Syriac and Mashriqi Arabic calendars. Ḥijāzī's choice of Tammūz as the title of a poem that praises Nasser and the UAR is neither arbitrary nor original: its Syrian association makes it very appropriate, and many distinguished modern Arab poets employ the symbol of Tammūz in their works.[27] Naming Tammūz the season of uprising and revolution, Ḥijāzī suggests that Nasser's nationalization of industry in Egypt and Syria, begun in July 1961, is a step toward Arab uprising and nationalism. Ḥijāzī supports this nationalization and considers it a necessary step toward the rebirth of the spirit of nationalism in the Arab world in general and in the UAR in particular. Ironically, the nationalization of industry and the destruction of the "organizational independence of trade unions" were among the main reasons leading to the UAR's collapse.[28] Although this poem was so close to the collapse, it can be interpreted as the poet's last call and hope for the preservation of the UAR. Tammūz is an extended metaphor for Nasser himself, who was known for this nationalization and its role in the development of the Egyptian economy. Despite the collapse of the union, Nasser become the poet's Tammūz, who would bring rebirth and change through his accomplishments. Furthermore, Ḥijāzī mentions more than once in this poem that the singer will always remember Tammūz. Thus, Ḥijāzī asserts that neither Nasser nor the nationalization of Egypt and the notion of the UAR will be forgotten. His poem becomes his means of documenting the hero's attempts to advance his country's economy and unite it with Syria. Using Tammūz as a symbol for rebirth and revolution, Ḥijāzī encourages his people to place their faith and trust in the nation's hero, Nasser.

Ḥijāzī also treats the notion of love for one's homeland and beloved in this poem. He emphasizes the relationship between patriotism and politics. Ḥijāzī expresses his love for his beautiful beloved and green fertile countryside and then follows it with praise for Tammūz and his relationship to Syria, as we see in the last stanza.

تموز

[. . .]
دمشق! يا نشوة البطولة، يا   معنى أعاني ولا أحاكيه
يا وردة عطرها لصاحبها   وشوكها للدخيل يدميه
يا أخت تموز! يا حبيبته   يا ملتقى نيله وعاصيه
تموز في العين .. لا نضيّعه   نغدوه من عمرنا ونؤويه
نصيح في بدء كل ملحمة   "لم ينس تموّزَه مغنيّه."[29]

Tammuz

[. . .]
Damascus! O ecstasy of heroism
You are the meaning I suffer from but do not express

O rose who gives its scent to its owner
and its bloody thorns to its intruder

O sister of Tammuz! His beloved!
The juncture of his Nile and ʿĀṣī

Tammuz is in our eyes. We will not lose him
We nourish him with our lives and give him refuge

We shout at the beginning of every epic
"The singer of Tammuz has not forgotten him."

In this section, Damascus becomes a symbol of heroism, a rose, and a sister of Tammūz. Ḥijāzī sees Damascus as the core of the unity between Egypt and Syria and the juncture where the Nile and the ʿĀṣī (Orontes) rivers meet, at least politically. Furthermore, he sees Damascus as the sister of Tammūz, for whom Arabs will happily sacrifice their lives. Thus, he perceives in the unity of Syria and Egypt an ecstasy of heroism and leadership that welcomes its people and threatens its intruders. Images of the poet and the Arabs nourishing Tammūz, becoming his refuge, and shouting that they will never forget him make the poet's advocacy of Nasser and the UAR the key theme in the poem.

This excerpt from the last stanza shows the form of the entire poem, in which Ḥijāzī blends modern content and classical form. Furthermore, Ḥijāzī treats this modern issue by employing new literary devices, such as Near Eastern mythology. It is interesting how in this collection Ḥijāzī uses the classical form of poetry to treat a political idea, and also that he does not use the classical form when he treats romantic notions.[30] It is as if he finds this topic so serious and important that he distinguishes it from the poems on love and the countryside by changing the form. Ḥijāzī then mixes free verse with the classical form in another poem on politics, "Rithā' ilā al-Mālkī" (Elegy to al-Malki). When Ḥijāzī uses the classical form, he excels at it; it is as if he wants to prove to his opponents that he has not lost his ability to do so. Furthermore, Ḥijāzī mentions in the interview included as an appendix to this volume that he used the classical form in some of his earlier collections when he wrote *marāthī* (elegies). Ḥijāzī maintains that poems such as "Rithā' ilā al-Mālkī" are written to be read orally, and since people prefer classical poetry to free verse poetry (for auditory reasons), he makes use of the classical form in such poems.[31]

"Rithā' ilā al-Mālkī" was written in 1959 to memorialize a Syrian colonel, ʿAdnān al-Mālkī, who was assassinated in 1955 while watching a soccer match between the Syrian military police team and the Egyptian coast guard team in Damascus.[32] The poem is an elegy, one of the main genres of classical Arabic poetry. Thus, to treat political ideas and classical genres in one poem, Ḥijāzī uses two forms, classical and free verse. The classical form suits the elegy, and the free verse form gives the poet more freedom to express his political views. In the poem, ʿAdnān al-Mālkī's assassination signals the rebirth of Arab unity. Ḥijāzī considers al-Mālkī a martyr who sacrificed his life for the dream of Arab nationalism and unity. The significance of the assassination of a Syrian colonel by a pro-Western sergeant from the Syrian National Party is political. Ḥijāzī sees in this assassination an attack on Arab unity and an opportunity to call for its preservation. In this poem Ḥijāzī says:

رثاء المالكي

[. . .]
وفي رياح الدجى أشلاء أغنية
وفي رياح الدجى شوق لميلاد
الوحدة .. الوحدة الكبرى وحلم غد
عدل وحرية
أشلاء أغنية
[. . .]
يا من سترثينا
لا تبكنا .. إن يوم النصر يحيينا
يوما تعود به الأشلاء للجسد
يوما تعود به البلدان للبلد
الوحدة .. الوحدة الكبرى وحلم غد
عدل وحرية

[. . .]
عدنان! حلم الغد الرفراف أرداه
أرداه، أحياه للأبد
[. . .]
بفكرة الوحدة الكبرى مشى دمه   يدق لي الباب حتى لان و انفتحا![33]

Elegy to al-Malki

[. . .]
And in the winds of the dawn, there are remnants of a song
And in the winds of the dawn, there is a longing for birth
Unity . . . the great unity and a dream for tomorrow
Justice and freedom
Remnants of a song
[. . .]
You, who are going to lament us
Do not weep for us . . . the day of victory will revive us
A day when the severed limbs return to the body
A day when countries return to the country
Unity . . . the great unity and a dream for tomorrow
Justice and freedom
[. . .]
Adnan! The waving dream of tomorrow killed him
Killed him, revived him forever
[. . .]
His blood walked with the idea of the great unity
Knocking on the door for me until it was opened.

In this poem, Ḥijāzī laments al-Mālkī and maintains that despite his death, he will always be remembered for his faith in and inspiration for the great Arab unity. Nasser, too, called for justice and freedom to achieve Arab nationalism and unity with Syria. The dark images used to describe al-Mālkī's assassination, like severed limbs and weeping people, are juxtaposed with pleasant images that reveal a great deal of optimism, aspiration, and faith in Nasser's project. Writing this poem, Ḥijāzī takes the opportunity not only to express his grief and sorrow for the death of a fellow nationalist, but also to strengthen people's faith in Nasser. Al-Mālkī's blood revives the dream of Arab nationalism, and Ḥijāzī's poem documents al-Mālkī's sacrifice and provokes people to celebrate Nasser as their last remaining hope for freedom and justice.

THE DEFEAT

In 1972, seven years after his third collection and five years after the humiliating defeat in the Arab–Israeli war of 1967, Ḥijāzī published his fourth collection: *Marthiyat al-ʿUmr al-Jamīl* (Elegy of the Beautiful Life). In 1974 Ḥijāzī would leave for Paris after being harassed by Anwar Sadat's regime. In *Marthiyat al-ʿUmr al-Jamīl*, Ḥijāzī laments the death of Nasser, whom he regarded as the hero and savior of Arab nationalism. Most of the poems in this collection are songs for Palestine and elegies to Nasser, to other political figures, and to Arab countries. Among the key poems in this collection are "Marthiyat Lāʿib Sīrk" (Elegy of a Circus Performer), "ʿAbd al-Nāṣir 3" (Nasser 3), and "Marthiyat al-ʿUmr al-Jamīl" (Elegy of the Beautiful Life).

مرثية لاعب سيرك

في العالم المملوء أخطاء
مطالب وحدك ألا تخطئ
لأن جسمك النحيل
لو مرة أسرعَ أو أبطأ
هوى، وغطى الأرض أشلاء
في أي ليلة ترى يقبع ذلك الخطأ
في هذه الليلة! أو في غيرها من الليال
حين يغيض في مصابيح المكان نورها وتنطفئ
ويسحب الناس صياحهم
على مقدمك المفروش أضواء
حين تلوح مثل فارس يجيل الطرف في مدينته
مودعا· يطلب وجد الناس، في صمت نبيل
ثم تسير نحو أول الحبال
مستقيماً مؤمنا

وهم يدقون على إيقاع خطوك الطبول
ويملأون الملعب الواسع ضوضاء
ثم يقولون: ابتدئ.[34]

Elegy of a Circus Performer

In a world full of mistakes
You alone are asked not to err
Because your frail body,
If it speeds or slows once,
Will fall, and overlay the earth
With its dismemberment
In what night do you think this mistake lies?
This night! Or any other
When the lamplights dim and go out
And people raise their shouting voices
At your arrival drenched in light,
When you appear like a knight who roams his city
With sights set upon his farewell, asking for people's love,
in noble silence,
Before you move toward the first rope,
Gesturing on high
As drums beat to the rhythm of your stepping
And fill the spacious arena with sound
And then signal: Begin![35]

In this poem, Ḥijāzī uses the metaphor of a circus performer to treat Nasser's role as a politician and leader of the Arab nation and his political downfall. In a world full of mistakes, Nasser is the circus performer who is not expected to err. If he falls, his dismembered (and thus dead) body will cover the earth. Ḥijāzī composes this poem to remind his readers of the burdens and challenges of Nasser's leadership and his responsibility toward the public, which placed its utmost trust in him. Ḥijāzī's speaker asks Nasser in line 7, "In which night do you think this mistake lies?" He blames Nasser for the defeat and considers it the sole reason for his political downfall. The circus performer walks toward the first rope in the middle of the circus ring. His steps are straight, and the audience beats the drums to the rhythm of his steps, shouting, "Begin!" Likewise, the Arab public eagerly watched Nasser moving forward toward his dream of Arab nationalism and the UAR, only to be disappointed when he lost the war against Israel and humiliated them by putting an end to their dream. The circus performer analogy enables Ḥijāzī to compare the challenges Nasser had to overcome to those of a circus performer, who is not supposed to err and whose steps are carefully calculated and watched by the public.

In "ʿAbd al-Nāṣir 3," Ḥijāzī laments Nasser's death in 1970.[36] This poem is also a sequel to "ʿAbd al-Nāṣir 2," which was published in *Lam Yabqā illā al-Iʿtirāf*.[37] Ḥijāzī says in this poem, "My voice is one among many other voices, which conveys but little / of my deep love for you / but when words become sacrifices / I will repay my heavy debt to you."[38] These lines are among the many in this poem that express Ḥijāzī's continued love for and devotion to Nasser, even after his death and the collapse of Nasserism. Although an earlier poem questions Nasser's preparedness for the 1967 war, Ḥijāzī expresses his love for him in this one. His love for Nasser is in conflict with his disappointment in him.

In another stanza, Ḥijāzī questions whether his love for Nasser is derived from fear: "What do I say? / I am afraid that my love for you is because of fear / stuck in me from bygone centuries."[39] In neither the first nor the second in this series of three poems—each in a different collection, and all with the same title except for the number—does Ḥijāzī question his love for Nasser or criticize him. It is only in this third poem that we see the poet wonder if his love for Nasser is based on fear, and if Nasser has humiliated the Arabs and disappointed them. It is as if after Nasser's death and the political downfall of his oppressive administration, Ḥijāzī starts to question his own stand on Nasser and his regime. In a 2011 interview, Ḥijāzī mentioned that he came to realize after the death of Nasser that Arabs were defeated "in the 1967 War not because of a shortcoming in weapons or armies, but because of the absence of democracy under the rule of Nasser."[40] Thus, Nasser's death and the 1967 defeat enabled Ḥijāzī to better evaluate Nasser's regime and unjust practices in Egypt. It is perhaps for this reason that this collection is the last in which Ḥijāzī praises or laments Nasser.

THE SEARCH FOR POETIC VOICE AND LEGACY AFTER THE DEFEAT

Another poem among the many lamenting the death of Nasser carries the title of the collection itself: "Marthiyat al-ʿUmr al-Jamīl" (Elegy of the Beautiful Life).[41] In it Ḥijāzī considers Nasser's time a bygone era that will never return: "The age of battles has passed and the friends / went and we are orphans again."[42] In another stanza, he says, "I have followed you since the beginning of the dream / from the beginning of hopelessness to its end."[43] Ḥijāzī addresses Nasser directly in this elegy and tells him that he has followed him in his pursuit of nationalism and Arab unity since its beginnings, even though it was a hopeless dream. Furthermore, Ḥijāzī questions if his love for Nasser was taboo because he mentions that some people asked him not to follow Nasser, but he did not listen to them: "A friend screamed: 'Do not believe'" and "A friend screamed: 'Do not pledge allegiance.'"[44] However, Ḥijāzī ignored these calls and followed Nasser from "one impossible to another."[45] In this poem, Ḥijāzī addresses Nasser with questions such as "who of us carries the burden of the defeat now?"; "did my song deceive you and you waited for what I promised you, but you did not win?"; "or was I deceived by your ruling until I thought you are our savior?"; and " or were we both deceived by the mirage of the beautiful time?"[46] This collection in general and this poem in particular mark a turning point in Ḥijāzī's poetry where he questions not only his allegiance to Nasser but also the legacy of his own work. At this point in the poem, Ḥijāzī shows up, voicing his rejection of the past and his intent to make a change in his poetry without need of a speaker or a persona. This stage is significant because in this collection, unlike his earlier ones, we see the poet posing questions about Nasser and his regime more than making political statements in their favor. We find Ḥijāzī searching for his own voice after the 1967 defeat and the collapse of the Nasserist regime.

In the following stanza in "Marthiyat al-ʿUmr al-Jamīl," Ḥijāzī expresses his frustration and loss of faith in Egypt:

مرثية العمر الجميل

[. . .]
إنني ضائع في البلاد

ضائع بين تاريخي المستحيل،
وتاريخي المستعاد
حامل في دمي نكبتي
حامل خطئي وسقوطي.[47]

Elegy of the Beautiful Life

[. . .]
I am lost in this country
Lost between my impossible history
And my restored history
Carrying my *nakba* in my blood
Carrying my mistake and fall.

Distinction between Ḥijāzī and his speaker becomes impossible in this poem. The collapse of the Nasserist regime disorients the poet, who lost the dream he had lived for and believed in all his life and to which he dedicated his poetry. Ḥijāzī realizes his mistake in standing behind Nasser and his regime and decides to continue his journey, carrying the pains of the defeats of 1948 and 1967. The title of the poem, "Marthiyat al-ʿUmr al-Jamīl," is an elegy for Ḥijāzī's life, which he believed to be beautiful. By writing an elegy for a past era, Ḥijāzī announces a new beginning in his poetry. At this stage of his career, Ḥijāzī regrets standing behind a political leader and using his poetry to support that position. This poem ends with Ḥijāzī's speaker wondering:

هل ترى أتذكر صوتي القديم،
فيبعثني الله من تحت هذا الرماد
أم أغيب كما غبتَ أنت،
وتسقط غرناطة في المحيط[48]

Will I ever remember my old voice
So that God will resurrect me from under these ashes?
Or will I disappear as you disappeared?
While Granada drowns in the sea!

Questioning whether he will be able to regain his old voice indicates Ḥijāzī's intent to make a change in his poetry by restoring the poetic voice he had before writing about Nasser and his regime. Ḥijāzī gives himself two choices: accept failure and disappear like Nasser or rise from the ashes. Changing the direction of his poetry and restoring his poetic voice will resurrect the poet and his poetry. Thus, in this collection Ḥijāzī no longer wants to make Nasser and his dreams the core of his poetry. He realizes that if he did so, as a poet he would disappear in the ashes of a bygone era. Although he sympathizes with Nasser and writes elegies to him, Ḥijāzī realizes that if he wants to create a poetic legacy, he has to move beyond his committed Nasserist phase.

Ḥijāzī mentions in a 2011 interview that he and other intellectuals believed in Nasser and were loyal to him because they thought they believed in a revolution. However, this all changed after the 1967 defeat "I used to believe that Nasser's regime would correct itself when it felt safe, but this did not happen and the regime continued to be a dictatorship, which lost contact with the public . . . and which finally led to the 1967 defeat that put an end to my relationship to this regime despite the fact that I continued to love Nasser, sympathize with him, and lament him after his death."[49] Ḥijāzī then began to question Nasser's regime and despise its dictatorship and shortcomings.

In *Marthiyat al-ʿUmr al-Jamīl* Ḥijāzī uses lyrical, free verse, and classical forms. "Min Nashīd al-Inshād" (From the Song of the Songs) is a lyric elegy to Nasser. "Al-Riḥla Ibtada'at" (The Journey Has Begun) is written in lyrical, free verse, and classical forms.[50] Ḥijāzī mixes these three forms together in one poem to express a kind of confusion and frustration from not only a personal perspective, but also a poetic one. This elegy expresses the challenge Ḥijāzī faces in dealing with his conflicting emotions toward Nasser and his past. He uses different forms of poetry to treat one topic, elegy, and yet these forms combined do not seem able to express his loss and disorientation. This collection as a whole expresses a great deal of emotional distress, which seems to force the poet to express himself without a persona or speaker. Although this collection speaks of the poet's inability to deal with the new reality, it marks a new stage in his poetry, a movement toward a more critical, objective, and sophisticated poetry. It is as if Nasser's death and the collapse of his regime have awakened the poet from his beautiful dream to a different reality. This reality requires a different kind of poetry, a poetry that no longer idolizes political figures. Lamenting the death of Nasser and realizing the need to move beyond the Nasserist era and its false promises, Ḥijāzī learns from his mistake and begins a new phase in his poetry, one marked by his realization that he is standing at the border between a bygone era and a new era.

With his move to France in 1974, after being forced to resign his job by Sadat's regime, Ḥijāzī distances himself from direct involvement in political life in Egypt and looks at things from a different perspective, watching from a distance and evaluating situations critically. With this change in Ḥijāzī's life, we expect to see some changes in his poetry. Ḥijāzī's use of free verse and lyrical romantic poetry to treat personal and political issues in his four past collections suggests his search for the appropriate poetic form. In his fifth collection we witness a change not only in content, but also in form.

Kā'ināt Mamlakat al-Layl (Creatures of the Night Kingdom) was published in Beirut in 1978. It is worth noting that none of the poems in this collection praise Nasser or lament his death. Ḥijāzī's poetry is no longer a platform for Nasserist propaganda; rather, it is about and for the people and their revolution. Although some might argue that Ḥijāzī continued to write about politics, I argue that his whole perspective on politics changes in this collection and his two latest collections, *Ashjār al-Ismint* (Cement Trees, 1989) and *Ṭalal al-Waqt* (The Standing Ruins of Time, 2011). He gradually moves from *iltizām* in its traditional sense to a commitment to people and his poetry. For Ḥijāzī, the revolution is no longer a Nasserist revolution or a regime revolution. Instead, it is the people's revolution because, as he puts it, "the individual will eventually die but the revolution will remain."[51]

Ḥijāzī has concluded that his poetry no longer has to support a regime or its leader; he no longer perceives it as a tool whose sole purpose is to serve a regime's revolution. Thus, the limitations he created and was challenged by in his previous four collections are no longer present in *Kā'ināt Mamlakat al-Layl.* Although he treats some political and social topics in his poetry from 1978 onward, not only does his perspective change, but so do his stylistic devices. To treat human anxieties in the modern world and in exile, Ḥijāzī takes a deeper and more mature approach. Among the major themes addressed in this collection are alienation, exile, and the anxieties of the poet in Paris, the city of others. Furthermore, Ḥijāzī begins to employ masks and imagery in a way we have not seen in his previous collections.

THE POET OF THE PUBLIC

The night kingdom in "Kā'ināt Mamlakat al-Layl," the title poem of this collection, refers to Sadat's dictatorship. In this poem, Ḥijāzī uses a mask of a god of sex to explore darkness, anxieties, fear, and death in modern life. He gives shape to the feelings of loss and despair in a life characterized by fear, where he "is at his closest to modernist dramatization."[52]

كائنات مملكة الليل

إله الجنس و الخوف، وآخر الذكور أنا
[. . .]
تركت مخبأي لألقي نظرة على بلادي
ليس هذا عطشا للجنس
إنني أؤدي واجبا مقدسا
وأنت لست غير رمز فاتبعيني
لم يعد من مجد هذه البلاد غير حانة
ولم يبق من الدولة إلا رجل الشرطة
يستعرض في الضوء الأخير
ظله الطويل تارة
وظله القصير!
[. . .]
الخوف صار وطنا
وصار عملة
وصار لغة قومية
صار نشيدا و هوية
وصار مجلسا منتخبا
والخوف صار حاميه.[53]

Creatures of the Night Kingdom

I am the god of sex and fear and the last male
[. . .]
I left my hiding place to take a look at my country
Not out of lust
I am performing a holy duty
And you are only a symbol, so follow me
Nothing remained of the glory of this country but a bar
Nothing remained of the state but a policeman
Showing off under the last light
His long shadow one time
And another time his short shadow
[. . .]
Fear has become a homeland
A currency
A national language
Anthem and identity
An elected council
And fear has become its savior.

In this poem, the speaker is the god of sex and fear and the last male who, in a dialogue with a woman, explores the fear and humiliation dominating life in his night kingdom. Using this mask, the speaker journeys to his homeland, Egypt, to explore the state of his country after his departure, not out of lust, he tells her, but because this is his sacred duty. Although he has left his country and distanced himself from its social and political scenes, the speaker is still concerned about his people. He flies to Cairo and laments what he finds there, for the country that once led Arab nationalism has been reduced to a bar populated by chattering drunks and the state to a policeman. Thus, there is nothing to be proud of about Egypt, which has become a wasteland devoid of democracy, freedom, morals, ethics, and security. Ḥijāzī's readership immediately recognized that he was talking about Sadat's Egypt.

Ḥijāzī complicates the images of his wasteland by projecting fear into the scene. Fear has become the dominant theme in every aspect of life in his country: its currency, national language, anthem, identity, and elected council, as well as what protects that council. More importantly, it has become homeland itself. Dominating every aspect of life in the night kingdom, fear is now the religion and the god everyone worships and fears in Sadat's Egypt. Instead of promoting security, Sadat uses fear and oppression to terrorize Egyptians and impose his authority over them. Failing to maintain an identity or speak a language that doesn't involve fear, the speaker distrusts and despises everything he sees and hears. In addition, seeing fear in the eyes of his people from their defeated past and their unknown future, as well as from their regime, complicates the mission of the god of sex and fear. He feels paralyzed, and he "decides to cut his neck with a knife and bleed" until he dies at the end of the poem.[54] This end intensifies the dramatic tone of the poem and creates a state of pessimism.[55] This god is the poet himself, who tries to save his country but is paralyzed. This poem, written in free verse form, reflects Ḥijāzī's successful attempt to employ masks and extended poetic images to give shape to the feelings of humiliation, frustration, and fear in his homeland.

Ḥijāzī is no longer the pro-regime poet of his previous four collections. On the contrary, his voice is critical and his judgment candid. Ḥijāzī expresses his dissatisfaction with the regime in Egypt not only by opposing Sadat—paying the price of his career as a result—but also by criticizing it in his poetry. The poems in this collection gives shape to the feelings of loss, oppression, terror, and fear people feel under the Sadat regime. Ḥijāzī is still "committed," however, to the extent that his poetry expresses his concern for the state of his homeland and his need to openly condemn Sadat's regime. Because his poetic voice is independent now, neither politicians nor regimes can control what he says or writes. Besides, his experiences in Paris have enabled him to treat the city and themes of alienation and loss from a more mature perspective. Thus, Ḥijāzī starts employing stylistic devices such as the masks to enrich his poetry and better express and shape his feelings, as we will see in other poems in this collection.

Eliot's influence on Ḥijāzī becomes clearer in this collection when Ḥijāzī begins to distance his direct personal emotions from his poetry. Ḥijāzī maintains in *Al-Shi'r Rafīqī* that "the more mature his tools are and the more they are able to depict more than his direct needs, the poet realizes that he is facing the whole universe. . . . This way, the poem goes beyond being a tool to express an individual case."[56] Ḥijāzī begins a new journey, one in which he occupies himself with issues and concerns beyond his personal and direct emotions or his allegiance to the regime. He concerns himself with the public and their demands and aspirations. He realizes that he needs to develop new tools in his poetry to treat these new issues and concerns.

Moving from the personal to the universal, Ḥijāzī makes a transition toward a poetry that employs modern techniques to treat issues concerning humans in the modern world. The shift in Ḥijāzī's poetry begins in the late 1970s after a genuine commitment to *iltizām*. His "Kā'ināt Mamlakat al-Layl" can be applied more broadly than just as a critique of Sadat's regime in Egypt. Ḥijāzī's night kingdom refers to all oppressive regimes, and their creatures are the oppressed people of the world. In the night kingdom, darkness, oppression, injustice, death, and fear leave no space for hope, freedom, and peace. People have become creatures in this kingdom because their basic human rights and dignity have been stripped away. Ḥijāzī's creatures have to deal with their "overwhelming sense of failure, decline, and despair," which "keeps the Arab poet closer to the Eliotic modernist model."[57] Ḥijāzī's "Creatures of the Night Kingdom" resembles Eliot's "The Waste Land." Ḥijāzī's poem also ends on a pessimistic note when the last male commits suicide, a manifestation of defeat, failure, and surrender. Ḥijāzī's decision to employ the mask of a god of sex and lust is interesting. In the collections he published when he was in France, he explored the topic of sex and lust and wrote several poems in which the city of Paris becomes a prostitute and the countryside in Egypt becomes his faithful beloved.

Another key poem critical of the status quo is "Girnīkā" (Guernica). It takes its title from Picasso's *Guernica*, painted in the months after the Germans and Italians bombed and wiped out the Basque city of Guernica in April 1937, during the Spanish Civil War. The painting depicts the tragedies of war and the destructive power of modern technology, and presents the wasteland the war has made of Guernica. Like Ḥijāzī, Picasso experienced tragedy from afar: "In Paris, Picasso read, saw pictures, and heard similar reports . . . [and then] created *Guernica*, which is a testimony to his genius, after several weeks of intense work in Paris."[58]

When Ḥijāzī saw *Guernica* in Madrid, he was very impressed because he believed that "despite the artistic value of *Guernica*, one cannot help but think of Franco, the Civil War in Spain, and one's own culture and knowledge."[59] Ḥijāzī found another Guernica in his country, Egypt, and felt responsible for telling the world about his people's ordeal by writing his own *Guernica*.

Ḥijāzī attempted to imitate and recreate Picasso's genius and create a similar influence by using new means of expression. "Girnīkā" consists of four parts, each with a different title. Using different images and masks, the four poems combine notions of war, destruction, and death into a collage. This poem is Ḥijāzī's painting, drawn with words that depict universal despair, tragedies, and the destruction of war. The collection's 1978 publication date carries further political significance: in September of that year, Sadat signed the Camp David Accords. Ḥijāzī, like many other Arab intellectuals, opposed Sadat's decision to sign the peace treaty with Israel and called him "a traitor."[60] Therefore, writing this poem, Ḥijāzī treats the destruction of war not only universally, but also locally. Egypt becomes another Guernica, whose suffering and destruction are summed up by Sadat's peace accord with Israel.

The titles of the poem's four parts are, in order, "Khuṭbat Lūsiyās al-Akhīra" (Lucian's Last Sermon), "Baḥḥārat Magillān" (Magellan's Sailors), "Pāblū Nīrūdā" (Pablo Neruda), and "Al-Mashhad al-Akhīr min al-Fīlm Z" (Last Scene of the Movie *Z*). Lucian of Samosata (AD 125–AD 180) was a Greek politician and rhetorician, Ferdinand Magellan (1480–1521) a Portuguese explorer, and Pablo Neruda (1904–1973) a Chilean poet and politician; the film *Z*, released in 1969, is a French political thriller directed by Costa-Gavras that treats repression and the corruption of morals under the military dictatorship in Greece in the late 1960s. Ḥijāzī brings these four poems together by linking each to tragedies of war, military dictatorships, and corruption, which are key ideas in Picasso's painting.

In "Khuṭbat Lūsiyās al-Akhīra," Lucian lies dead after giving his speech.

خطبة لوسياس الأخيرة

كان لوسياس على سجادة البهو قتيلا
هذه خطبته الأولى

التي توّج فيها بإمتشاق السيف أغنياته للحق
لكن بعد أن فات الآوان
سقط السيف من الكف التي رفرفت
فوق رؤوس الناس بالحكمة!
في الستين يا لوسياس
لن تحسن تلك المهنة الأخرى
ولو صرت اشتراكياً
وقاسمت أرقاء أثينا الخمر و الخبز
وهل كنت أخذت القصر بالسيف
لكي تمنعه بالسيف؟
لا بأس إذن
أن يقتل الجند خطيباً
تحت سقف البرلمان![61]

Lucian's Last Sermon

Lucian lies dead in the carpeted hallway
This was his first speech
In which he exalted the raised sword with his songs of truth,
But only after it was too late
The sword fell from the hand that fluttered many times
With wisdom over the crowd
At sixty, Lucian,
You will not be able to master this new profession
Even if you become a socialist
And share bread and wine of Athena's slaves
Did you take the palace by sword
So you could annul it with the sword?
It is fine then
That the soldiers kill an orator
Under the dome of the assembly.[62]

In the first section of "Girnīkā," Ḥijāzī addresses Lucian of Samosata, a Greek politician and rhetorician who was known for his satire, in an ironic tone. Known for his wisdom and speeches that impressed the public, Lucian here finds himself unable to move the crowd with his speech. This sermon is different from his previous sermons in that now he tries to impose his orders and authority on people by force. For this he pays with his life. Images of Lucian lying dead on the assembly-hall carpet are juxtaposed with images of his past, when he was celebrated, honored, and followed by the crowds. In this poem, Lucian becomes the corrupt orator who, instead of using his wisdom and rhetoric to influence people, turns into a dictator who threatens to kill his people. The orator represents Sadat, who, despite being known for his charismatic personality and influential speeches, terrorized Egyptians and tortured them during his oppressive regime and dictatorship. In 1979, one year after the publication of this collection and the signing of the Camp David Accords, Sadat signed the Egypt–Israel peace treaty. This act outraged the Egyptian public and made Sadat even more despised by his people. In 1981 Sadat was assassinated by fundamentalist army officers, just as Lucian was assassinated by his soldiers.

The second part of Ḥijāzī's "Girnīkā is "Baḥḥārat Magellān" (Magellan's Sailors). Magellan, a Portuguese explorer, is most famous for organizing the first circumnavigation of the earth, though he was killed before it was complete.

بحّارة ماجلان

كانت الشمس التي تلفحنا فوق مدار السرطان
زهرة مقرورة
فوق مدار الجدي
ليست هذه الأرض إذن تفاحة
بل صخرة تفلت منّا
في التقاويم التي لم نكتشف إيقاعها الصعب
فمن يوقف هذا الدوران
ساعة
ندفن ماجلان فيها
ونشم الريح، هل تحمل طعم الشاطئ الآخر
كم تبعد شيلي عن نيويورك؟
وعن موسكو؟
وكم قبر من الساحل للساحل!
كم ميل ترى بين الكلاشنكوف و الأيدي!
وكم يبعد مبنى البرلمان
عن سلاح الطيران.[63]

Magellan's Sailors

We were burned by the sun in Scorpio,
A flower blossoming
Above the orbit of Capricorn
So this earth is not an apple
But a stone we lose
In a calendar whose difficult rhythms we've not discovered
Who can put a stop to this turning
For an hour
In which to lay Magellan to rest
And to smell the wind? Does it carry the fragrances
of the other shore?
How far is Chile from New York?
From Moscow?
How many graves are there from one coast to another?
How many miles between a Kalashnikov and the hands,
How far are the warplanes
From the halls of the parliament . . . ?[64]

This poem depicts the tragedy of Magellan's sailors, who are lost in the middle of the sea, carrying the corpse of Magellan on their ship. These sailors are unable to stop their ship even for an hour to bury their captain. Ḥijāzī's speaker, one of the sailors, says that the sphere of the earth is not an apple (living) but a stone (lifeless). Magellan's sailors will not find the shores they seek because they are in the middle of death. They will be forever lost in the middle of the sea, destined to circumnavigate the earth, wondering if they will be able to reach any shore. The speaker is also the Egyptian citizen, who is destined to be forever lost because of Sadat's rule. Ḥijāzī predicts that Sadat will die long before he can bring peace, democracy, and freedom to Egypt. For Ḥijāzī, Sadat's political decisions, military dictatorship, and oppressive regime made Egypt a wasteland crammed with graves from one coast to another. In the last two lines, the speaker, Ḥijāzī's mask, wonders how far the parliament building is from the warplanes, depicting the violent repression and lack of democracy in Egypt. In the previous section, the orator rules by the sword instead of by wisdom; in this section, arms and warplanes rule instead of democracy. Sadat is a politician who dragged his country into an eternal state of loss, oppression, and violence.

This section also portrays the destruction and damage modern technology has brought to mankind. The weapons of war erase cities from the map. Like Guernica in 1937, Egypt endured a great deal of destruction because of Sadat and his political decisions. For Ḥijāzī, Sadat was living an illusion and would never steer Egypt to the shore. Egypt was sinking deep in the ocean under his rule. This poem expresses Ḥijāzī's abhorrence of war and dictatorships like Sadat's, which sink nations in pain, distress, agony, and anguish. Magellan's sailors are lost in the middle of the ocean after his death, and the Egyptians are likewise forever lost and alone in the middle of the oppression and terror Sadat created. This poem attempts to provoke the Egyptians to voice their opposition and put an end to Sadat's regime.

These masks and images of war in modern times extend in the other two parts of in this poem. In "Pāblū Nīrūdā" (Pablo Neruda), we see the Chilean communist poet and politician, dying in his bed, alone:

بابلو نيرودا

ها هو الثور الخرافي يقوم الآن من لوحات بيكاسو
ومن أشعار لوركا
بينما أصبحتَ شيخاً
عاجزا عن أن ترى روعته الوحشية البكر
وتلقاه بذات العنفوان
في الثلاثين التي لم تتكرر أبدا، كنت تناديه
وتغويه بزخّات السهام الحمر أن يأتي
وتعطيه الأمان
واقفا في ليل غرناطة بالجيتار
أطلعتَ رياحين الشبابيك
وأيقظت عصافير الكتدرائية الخضراء
في تلك الثلاثين التي لم تتكرر
من يغنيّكَ النشيد الأممي الآن
من يدنيك من أرض الهنود الحمر
من رائحة النترات والخبز و من ليل المراعي

لتشمّ النار في العشب الشتائي
ومن يعطيك أسماء الذين استشهدوا قبلك؟
في الستين يأتي الثور في هيئته العصرية النكراء
في حلّته الصفراء يأتي
بينما انت هنا وحدك
ملقى في فراش المرض الملعون
ماذا؟
قد تأخرت كثيرا أيها الثور الخرافي
تأخرت كثيرا
أيها الثور الجبان.[65]

Pablo Neruda

The mythical ox rises now from Picasso's paintings
And from Lorca's poetry
And you have become an old man
Unable to see his beastly virginal magnificence
And to meet him with equal violence
In the thirties that never came again, you used to beckon to him
Tempting him, with a poke of red arrows, to come
And you'd make him feel safe
Standing with a guitar in the night of Granada
You sent out lavender from the windows
And awakened the birds of the green cathedral
In those thirties that never came again
Who will sing you the anthem now?
Who will bring you closer to the land of the Red Indians,
To the smell of nitrates, and bread and the pastures at night
And the smell of fire in winter grass
And who will tell you the names of those who were martyrs
before you?
At sixty, the ox comes in his horrible modern form,
He comes in his yellow costume
While you are all alone,
In the bed of a fearsome disease
What?

Mythical ox, you've come too late,
Too late,
You cowardly ox . . .[66]

In this section, the speaker addresses Neruda on his deathbed and reminds him of his old days. He tells Neruda that the mythical ox rises from Picasso's paintings and Lorca's poetry once again, while Neruda is unable to see it in the same way he used to see it in his thirties. The ox in Picasso's *Guernica* suggests brutality and darkness.[67] In his sixties, Neruda is now old, fragile, and unable to meet the ox with equal vigor ("vigor" in Arabic text, "violence" in English translation). Although Neruda fought his enemy in his thirties, he must now fight him in his current form: the coward enemy has returned because Neruda is sick and too old to fight. Neruda also is a stand-in for the poet himself. Ḥijāzī is horrified at the status quo in the Arab world in general and in Egypt in particular, and he is unable to do anything. The ox takes the vile modern form of dictatorships and wars whose weapons are monstrous, and of the darkness and brutality that Picasso spoke of and that his painting embodied. Thus, Ḥijāzī adds another significant symbol to his collage of images: the ox. Ḥijāzī revolts against what Sadat brought to Egypt: pain, violence, despair, loss, and anguish. Furthermore, Picasso, Lorca, and Neruda become masks/doubles of Ḥijāzī himself, for the work of these three artists serves their politics, and so does Ḥijāzī's serve his.

In a letter dated May 1, 1937, less than a week after the attack, Picasso wrote, "I am full of incommensurable rage at the massacre in Guernica. But I do not know what to do."[68] In the next months he painted *Guernica* to present his outrage at this massacre. Likewise, Ḥijāzī wrote his poem to condemn the oppressive regime of Sadat. Although Ḥijāzī is aware of the terror Sadat imposed on Egypt, he is unable to stop him. However, Ḥijāzī writes poetry that criticizes Sadat and encourages his people to revolt against Sadat's regime, expressing his and his people's frustration and voicing their opposition. The ox in this poem is Sadat's castrated regime, and its modern form is its violent and repressive side. Like Neruda, Egypt is bedridden by a cursed disease, caused by Sadat, whose armed authoritarian regime is cowardly for using violence and force against its civilians.

The last part of this poem is "Al-Mashhad al-Akhīr min al-Fīlm Z" (The Last Scene of the Movie *Z*), drawing on Costa-Gavras's 1969 French political thriller about the military dictatorship in Greece in the late 1960s. The poem reads as follows:

المشهد الأخير من الفيلم ز

كان نوّاب الأقاليم يشدّون على الأعين ظلّ القبعّات
السود في خوف فكاهيّ
وينسلّون في الليل فرادي
تلك سياراتهم مذعورة تمرق كالفيران
في منعطف الوادي الذي يمتد مثل الأفعوان
والرئيس الإشتراكي على سجّادة البهو
بنظّارته، شيخ وحيد
هجرته هيبة المنصب
والحرّاس قتلى حوله
والدم مازال طريا
وجنود الانقلاب الجامدو الأوجه
يلقون على جثته القبض
ويصطفون كالأعمدة الجوفاء في البهو
ولن تمضي سوى بضعة أيام
وتأتي فرق التنظيف كي تغسل هذا الدم بالماء
وتمحو من على الجدران
آثار الدخان![69]

Last Scene of the Movie *Z*

The MPs of the provinces pulled the shadows of their black hats
over their eyes
In laughable fear
And they slipped one by one into the night
These are their terrified cars, passing like mice
Through the snaking curves of the valley
The socialist president lies on the fine carpet in the hallway
Clutching his glasses, a lone sheikh
Abandoned by the glory of his station,

the guards around him dead,
Their blood still warm,
And the henchmen of the coup with their solid faces
Are arresting his corpse
They fall in line like hollow columns in the hall
In just a few days
The cleaning crew will come to wash away all this blood
with water,
To scrub smoke
From the walls . . .[70]

The movie *Z* treats the corruption of the right-wing government that was firmly controlling Greece in the early 1960s. Gregoris Lambrakis, a left-wing member of parliament, died five days after voicing his opposition to the government in a rally. He was run down in the middle of the street by right-wing officials. Half a million people shouted at his funeral "Lambrakis zi!" (Lambrakis lives), so "Z" became a symbol for resistance against the regime. The film is based on the novel *Z*, by Vassilis Vassilikos, which was published in 1966.

Ḥijāzī's "Al-Mashhad al-Akhīr min al-Fīlm Z" depicts the film's last scene, in which the military police assassinate the socialist president and flee. Ḥijāzī uses ekphrasis by taking this last scene and capturing in poetry what is captured in film. Ḥijāzī presents the image of the MPs right after they assassinate the president. Pulling their black hats over their eyes in disguise, they slip away into the darkness of the night. The scene is charged with fear and terror; the MPs' cars flee the scene like mice, and death covers the murder scene. The socialist president lies dead on the fine carpet in the hall, where he was giving his last speech, and his guards are also dead. While their blood is still warm—a sign that the crime has just happened—the henchmen of the coup arrive on the scene to arrest not the president but his corpse. Ironically, the image of these henchmen, who are like hollow columns with their frozen faces ("solid" faces in English translation) and cold emotions, is juxtaposed with the image of the slain men lying on the ground, their blood still warm—warmer than the blood of the coup's henchmen. The cleaning crews follow the henchmen; after they clear the dead bodies from the scene, wash the blood with water, and scrub the remnants of smoke off the walls, it is as if nothing has happened. The crime has thus been covered up by the corrupt government, and justice is not served.

This poem is the last scene not only in the film *Z*, but also in Ḥijāzī's "Guernica." It is also the last scene under the rule of a dictatorship, where criminals slip into the night and go on as though no lives have been wasted and no cities destroyed. This is a universal scene in any war zone or country ruled by a dictator: the truth is covered up and criminals are saved. Although the hero in the film *Z* is a communist, Ḥijāzī's hero is a socialist. Ḥijāzī leaves Cairo and writes this poem because he opposes the regime in Egypt; thus, this socialist hero is Ḥijāzī himself, who challenges authority by voicing his opposition. His heroic socialist president is a lone sheikh, who lost his glory, standing against the regime and sacrificing himself so that truth prevails. He is assassinated after he delivers his speech. Likewise, Neruda dies alone and Magellan's sailors are forever lost in the middle of the ocean. All these three are masks of the poet himself. The poet is the voice of his nation, who defends his people against their dictatorial regime and calls for freedom and democracy. In "Al-Mashhad al-Akhīr min al-Fīlm Z" Ḥijāzī portrays a recurring scene in Egypt under Sadat's regime, where intellectuals and opposition leaders are assassinated and tortured.

Writing these four poems under the title "Guernica," Ḥijāzī aims to provide a bridge between art and politics. His poem speaks of universal human misery and the artist's opposition to Sadat's dictatorship in Egypt. Ḥijāzī uses a collage of poetic imagery, symbolism, masks, and myths and writes candidly about the struggle of not only civilians but also artists and poets under dictatorships.

Ḥijāzī's "Guernica," like Picasso's, is an original artifact that "combines myth and symbolism with realistic elements to transcend events as well as respond to them."[71] Picasso's painting succeeded internationally because of its ability to make the Spanish national misery, and the response to it, universal. Holding his personal feelings and emotions at a distance, Ḥijāzī depicts a universal human pain, much like the Eliotian notion of the poet's distancing his personal emotions from his poetry. We see neither Sadat nor Egypt directly in this poem. Ḥijāzī's "Guernica" becomes his statement on war and dictatorships and his dialogue with his fellow artists Picasso, Neruda, and Lorca.

In *Kā'ināt Mamlakat al-Layl*, whether it is Picasso, Neruda, or Ḥijāzī, the poet/artist is paralyzed in his confrontations with regime. Unable to change the status quo, the god of sex and fear commits suicide at the end of the title poem, screaming, "And then, I slashed my neck with a knife / so the blood ran around me like rivers / and the vultures screamed around my head."[72] The image of the speaker slashing his own neck emphasizes the image of vultures screaming next to the dead body because the "horrible and particular solar cry always approximates the scream of slaughter."[73] Thus, the reenactment of Ḥijāzī's speaker slashing his own throat symbolizes a life-giving sacrifice.

Picasso's life was a struggle "against reaction and the death of art," and *Guernica* expresses "abhorrence of the military caste."[74] Likewise, Ḥijāzī writes poetry as an expression of his struggle against reaction and the death of art. His poetry expresses his abhorrence of powerful dictatorships, those that have taken over Egypt in particular and in the Arab world in general. His poetry is also an attempt to protect art from death. In publishing "Guernica" in 1978, Ḥijāzī not only brings back to life the destruction of Guernica, but also reproduces another form of art, Picasso's painting, and brings it to life again after more than forty years. His recreation of Picasso's painting and the influence of modernist poets like Eliot suggest a clear development in his poetry. It also reflects the broader cultivation he has gained, perhaps especially since going to Paris.

Ḥijāzī's poetry can be seen as an extended dialogue with Eliot's "Tradition and the Individual Talent." In *Kā'ināt Mamlakat al-Layl*, he moves a step past his Nasserist committed poetry and makes a significant change in his poetry. All the poems in this collection are written in free verse, even the elegies. These elegies lament either the lost past, as in "Al-Marāthī aw Maḥāṭṭat al-Zaman al-Ākhar" (Elegies or Stations of the Other Time), or literary or political figures, as in "Marthiyya ilā Victur Hūgū" (Elegy to Victor Hugo) and "Marthiyya ilā Kārl Mārks" (Elegy to Karl Marx).[75] The idea of writing elegies to long-dead literary and political figures suggests the poet's desire to be associated with these figures, to whom he pays tribute.

THE CRITIC: MUBARAK'S EGYPT

In 1981, after the assassination of Sadat, Hosni Mubarak became Egypt's fourth president. He was appointed as vice president in 1975 by Sadat. He would be ousted in 2011 as a result of the Egyptians' January revolution. When Mubarak became president, Ḥijāzī was living in Paris and watching as his country was handed from one dictator to another in a monopoly of power. The first collection Ḥijāzī published after Mubarak assumed the presidency is *Ashjār al-Ismint* (Cement Trees, 1989). In it, Ḥijāzī treats a variety of themes and subjects similar to those explored in *Kā'ināt Mamlakat al-Layl*, now turning his criticism to Mubarak's regime. All the poems in this collection are written in the free verse form.

Ḥijāzī dedicates seven of the sixteen poems in this collection to some of the most influential twentieth-century Arab poets and novelists, such as the Egyptian poets Ṣalāḥ ʿAbd al-Ṣabūr (1931–1981) and Amal Dunqul (1940–1983) and the Saudi novelist ʿAbd al-Raḥmān Munīf (1933–2004). Ḥijāzī identifies with the modern Arab poets and novelists who treat social and political ills in the Arab world. In his dedications and elegies to these poets and novelists, Ḥijāzī is mainly melancholic and pessimistic, especially in his elegies to his fellow poets al-Ṣabūr and Dunqul. *Ashjār al-Ismint*, a depiction of the artificiality and cruelty of the Parisian landscape, becomes a metaphor for the Arab dictatorships. In it Ḥijāzī reveals a great deal of sympathy for the struggle of Arab poets and writers in the twentieth century. Ḥijāzī identifies with the poets and writers who withstood much harassment from oppressive Arab regimes. In so doing, he begins to seriously treat metapoetic themes, though not in the same way al-Bayātī does.

In the collection's title poem, "Ashjār al-Ismint," Ḥijāzī expresses feelings of frustration and criticizes oppressive Arab regimes that not only spy on writers and challenge them, but also create a submissive, defeated generation. It is worth noting that although Ḥijāzī in this collection is critical of some of the regimes' practices, and of the Arabs' passivity, his voice remains exhausted, pessimistic, and frustrated. His is the voice of a broken poet uttering his last words, neither revolutionary nor inspiring or evocative. Ḥijāzī sounds defeated and betrayed. He laments his fellow poets and questions the public's role in setting themselves free. He also criticizes the despotic Arab regimes for oppressing writers and banning them from expressing the ordeal of these crushed individuals, whose pains and struggles are passed on from one generation to the next:

أشجار الأسمنت

تقبل الريح وتمضي
دون أن تعبر هذا الصمت،
أو تقوى على حمل استغاثات القرى
والسفن الغرقى،
وهذا شجر الأسمنت في كل مكان
يتمطَى ، ويخورْ
كالشياطين،
ويصطاد العصافير التي تسقط كالأحجار،
في أجهزة الرادار،
أو تشنق من أعناقها الزّغب،
على أسلاك آلات استراق السَمع،
في تلك السموات التي نعرف من شرفاتنا
أن العصافير تموت الآن فيها
حينما يرتطم السرب.[76]

Cement Trees

The wind comes and goes
Without crossing this silence
Or being able to convey the villages' distress
And the shipwrecked vessels
And these cement trees are everywhere
Showing off and roaring
Like demons
And hunting birds, that fall like stones
In the radars
Or hanging them from the fuzz of their necks
On the wires of the spying machines
From our balconies, we know that
The birds are dying now in these skies
When the flock crashes.

The speaker watches the villages in distress and shipwrecked vessels while the wind comes and goes, uncaring. Life seems to go on without sympathy for the ordeal of the speaker, a poet, who is likened to the bird. Writers express the struggle of the individual in their societies and oppose their oppressive regimes. These regimes are like cement trees: they suffocate the individual and hide his screams between closed doors. They are like demons, which hunt human beings and throw them mercilessly to the ground. The speaker criticizes the Arab regimes for spying on writers, torturing them, and censoring and banning their works from the public. This poem reflects the disappointed, pessimistic, and depressed tone of the whole collection. Ḥijāzī expresses his opposition to the lack of freedom of expression throughout the Arab world, particularly Egypt. Writers are hunted down and their lives are monitored. Furthermore, the oppressive regimes' attack on writers is reinforced by their assassination of young writers. Whether under the rule of Mubarak or the Saudi monarchy, which banned Munīf's works for criticizing it, Ḥijāzī sees the Arab world as a wasteland that oppresses its citizens and silences their voices.

In another stanza in this poem, the speaker looks at the dynamics of life in his country and sees no hope in the Arab public, which is not willing to oppose the regime and fight back.

يقبل الليل ويمضي
دون أن نشبع من نوم،
وهذا شجر الإسمنت يلتف علينا
والمواليد الذين اعتاد آباؤهم الصمت
يجيئون قصارا
ناقصي الخلقة،
لا يخرج من أفواههم صوت
ولا تنمو خصاهم.[77]

The night comes and goes
And we do not sleep enough
While these cement trees wrap us
And the offspring whose parents are used to silence
Are born short

Deformed
No sound comes from their mouths
And their testicles do not grow.

In his wasteland, the speaker expresses the agony of his people, who are unable to find comfort in their lives. The night is incapable of alleviating their pains, and their attempts to escape from stark reality through sleep are fruitless. Fear of the regime follows them in their dreams, and no one escapes its grip. In a life governed by fear of the authorities, the restless, silenced, depressed, and suffocated nation gives birth to deformed offspring, the result of a defeated generation of Arabs accustomed to seeing their lives snatched from them. These offspring, like their parents, will neither oppose the authorities nor speak out. Ḥijāzī's pessimistic outlook is justified by the status quo in Egypt during Mubarak's rule. He sees no hope of setting Egypt free because Mubarak's grip is strong and Egypt's people are defeated.

Ḥijāzī's becomes a lone voice against the current. This explains his melancholy, and it also explains why he kept a low profile for twenty-two years after the publication of this collection. After bearing witness in *Kā'ināt Mamlakat al-Layl* to his people's failure to oppose the regime and speak out, Ḥijāzī watches Egypt from a distance and laments the death of his fellow poets and writers, who get no response to their writings. Almost ten years later, Ḥijāzī questions the role of poetry in society in *Ashjār al-Ismint*. Having for many years written poetry that opposes the oppressive regimes in the Arab world and seen no change in people's attitudes and positions, Ḥijāzī's voice loses its power, which results in losing hope for his people. This explains the pessimistic tone of this collection and the poet's desire to be identified as a critic more than as a poet in the one that arrives more than two decades later. It seems as though great events such as the Arab Uprising might be able to bring poets and their voices back to life. While al-Bayātī turned to metapoetry and enriched his poetry by reinventing his language and creatively using masks and myths, Ḥijāzī's voice was gradually losing its power. Seeing no change or even potential for a revolution, Ḥijāzī loses his inspiration and refrains from publishing poetry collections for over twenty years and focuses on journalism to voice his opposition.

THE ARAB UPRISING AND THE RESURRECTION OF POETRY

Shortly after the eruption of the Egyptian revolution, *Ṭalal al-Waqt* (The Standing Ruins of Time) was published in 2011. In this collection Ḥijāzī is no longer content to merely express frustration and pose questions. His critical voice rises and inspires the public to take a similar stand. The poet uses his critical voice to express universal and national concerns using free verse and advanced poetic techniques. Published twenty-two years after *Ashjār al-Ismint*, this collection presents the culmination of the transformation in Ḥijāzī's poetics that began to develop in *Kā'ināt Mamlakat al-Layl*.

The thirteen poems in this collection can be thematically divided into two categories: the political and revolutionary, and the dedicatory. Both categories consist of poems that point in one direction: the past is behind us and we are the ones who make the future. It is interesting how metapoetry and politics intertwine in this collection. However, this becomes less surprising if we read Ḥijāzī's earlier statements on the relationship between the new poetry and Nasser, which are two sides of the same coin:

> Nasser and poetry have one thing in common: both of them address the nation. Nasser, until now [1971], is the only Arab leader who could break the barriers and speak to the Arab public and evoke its feelings of its unity. Likewise, Arabic poetry is the only kind of art, until now, which addresses the national feelings of the nation. . . . Nasser, the revolution, was born in the catastrophe of Palestine, and thus was born the new poetry. Nasser and the new poetry were born together, and they rebelled against the institutions of our old society, which created misery in our spiritual and material life. . . . From here, Nasser, as a revolution and a man, was an ideal subject for the new poetry. An ideal subject but not a traditional one. . . . The new poetry treated Nasser as a dream and a companion.[78]

Ḥijāzī maintained in 1971 that poetry was written to serve Nasser and the revolution, which made Nasser the ideal subject for the new poetry. However, after the eruption of the Arab Uprising, the people's revolution inspired poets to resume writing poetry, so poetry is reborn, but not to serve a specific leader or regime. The difference between the two stances lies in the poet's realization that his poetry needs to be critical of those in power and supportive of the people. Ḥijāzī's later poetry, as we see in this collection, makes some use of myths, masks, and extended poetic images that enrich his poetry and make it less direct or personal. In *Ṭalal al-Waqt*, Ḥijāzī moves beyond *iltizām* in its traditional sense toward a new kind of *iltizām*. His poetry, at this stage, empowers poets and people alike and situates itself in the Arab literary tradition.

Here Ḥijāzī identifies himself with critics more than with poets in order to inspire the public to be critical of the sociopolitical scene and of its own roles in society. The role of the reader, like that of the poet, shifts from observing history to making it. Ḥijāzī invites his readers to reevaluate their role in and contribution to society, and to lead a revolution in thought and culture by rebelling against the past. In this collection, Ḥijāzī adds another dimension to his poetry: the metapoetic. For Ḥijāzī to occupy himself with politics in his poetry is not new. What is new is treating metapoetic concerns and intertwining them with politics. Ḥijāzī now assumes the role of critic-poet.

Ṭalal means "a portion still standing of the remains of a dwelling or house."[79] *Ṭalal al-Waqt* means "the standing ruins of time." This collection is a manifestation of man's struggle through time, whose ruins stand as a witness. Politics and poetry intertwine through Greek and Near Eastern mythology to treat the universality of death and pain, the quest for freedom and dignity, the inevitability of destruction and suffering as a precondition for rebirth and resurrection, and the celebration of poetry of high quality. Publishing this collection a few months after the eruption of the Egyptian revolution and after twenty-two years of keeping a low profile, Ḥijāzī delivers a statement on the current political, social, and literary scenes in the Arab world in particular and the world in general. It is worth noting that although Ḥijāzī did not publish poetry collections for two decades after his return to Egypt from France, he published occasional poems, and he openly expressed his opinions about politics, religion, education, and literature through his column in *Al-Ahrām Weekly*. In this weekly column on issues of concern to both Egyptians and Arab citizens in general, Ḥijāzī reached millions of readers across the Arab world, through journalism rather than poetry. Ḥijāzī defended freedom of speech and called for secularizing the political and educational systems. The revolution in Egypt revived Arab citizens' faith in themselves, and Arab poets and artists were no exception. Publishing *Ṭalal al-Waqt* amid the revolution in 2011, Ḥijāzī's faith in the vocation of poetry and the people's will to change is restored. It is worth noting that the majority of the poems in this collection were written between 1990 and 2010. Ḥijāzī wrote a few poems after the eruption of the Arab Uprising, added them to the poems he had already published, and collected them all in one book.

In this collection, whether directly or indirectly, politics and metapoetry are present in every poem. Politics is represented as a tool of destruction and poetry as the poets' means of maintaining order in a world governed by chaos. The world in this collection is a wasteland. Without people's consent and will to sacrifice their lives and die for their principles, there is no hope for rebirth and resurrection. Interestingly, this collection is not typeset; instead the poet's own handwritten texts are reproduced to reflect a direct relationship between the poet and the reader. The collection also contains thirteen illustrations by the contemporary Egyptian artist Wajīh Wahba, a member of the expressionist school. Most of these depict meditating human figures.

This collection's thirteen poems can be divided into two major categories, despite some overlapping themes. The first category is the political and revolutionary, which includes "Danse Macabre" (The Death Dance) and "Al-Tughāt" (The Tyrants). The second category consists of a series of metapoetic dedications to six giants of twentieth-century Egyptian literature and the Tunisian Romantic whose poem became the motto of the Arab Uprising. These six poems are "Shafaq ʿalā Sūr al-Madīna: ilā Faraj Fouda" (Twilight on the City Wall: To Faraj Fouda), "Al-Karawān: ilā ʿAbbās Maḥmūd al-ʿAqqād" (The Curlew: To Abbas Mahmoud al-Aqqad), "Al-Sāʿa al-Khāmisa Masā'an: ilā Najīb Maḥfūẓ" (Five P.M.: To Najib Mahfouz), "Laka al-Khulūd: ilā Amīn Nakhla" (May Eternity Be Yours: To Amin Nakhla), "Irādat al-Ḥayā: ilā Abī al-Qāsim al-Shābbī" (Will to Live: To Abu al-Qasim al-Shabbi), "ʿAwdat al-Rūḥ: ilā Tawfīq al-Ḥakīm" (The Return of the Soul: To Tawfiq al-Hakim), and "Sāriq al-Nār: ilā Ṭāha Ḥusayn" (The Fire Stealer: To Taha Husayn). Most of the poems in both categories employ images of death and corruption and convey a message of defiance, resistance, and change. The only three dated poems in this collection are "Al-Tughāt," "Irādat al-Ḥayā: ilā Abī al-Qāsim al-Shābbī," and "ʿAwdat al-Rūḥ: ilā Tawfīq al-Ḥakīm," all of which were written after the eruption of the Egyptian revolution in January 2011 and published in *Al-Ahrām Weekly*. "Sāriq al-Nār: ilā Ṭāhā Ḥusayn" (The Fire Stealer: To Taha Husayn), which is not dated in the collection, was first published in *Al-Maṣrī al-Yawm* on January 31, 2011.

In "Ṭalal al-Waqt," the first and title poem in this collection, Ḥijāzī refuses to sing and maintains that "we should all remain standing in the wilderness":

طلل الوقت

آه!
لا توقظ الدفوف
فما آن لنا بعد أن نهز الدفوفا
بين أرواحنا و أجسادنا ينكسر الإيقاع
فلنبق في العراء وقوفاً.[80]

The Standing Ruins of Time

Oh!
Do not wake the tambourines up
The time has not come yet to shake the tambourines
The rhythm between our bodies and our souls is broken
So let us remain standing in the wilderness.

This poem gives shape to the poet's frustration and disappointment with the status quo in Egypt. The title refers to the time during which the poet lives in a wasteland that has not yet seen change or hope. This time is the standing ruins of the past; the hoped-for future has not come yet. Thus, Ḥijāzī maintains that his people should neither sing nor dance because their bodies and souls cannot keep the same rhythm, and therefore they should remain standing in the wilderness until a change takes place. This indicates the gap between what the people do (their bodies) and what they feel and believe (their souls). Ḥijāzī provokes his people to realize that there is a discrepancy between their beliefs and actions. Thus, because there is nothing worth being happy for in their lives, they should not sing or dance until they live the life they want and deserve. The past political events and defeats in the Arab world are the standing ruins of time, which have proven to Arabs that they are still living the same humiliating life despite the change of rulers. Whether headed by Nasser, Sadat, or Mubarak, the same regimes have ruled and terrorized the Egyptians, and their promises of democracy and a better life and future are mere lies. Ḥijāzī asks his fellow citizens to remain standing in the wilderness until their life changes. To do so is to face cruel reality without fearing death until change takes place. Ḥijāzī speaks of this change and the status quo in Egypt and the Arab world in the other poems in this collection as well. This poem suggests the brief calm before the storm in the Arab world.

"Danse Macabre" (The Death Dance) and "Al-Tughāt" (The Tyrants), which belong to the political and revolutionary category, also speak of the status quo, projecting the political and social scenes in the Arab world as a wilderness corrupted by tyrants. In "Danse Macabre," Ḥijāzī employs death images and mythology to convey the disappointment, frustration, and loathing that preceded the Egyptian revolution. The first two stanzas read as follows:

Danse Macabre

اشربو للردى!
وكلوا للردى!
فالوليمة ما أولم القبر للدود
من لحمنا و دمانا غدا
والحياة! انظروا للظلال، وقولوا سدى!
لم نكن غير ظل على حائط صعدا!
ثم دبّ دبيباً، وأدركه الوقت فارتعدا
وانتهى بددا
نحن ياسيدي لم نكن أبدا
أبدا أبدا!
من أين يأتي كل هذا الموت؟
أيّ خطيئة عمياء لوّثت المدينة

فاستحقت ان تُعاقب بالظلام السرمدي
تعيشه، والشمس طالعه
تزف له، وتنجب منه نسلا شائهاً
وجه، ولا عينان
وفم، ولا شفتان
لغو، ولا لغة
وأشعار بلا معنى ولا ميزان.[81]

The Death Dance

Drink to death!
And eat to death!
Because this feast is what the grave has prepared for the worms
Of our flesh and blood for tomorrow
And for life! Look at the shadows and say: "In vain!"
We have never been but a shadow ascending a wall!
Then it walked slowly until there was no time left so
it was terrified!
And it vanished
We, sir, have never been before
Never never!
Where does all this death come from?
Which blind sin corrupted the city
So it deserved to be punished with absolute darkness?
It lives in it while the sun shines
It is wedded to him and it gives birth to a deformed offspring
A face and no eyes
A mouth and no lips
Chatter and no language
And poetry without meaning or rhythm.

The "danse macabre" is a symbol for the Black Death, "with its writhing skeletons dancing arm-in-arm with soon-to-be dead men, women, and children."[82] In this poem, the speaker asks his people to drink and eat before they dance their last dance of death, in which they offer their bodies to the worms. The speaker asks his people to look at their past, worthless lives, which they lived in vain, and realize that they "have never been before." The image of death coming from everywhere in the city is followed by an image of darkness covering the city and preventing the sun from shining. The speaker wonders why has the city been so punished, cursed, and corrupted. The city is wedded to absolute darkness, and their offspring is a deformed creature with no face, eyes, mouth, or lips. This creature's language is chatter, and its poetry is void of meaning and rhythm. This deformed creature is the offspring of the nation Ḥijāzī criticized in "Ashjār al-Ismint." Egypt's defeated and submissive nation is responsible for its new, deformed generation. The city is a wasteland, and its inhabitants are deformed creatures who live and die in ignorance and darkness while the sun shines somewhere else. Ḥijāzī here questions the state of Egypt under the rule of Mubarak. Egypt is ridden by the Black Death, which suggests the dictatorship of Mubarak's regime. Ḥijāzī sees his plague-ridden country marching toward defeat while its people dance their last dance of death. Egypt's deformed nation neither sees, nor hears, nor speaks out. Ḥijāzī criticizes not only Mubarak's dictatorship, which brought darkness and deformation of nation, culture, and literature to Egypt, but also his fellow Egyptians.

For Ḥijāzī, although Mubarak's regime is responsible for the deterioration of Egypt, Egyptians also share some responsibility for this decay. The image of the dancers drinking and dancing is interrupted by another image of them looking at their shadows and realizing that they have lived their lives in vain and that their dance is the danse macabre. Ḥijāzī wants his fellow Egyptians to realize that they have wasted their lives without accomplishing anything and that the regime, like the plague, sweeps away all their dreams and feasts upon their corpses. He incites the Egyptians to reject and take action against humiliation, oppression, and the deformation of their offspring and literature under the rule of Mubarak, who will continue corrupting the country. Mubarak's dictatorship has imposed its order by violence and not only tortured and oppressed people, but also reduced their language to chatter and their poetry to words devoid of meaning or rhythm. Thus, this poem expresses Ḥijāzī's opposition to Mubarak's regime and his call to his people to fight this Black Plague to death because "when vulnerable mortals could depict, narrate, and enact the Dance of Death, they gained a subtle sense of control."[83] Writing this poem, Ḥijāzī depicts the state of horror and decay and narrates and enacts the dance of death in Egypt under the rule of Mubarak. In so doing, he tries to convey and transmit "a subtle sense of control" over the deterioration of Egypt. This sense of control is only gained when people change their attitudes by realizing that they should not agree to being the regime's feast; instead, they should fight it. In this poem, as in many others in this collection, Ḥijāzī attacks Mubarak's regime and urges his people to revolt.

In "Al-Tughāt" (The Tyrants), Ḥijāzī represents dictatorships with images of snakes, aliens from other planets, monsters dyeing their hair, and their bodies hanging between the sky and earth. These monsters and tyrants have corrupted and cursed the city.

الطغاة

والطغاة
الغزاة
الولاة
الجباة
هذه الكائنات الخرافية
الأفعوانات
قائدة الإنقلاب
مزورة الانتخاب
المسوخ التي صبغت شعرها
ونفت نفسها خارج الوقت كيلا تموت
تتأرجح بين السموات و الأرض
تسترق السمع بين مقابرنا والبيوت
[. . .]
ونحن الظماء
ونحن الجياع العراة
وقوف هنا لا نزال على شرفات مآذننا
وسطوح منازلنا
نستغيث، ونرفع أيدينا بالدعاء
وهي تصغي لنا من بعيد، وترمقنا بازدراء
وتهشّ على رأسنا بعصاها![84]

The Tyrants

And the tyrants
The invaders
The governors
The tax collectors
These mythological creatures
The snakes
The coup leaders
The election falsifiers
The monsters who dyed their hair
And exiled themselves outside time so they do not die
Swinging between heaven and earth
Spying on us between our graveyards and houses
[. . .]
And we are the thirsty
And we are the naked hungry
Still standing here on the balconies of our minarets
And the roofs of our houses
Asking for help and raising our hands to pray
Listening to us from afar, they glance at us with contempt
And strike us with their stick.

In "Al-Tughāt," Ḥijāzī juxtaposes images of the tyrants in the Arab world with images of their citizens. The tyrants are the coup leaders and invaders of their own countries who force their rule on their people with dictatorships and falsified elections. They are also the governors and the tax collectors who suck their people's blood and money. They exploit citizens and steal their money until they and their families die of hunger. These mythological creatures present themselves as gods who are above everybody. They are snakes and monsters who dye their hair and exile themselves outside time to remain young, images aimed squarely at Mubarak, who was known for dyeing his hair, and other dictators who used such tricks to remain young in the eyes of their people. Such tyrants refuse to accept that they are old and no longer fit for their positions, so they terrorize their people in order to remain in power. The depiction of tyrants as snakes, monsters, and mythological creatures also indicates their attempts to constantly change form in order to stay in power. They swing between heaven and earth by spreading their forces everywhere to spy on people and terrify them. The dictatorship of tyrants creates a mortified, horrified nation that fears its leaders in life and death.

These ugly images of the tyrants are juxtaposed with those emphasizing the suffering of their people, especially the Egyptians. The speaker screams that his thirsty, naked, and hungry people remain standing against Mubarak, who glances at them with contempt from afar and strikes them, like animals, with his stick. Ḥijāzī directs his people's feelings of rage and aversion toward Mubarak and his crimes. This poem is dated March 8, 2011, which means it was written after the January 25 Egyptian revolution.[85] Ḥijāzī expresses the public's feelings and emotions toward the end of another extended era of oppression and defeat in Egypt's history, and gives shape to the feelings of a whole nation in the making. In this last stanza of this poem, Ḥijāzī announces the resurrection of Egypt as a result of the revolution:

ولقد آن يا مصر، يا غالية!
آن أن تستعيدي شبابك
آن أن تولدي مرة ثانية
آن أن يسقط العبد فيك
وأن تسقط الجارية
لكي يسقط الطاغية.[86]

And it is time, Egypt, O my dear!
It is time to restore your youth
It is time to be reborn again
It is time for the slave in you to fall
And for the slave girl to fall
So the tyrant will fall!

Ḥijāzī ends this poem on a high note and with an optimistic tone. He perceives the revolution as the rebirth of Egypt, whose past rule of slavery and corruption will come to end after the fall of its dictator, Mubarak. On February 11, 2011, the day Mubarak resigned, Ḥijāzī wrote "'Awdat al-Rūḥ: ilā Tawfīq al-Ḥakīm" (The Return of the Soul: To Tawfiq al-Hakim). The poem takes its title from the novel *'Awdat al-Rūḥ* (The Return of the Soul, 1933), by Tawfīq al-Ḥakīm (1898–1987), a prominent Egyptian playwright and novelist. The novel became immensely popular during the Nasserist revolution for its vision of national rebirth, and its title was revived again in popular usage to describe the January 2011 Egyptian revolution. Writing this poem on the same day Mubarak was ousted, Ḥijāzī celebrates the revolution, the national rebirth of Egypt, and its offspring, freedom:

عودة الروح
إلى توفيق الحكيم

إنّ سبعين قرنا تطل عليكم
وأنتم بقلب المدينة
بل أنتمو قلبها النابض الآن
أنتم مدينتكم
هذه القاهرة
لم تكن غير سجن
وهاهي ساحاتها و شوارعها العامرة
جنة حرة
ومدى
وفضاء!
[. . .]
إنها عودة الروح!
عودة مصر إلى نفسها
عودة الشعر إلى الشعراء
عودتنا كلّنا للغناء![87]

The Return of the Soul: To Tawfiq al-Hakim

Seventy centuries are indeed overlooking you[88]
While you are in the heart of the city
You are its beating heart now
You are your own city
This Cairo

Has been but a prison
And here its squares and prosperous streets
Have become a free heaven
And a horizon
And a space!
[. . .]
It is the return of the soul!
The return of Egypt to itself
The return of poetry to poets
The return of all of us to singing!

Ḥijāzī shifts his pessimistic tone to an optimistic one when he sees the return of the soul to Egypt coming true through the 2011 revolution. The wasteland we see in "The Tyrants" and "The Death Dance" becomes heaven on earth. Cairo, which has been a prison for centuries under the rule of dictators, opens its heart to its people and becomes their heaven, horizon, and space. Ḥijāzī promises his people a better, brighter future and a return of life to Egypt and to them because their revolution has made them their city's beating heart. It is hoped that the revolution against Mubarak's regime will resurrect Cairo and bring Egypt back to its people, so the Egyptians may be able to sing and the poets to write. Ḥijāzī intertwines poetry with politics in line 57, where poetry returns to poets like the soul returns to the body. This is a statement on the lack of freedom of expression under the rule of Mubarak, which explains the poet's lengthy absence from the poetic scene. Unlike "Ṭalal al-Waqt" and "Danse Macabre," "'Awdat al-Rūḥ" announces that now is the time to dance and celebrate. In "'Awdat al-Rūḥ" Ḥijāzī also celebrates the influence of the Egyptian revolution on his poetry. By revolting against Mubarak and announcing the beginning of a new era in Egypt, the Egyptians inspired Ḥijāzī to write poetry. For the first time, the public plays a positive and active role in Ḥijāzī's poetics and becomes the force behind the revival of poetry. This is a significant change in Ḥijāzī's work. His relationship to his reader is no longer one of giver and recipient: his readers are no longer passive because they are not only the reason for the liberation of Egypt, but also the inspiration of poets like Ḥijāzī himself. Ḥijāzī's voice is no longer the defeated and exhausted one we heard in

Ashjār al-Ismint. Instead, it is loud, strong, and full of life, pride, and hope. It is worth noting that the military commander ʿAbd al-Fattāḥ al-Sīsī overthrew and led on July 3, 2013, the military coup against Muḥammad Mursī, the first and only democratically elected president of Egypt. Therefore, the military continues to control the state, and neither democracy nor freedom of expression are among its goals. For Ḥijāzī, the fact that his people revolted against the regime of Mubarak indicates the return of the soul to Egypt. Furthermore, despite not realizing its goals of democracy and freedom in Egypt, the revolution signals a new beginning in the history of the politics of Egypt. The fact that the military overthrew Mursī and remains in power as of this writing reflects the complexity of the political situation in Egypt.

"Al-Karawān" (The Curlew), another poem in this collection, is dedicated to Egyptian poet, critic, and writer ʿAbbās Maḥmūd al-ʿAqqād.

الكروان
"إلى عباس محمود العقّاد"

1 "هل يسمعون سوى صدى الكروان
صوتا يرفرف في الهزيع الثاني"
[. . .]
7 الملك لك! الملك لك!
[. . .]
الملك لك! الملك لك!
صوت يجيء من النهاية، ناسخاً هذا الزمان
فكل شيء باطل
ما كان من بشر، ومن شجر، ومن بنيان
25 فنيت، وهذا الليل ليس بفان[89]

The Curlew: To Abbas Mahmoud al-Aqqad

"Do they hear anything but the echo of the curlew 1
A sound fluttering in the second part of the night?"
[. . .]
The power is yours! The power is yours! 7
[. . .]
The power is yours! The power is yours!

A sound that comes from the end, erasing this time
Because everything is in vain
What was of human beings, trees, and buildings
Perished while this night is not perishable. 25

The first two lines in "Al-Karawān" are the first verse from a poem by al-ʿAqqād with the same title, "Al-Karawān" (The Curlew). In al-ʿAqqād's poem, this bird, the curlew, is criticized for repeating the same sounds. Al-ʿAqqād uses the call of the curlew, praising and praying to Allah when people are asleep, to question whether people realize that despite sounding redundant, the curlew always has something new in its essence. Ḥijāzī's poem challenges the religious aspect of al-ʿAqqād's poem by provoking people to revolt and decide their own destiny. Al-ʿAqqād's Karawān is his poetic voice, which was criticized for being redundant in treating the same set of issues in his poetry. Ḥijāzī writes this poem as a *muʿāraḍa* of al-ʿAqqād's poem to reflect on and challenge the earlier poet's stance on religion and poetry.[90] Ḥijāzī treated social and political issues in his earlier as well as his later poetry, and his "Al-Karawān" is thus an attempt to reaffirm the novelty of his poetry. Ḥijāzī's use of the curlew differs from that of al-ʿAqqād in that al-ʿAqqād's curlew praises Allah throughout the night, whereas in his lines 23–25, Ḥijāzī shifts the focus from religion to humankind and their struggle against darkness: dictatorships. Everything perishes except for man's struggle. In "Danse Macabre," Ḥijāzī states that the human being is the core of everything:

Danse Macabre

26 الملك لك! الملك لك!
الملك لك! الملك لك!
[. . .]
38 الملك لك! لك!
[. . .]
"هل يسمعون سوى صدى الكروان
صوتا يرفرف في الهزيع الثاني"
الملك لك!
55 الملك للإنسان!
الملك للإنسان![91]

The Death Dance

The power is yours! 26
The power is yours!
[. . .]
The power is yours! yours! 38
[. . .]
"Do they hear but the echo of the curlew
A sound fluttering in the second part of night?"
The power is yours!
The power is Man's! 55
The power is Man's!

The repetition of "The power is yours" in "The Curlew" and "The Death Dance" and "the power is Man's!" in "The Death Dance" reflects an ironic tone toward religion. Ḥijāzī's statement that "the power is Man's" represents the victory of the human will to change over religion. Instead of praying and waiting for change to happen, Ḥijāzī shifts the agency to his people and provokes them to be the change makers. Instead of staying awake through the night to pray and praise Allah, Egyptians should take action and respond to the humiliation of their nation by revolting against the status quo. Al-ʿAqqād attempts to change what people think of his poetry, but Ḥijāzī wants to change how people see themselves. Ḥijāzī provokes the Egyptians to realize that the solution to their ordeal lies in their hands: the change has to come from within. Neither their religion nor tyrants are going to change their lives. Thus, he calls for a people's revolution.

Ḥijāzī himself criticized al-ʿAqqād for his rejection of free verse as a legitimate form of poetry. Ḥijāzī maintains that al-ʿAqqād revolted against the poets of his time, so Ḥijāzī and other poets revolted against him by writing in the free verse form and viciously attacking the neoclassicists. Al-ʿAqqād wanted to see change take place in the prosaic poetry of his age, and he had a vision about free verse poetry, but he also attacked those who wrote free verse poetry and declared their poetry to be prose.[92] However, Ḥijāzī maintains, "I have never been excited about the prose poem. I have always considered it lacking, and I have not changed my mind because I have not found yet an example that would convince me that the prose form is one of the poetic forms."[93] In addition, Ḥijāzī attacks the prose poem and defines poetry: "Rhythm is the other wing in the poetic figurative language, next to the poetic image. And with the image and the rhythm, language is transferred from the world of waking to the dream world or it changes from walking to dancing, as the French poet Paul Valéry used to say. And if this is the function of rhythm, then poetry cannot be without rhythm."[94] This explains why Ḥijāzī neither writes prose poetry nor accepts it as a legitimate poetic form. This distinguishes him from other twentieth-century Arab poets, including Adūnīs, who wrote and supported the prose poem and considered it a development of the free verse poem. Adūnīs criticized poets who wrote exclusively in one form and defended the poet's duty to reinvent himself by being creative and innovative. Freedom for Adūnīs lay in the ability to write in whichever form the poem dictates. Likewise, al-Bayātī refused to identify a best form in poetry and maintained that innovation in language, regardless of form, is the measure of excellence in poetry.

In "Al-Sāʿa al-Khāmisa Masāʾan: ilā Najīb Maḥfūẓ" (Five P.M.: To Naguib Mahfouz), Ḥijāzī asks writer Najīb Maḥfūz to save Egypt:

الساعة الخامسة مساء
"إلى نجيب محفوظ"

وها أنت وحدك ياأيها الشاهد الفذّ
تخترق الظلمة الدامسة
عارياً، ناحلاً
لا تنوء بما حملت كتفاك
ولا تشتكي لعصاك
من الطعنات الخسيسة والأوجه الغطّة العابسة
بل تجود على الطرقات
بما عتّق الدهر والفكر من طيبات دماك
تدق بها فوق أبوابنا المغلقات
لنصحو في الساعة الخامسة
فانهضي الآن يا مصر! إن كنت ناهضه
ولك الشمس مركبة، والزمان حصان
أو إن ظلت هامدة فغدا لن يجيء
ولن يشرق الكوكبان![95]

Five P.M.: To Naguib Mahfouz

And here you are alone, O strong witness
Penetrating the absolute darkness
Naked, thin
Unable to bear what your shoulders carry
And never complaining to your cane
Of the vile stabs and the despicable grim faces
Yet, you bestow on the roads
What time and thought have aged of the blessings
of your blood
You use them to knock on our closed doors
So we wake up at five o'clock
Rise now, Egypt! If you are ever going to rise
The sun will be your carriage and time your horse
Or if you stay dead, tomorrow will never come
And the two planets will not shine!

Najīb Maḥfūẓ (1911–2006) was an Egyptian writer, critic, novelist, and thinker who survived an assassination attempt by Islamic extremists in 1994 for his controversial writings. The title of this poem, "Five P.M.," was the hour at which the attempted assassination took place. In the poem, it becomes the hour of awakening when Egypt rises and the sun shines. Images of Maḥfūẓ walking in the streets of Egypt to enlighten its people, despite being old and burdened, are juxtaposed with images of Egypt sinking in absolute darkness. Ḥijāzī addresses Maḥfūẓ and reflects upon his vision of the rise and rebirth of Egypt by revolting against dictatorships, ignorance, and oppression. Despite the vile stabs and the grim faces of Mubarak's regime, Ḥijāzī tells his fellow Egyptians that if they are ever going to rise, now is the time: if they do not revolt, tomorrow will never come and they will never see the sun. Thus assuming the role of the awakener of his people against their oppressive regime, Ḥijāzī becomes an extension of Maḥfūẓ.

In "Sāriq al-Nār: ilā Ṭaha Ḥusayn" (The Fire Stealer: To Taha Husayn), Ḥijāzī asks writer Ṭāha Ḥusayn, who becomes Prometheus, to guide Arabs toward freedom.

سارق النار
"إلى طه حسين"

آية أن يكحلّه الله بالظلمة السرمديّة
أم آية
أن يقود خطانا إلى النور
هذا النبي الضرير؟!
[. . .]
كان يسري بنا في الدجنة
يخرجنا من عصور
ويدخلنا في عصور
وكأنّا على رفرف من شعاع نطير
ونعرج في سلّم من سطور
والمعريّ يسبق طه
وطه يراه، ويركض في إثره
والمغنّي الأثيني في أول الركب يحضن قيثاره.[96]

The Fire Stealer: To Taha Husayn

Is it a miracle that God made absolute darkness
    the kohl of his eyes?
Or is it a miracle
That this blind prophet
Guides us toward the light?
[. . .]
He used to journey with us at night
Taking us out of ages
Into other ages
As if we were flying on wings of light-rays
And we ascend in a ladder of written lines
And Maʿarrī precedes Ṭāha
While Ṭāha sees him and follows him
While the Athenian singer is holding his guitar at the head
    of the riders.

Ṭāha Ḥusayn was an Egyptian novelist, writer, and critic. Although he was blind, his thought and writings made him one of the prominent

Arab writers of the twentieth century. In this poem, Ḥijāzī juxtaposes the image of absolute darkness as kohl in Ḥusayn's eyes with the image of the blind Ḥusayn guiding Arabs toward enlightenment. In the two images, Ḥusayn is portrayed as a blind prophet who guides his nation toward the light. Guiding the sighted, Ḥusayn becomes the discerning prophet whose blindness is only physical.

In lines 61–68, Ḥijāzī employs images of Ḥusayn's ascension journey with his people. Ḥusayn follows Abū al-ʿAlā' al-Maʿarrī and the "Athenian singer," Homer, toward the light. What these three poets have in common is that they were all blind. Ḥusayn wrote his Ph.D. dissertation on al-Maʿarrī and shared some of his skepticism toward religion. In this poem, Homer, the captain of the ship, holds his guitar and stands at the bow of the ship while al-Maʿarrī and Ḥusayn journey with him. Ḥusayn follows the in steps of al-Maʿarrī and Homer and guides his people on a night journey and ascension like that of the Prophet Muḥammad. We see images of these three riders journeying at night, leaving behind an age of ignorance to enter into an age of enlightenment, as if they are flying on a wing made of rays beaming from darkness into light.

The title of the poem, "Sāriq al-Nār: ilā Ṭāha Ḥusayn," compares Ḥusayn to the Greek god Prometheus, who defeated Zeus by stealing fire and giving it to humans. Al-Maʿarrī liberates his people by bringing them enlightenment and defying religion in his writings. Likewise, Ḥijāzī is an extension of these critics. He writes poetry to encourage his people to reject the status quo and revolt. He hopes to inspire his people to be active participants in the making of their history. He hopes his poetry will empower them to believe that they are capable of changing their fate and taking control of their lives.

Ḥijāzī's voice in the previous collection was very critical of the Arab individual. Instead of empowering and inspiring the individual to oppose his regime and stand up for his rights, Ḥijāzī announced his frustration and disappointment with him. This was the case for many Arab poets who were exiled for opposing their regimes and who wrote in support of their oppressed people for decades but saw no hope. This might explain why Ḥijāzī refrained from publishing collections for so long after 1989. However, an event as momentous and revolutionary as the Arab Uprising was enough to bring poetry to the forefront of society. It showed the power of the people who marched in protest against all the dictatorial regimes, against decades of violations of human rights in the Arab world. Watching the nation he had begged to protest and reject slavery waking up from its long sleep and transforming itself, children and young and old men and women alike, into fearless demonstrators in the midst of chaos, Ḥijāzī sees his prophecy coming true, and the poetry flows. By changing the way the world looks at Arabs, this political event also changed the way poets view their poetry. When asked if he believed there was a relationship between writing poetry and the Arab Uprising, Ḥijāzī said, "It is the substantial changes in life that awaken man and revive consciousness and existence, and provide him with new material to write about."[97] The revolution resurrected Ḥijāzī's poetic voice because it enabled him to say something new. This Arab awakening inspired another revolution in literature.

Ḥijāzī writes this new kind of poetry with a new revolutionary voice to give shape to his people's feelings of frustration and rebellion. *Ṭalal al-Waqt* also includes "Irādat al-Ḥayā: ilā Abū al-Qāsim al-Shābbī" (Will to Live: To Abu al-Qasim al-Shabbi). Al-Shābbī was a nationalist Tunisian poet and is best known for his poem "Will to Live," which was published in 1933; one of its verses was included in the Tunisian national anthem. The demonstrators in most of the Arab countries chanted this verse, "If people want to live, destiny will listen," after the Tunisian street vendor Moḥammad Bouʿazīzī immolated himself in Tunisia in December 17, 2010, igniting the spirit of revolution in the Arab world.

Ḥijāzī wrote this poem with a lot of excitement and hope. He addresses this poem to al-Shābbī to initiate a dialogue with "if people want to live, destiny will listen." Here, Ḥijāzī tells his people that if they want to live, it is not enough to just want to live; rather, they should carry their souls in their palms and walk in the middle of danger to make destiny respond. He demands that people stop relying on mere romantic dreams. In the following stanzas, Ḥijāzī reminds his people that a day and a year have passed but neither has destiny listened nor a stone been moved:

إرادة الحياة
”إلى أبي القاسم الشّابي“

”إذا الشعب يوما أراد الحياة“
فلا بدّ أن يتحرر من خوفه

ويحمل في كفه روحه
ويسير بها موغلا في الخطر
إلى أن يستجيب القدر
[. . .]
"إذا الشعب يوما أراد الحياة
فلا بدّ أن يستجيب القدر"!
وهاهو يوم يمر وعام
وجيل وجيل
ولم يستجب أحد للشعب
لم يتململ حجر
[. . .]
فلا بدّ أن نسترد شجاعتنا
وننادي جماعتنا
ونسير بأمواجنا العاتية
إلى الطاغية
نطالبه بالمقابل عن كل ماعرفته البلاد
من الجوع والقهر في ظله والهوان
أن يعيد الذي مات حياً
ومن خاف أن يشفيه من خوفه
ويعيد إليه الآمان
وما سفحته العيون من الدمع يجمعه دمعة دمعة
ويردّ الزمان إلى حيث كان
"إذا الشعب يوما اراد الحياة"
فلابد أن يقوم العبيد
قيامتهم
يصبرون على عضة الجوع
لكن على عضة القيد لا يصبرون
يموتون في أول الليل
إن كان لابد أن يموتوا
لأنهمو سيقومون في مطلع الفجر
كي يولدوا في غد من جديد!
[. . .]
"إذا الشعب يوما اراد الحياة"
فلابد أن يتحرش بالموت
أن ينزل الموت من عرشه
[. . .]

لا تخافوا من الموت
فالموت ليس سوى أن تخافوا من الموت
يغلبكم واحدا واحدا
فإذا ما اجتمعتم عليه مضى خاسئا
[. . .]
ولابد للشعب أن ينتصر.[98]

The Will to Live: To Abu al-Qasim al-Shabbi

"If one day, the people want to live"
Then they have to liberate themselves from their fear
And carry their soul in their palm
And walk with it in the middle of danger
Until destiny responds
[. . .]
"If one day, the people want to live
Destiny will surely respond!"
And here is a day passing and a year
A generation and a generation
While no one has listened to the people
No stone has moved from its place
[. . .]
Then we have to regain our courage
And call our people
And walk with our strong waves
Toward the tyrant
Demanding compensation for all that the country has known
Of hunger, oppression, and humiliation under his rule
To resurrect him who died alive
And to heal him who is scared
And restore safety to him
And to collect the eyes' tears one by one
And to restore time
"If one day, the people want to live,"
Then slaves should rise
To their resurrection

Patient with the bite of hunger
But impatient with the bite of the chain
They die in the beginning of the night
If they have to die
Because they will resurrect in the early dawn
To be born anew tomorrow!
[. . .]
"If one day, the people want to live,"
They should harass death
To bring death down from its throne
[. . .]
Do not be afraid of death
Because death is nothing but fear of death
Which defeats you one by one
If you fight it together, it leaves humiliated
[. . .]
And the people must win.

This poem empowers Arabs and affirms their faith in their revolution against dictatorships and the oppression that has governed their lives for ages. Ḥijāzī maintains that this is the perfect time to revolt and be resurrected into a new life. He gives shape to feelings of rage and disappointment, and he empowers his people by calling them to take matters into their hands if they aspire to live freely. In lines 1–20, Ḥijāzī juxtaposes two images of people calling for change. In the first, these people are carrying their souls in their palms and walking, reckless and fearless, in the middle of danger. In the second, these people do nothing except wait for destiny to change their lives, only to discover that time passes but no stone moves from its place and no one answers their calls. The significance of juxtaposing these two images lies in the poet's rejection of the people's surrender and their faith in destiny to bring change. Thus, the remainder of the poem becomes Ḥijāzī's manifesto of what people should do if they really want change. He reinforces al-Shābbī's vision of a nation fighting for its freedom, a nation whose will forces destiny to respond. Ḥijāzī provokes the people to break the chains that shackled them and their thought for centuries and to prove to their dictators that if they want to live, they will fear no one and they will fight until they win. The images in lines 37–103 are sometimes militant, sometimes empowering, and sometimes inspiring. In lines 37–47, the speaker calls for his nation to walk united like an army toward its tyrant, Mubarak, and to demand compensation for all the hunger, oppression, and humiliation the country has been subjected to under his rule. Also, he reminds his people that their tyrant is responsible for those who have suffered and those who are scared, for the tears that have been shed and the time that has been lost. Thus, "if they want to live," they have to rise from their slavery, as we see in lines 48–56, and despite being patient with the bites of hunger, they should be impatient with the bites of the chain. The speaker incites feelings of anger and frustration in his people and tells them to no longer accept humiliation and defeat. In lines 53–56, the speaker tells his people that if the price of rebirth and resurrection is death, they should be willing to pay it if necessary. Thus, in lines 63–75, he asks them to harass death and bring it down from its throne by fighting together and leaving it humiliated and defeated. If they do that, "the people must win." This marks the turning point in this collection: if people fight for life and no longer fear death, they must win.

It is worth noting that this poem also reinforces the role of poetry in politics and vice versa. The poet becomes the voice of his nation, who dedicates his poetry not only to express his nation's feelings, but also to empower and shape its actions during the Arab Uprising. His poetry becomes the weapon that provokes his people to fight for their freedom and articulates the public's opposition to the regime. In this collection, we hear the poet's voice rise from the turmoil of major political events. He carries on with long-dead critics a lively dialogue that engages his readers in current political events and the process of writing poetry. The relationship between the poet and his reader is at its best in this collection, with each inspiring the other. Ḥijāzī writes poetry that responds to contemporary social and political events inspired by and relevant to the Arab citizen, and the Arab citizen finds support and inspiration in poetry.

This assumption of the role of the critic-poet distinguishes Ḥijāzī's later poetry from his earlier work. In this collection in particular, we see a poet rebelling against the dictatorships, injustice, and humiliation of his people and of all mankind. Unlike Ḥijāzī's earlier collections, this one is neither direct nor personal. He begins to express some of his meta-poetic concerns, though not in the same way al-Bayātī does. Al-Bayātī's later poetry is more sophisticated and more carefully articulated than that of Ḥijāzī. This is in part due to the manner in which each poet responded to the lack of inspiration after the 1967 defeat. Al-Bayātī descended to the underworld, looking for inspiration, and became a mythmaker himself, one whose love for poetry kept him from leaving it behind. Ḥijāzī, however, waited for a revolution in society to ignite a revolution in his poetry. In this collection, we hear the poet's voice attacking the regime, questioning the people's will to revolt against it, and empowering his nation to make its own destiny. Ḥijāzī intertwines poetry and politics and invokes the critics who preceded him in order that he might have the same influence on his people. This reflects a mature kind of commitment in which his poetic voice is critical of both social and political ills, as well as the state of poetry. He is committed to literature as much as to politics. His poetic voice announces its independence from other voices by emerging as that of a critic-poet, one who writes poetry while assuming the role of the critic. His dedications to critics who preceded him attest to his poetic legacy and innovation. He even becomes an extension of the critics with whom he prefers to be associated. Being critical becomes the poet's goal. He encourages his people to be critical of the status quo. In this collection, we no longer hear the poet praising and advocating for a specific political leader or regime. On the contrary, we hear his voice indirectly shaping the feelings of the public and voicing his position on poetry and politics.

The publication of Ḥijāzī's latest collection in the midst of the Arab Uprising suggests the significance of the revolution for his poetic vocation. Having published no poetry collections for twenty-two years, Ḥijāzī regains his poetic voice and is reborn from the ashes of the past. The people's revolution he long called for in his poetry has returned freedom to Egypt and poetry to poets. Now, like his dedicatees, Ḥijāzī returns to the political scene through poetry in hopes of reaching his audience and inspiring them in the same way they inspired him.

Dedication in literature "raises problems and invites questions."[99] Ḥijāzī's "Irādat al-Ḥayā: ilā Abī al-Qāsim al-Shābbī" invites the reader and the Arab public to rethink their social and political lives. Ḥijāzī addresses the Arab individual and shifts the agency from destiny to mankind. By dedicating this poem to al-Shābbī, Ḥijāzī is extending al-Shābbī's poetry and politics into the current situation. Ḥijāzī's *mu'āraḍa* of al-Shābbī's most famous poem becomes a bold poetic, social, and political statement that questions the readers' understanding of their role as individuals responsible for their destiny, as well as poetry as an articulation of the people's aspirations and opposition to their ruler's apathy. Celebrated during the Arab Uprising, al-Shābbī's "Irādat al-Ḥayā" becomes Ḥijāzī's muse. Ḥijāzī's reflection on al-Shābbī's most powerful poem, in a poem written at this particular time, revives the Egyptian sense of nationalism and patriotism. In addition, it renews and inspires the public after decades of defeatist poetry.

Writing poetry of the revolution from a perspective of a fighter, Ḥijāzī turns into a critic and rebel. This collection treats pressing political issues in the Arab world and offers a critical perspective on modern Arab literary issues. In addition, some of Ḥijāzī's dedications, such as "Al-Karawān," shed light on other controversial poetic, religious, and political issues of his time. In dedicating this poem to al-'Aqqād, Ḥijāzī confirms his stance on literary issues. Al-'Aqqād rejected free verse form; Ḥijāzī rejected the prose poem. Thus, on one level, whether he admits it or not, Ḥijāzī identifies with al-'Aqqād because both of them are criticized for their attitudes toward new experiments with form in Arabic poetry. On another level, Ḥijāzī identifies with al-'Aqqād because Ḥijāzī does not want his people to criticize his poetry for being redundant and traditional. Ḥijāzī incites his people to think of their own ordeal and help themselves by revolting against their regimes. His karawān is a revolutionary that wants to awaken people and revive their will to revolt. Now that they are revolting against Mubarak, he is confident that they will be more responsive to his revolutionary poetry.

Ḥijāzī invites the Arab reader to read his poetry closely and engage with his poetics because "these poetic engagements emphasize both faith in the vocation of poetry and the commitment to transformation and change, fathomed and anticipated by poets."[100] Ḥijāzī's dedications to bygone critics who had a great influence on their people reflect his faith in the role of poetry in politics and society. In dedicating most of his poems in this collection to other critics, Ḥijāzī implies "that the poet, no less than the dedicatee, also suffers for embarking on innovation and change."[101] At this stage, Ḥijāzī's poetry, like the works of his dedicatees, reaches a point in which it empowers the public and calls for revolutionary change. He joins the group of riders—Ḥusayn, al-Maʿarrī, al-Shābbī, and Maḥfūẓ—and uses his poetry to enlighten his people and support their revolution against the dictator Mubarak, who ruled Egypt by the sword for decades. In *Ṭalal al-Waqt*, the dedicatees are the standing ruins of time. Time has changed, but their works and thought have outlived them and now inspire not only poets like Ḥijāzī, but also nations in the making, including the Arab world during the 2011 uprising. Ḥijāzī is like the classical Arab poet who stops on these standing ruins of time and hopes someone will join him on his journey.[102] By writing revolutionary poetry in such a critical time in the Arab world, Ḥijāzī joins his people's revolution by using his aesthetic weapon in the fight against Mubarak and his deformation of literature.

In *Ṭalal al-Waqt*, Ḥijāzī's dedications to dead critics create an extended dialogue between the poet, his people, and his dedicatees. The dedicatory poems resurrect the works of the dedicatees and evoke their writers' thought and influence for a new generation. Dedications may "entail a total identification with the dead, using the precursor to resurrect history as narrative from distortions and confusions."[103] Ḥijāzī's dedications, such as "Al-Sāʿa al-Khāmisa Masā'an: ilā Najīb Maḥfūẓ" and "Sāriq al-Nār: ilā Ṭaha Ḥusayn," entail an identification with his dedicatees. He identifies with Maḥfūẓ and Ḥusayn in their thought on the role of the critic-writer in his society. He praises them for their devotion to their profession and society and implies that he is following their example and devoting his poetry to his people and to the profession of poetry. These dedications add another, metapoetic dimension to his poetry. He hopes his poetry will influence his people in the same way the dedicatees' works and thought have influenced their readers, even though this influence or change might have to wait until after the death of the poet. Ḥijāzī seeks immortality through art.

Ḥijāzī's concern for achieving immortality through art is evident in his dedications. The long-dead critics to whom he dedicates these poems have outlived them and became the standing ruins of time. Like them, Ḥijāzī is alienated. He stands against the current and voices his opposition to the dictatorships of his time. His poetry signifies his role as a critic, poet, prophet, and visionary, like his dedicatees, and he calls his people to believe in the power of their will to transform their reality and impose order on their chaotic world. Treating distinct metapoetic themes in this collection, Ḥijāzī perceives poetry as a bridge between the past and the future. Poetry expresses the people's feelings and aspirations while at the same time giving shape to their revolution and opposition to oppression. The poet becomes the nation's voice, yet at the same time his individual voice is heard. He identifies with the long-dead critics whose influence and innovation touched their people' lives and left traces behind them.

Ṭalal al-Waqt is Ḥijāzī's own attempt to remain standing. It is the poet's contribution to the Egyptian revolution, in which the poet has become a critic, a fighter, and a historian. This collection will itself become a standing ruin of time and be read and appreciated by generations to come. *Ṭalal al-Waqt* also marks a turning point in Ḥijāzī's poetry. His dedications to long-dead critics, his treatment of contemporary issues and subject matter, and his mastery of writing poetry in the free verse form plot a change in the trajectory of his poetic career. His voice is candid, critical, and revolutionary, as well as aware of the literary tradition of those who preceded him, of his own individual talent, and of the interplay between literature and politics. Muhsin Jassim al-Musawi maintains that when a dedication "resurrects exemplary ancestors while opting for active participation in the current making of things, it assumes its other commitment to a 'forward trajectory.' "[104] Ḥijāzī's dedications resurrect exemplary literary ancestors while opting for active participation and engagement in current political events and literary movements in the Arab world. His engagement with universal contemporary issues is intertwined with metapoetic concerns; this in turn contributes to the development of his voice as a poet and a critic, concerned about the state of his nation and its literature. As a metapoetic poet, he revives "the spirit of the nation through his visionary poetry."[105] In fact, Ḥijāzī's poetry revives the spirit of every nation that had been subjected to decades of oppression. It is true that Ḥijāzī published this collection after the beginning of the Arab Uprising, which may suggest that he waited for a revolution to spark him instead of sparking it. However, in reviving the spirit of defiance in the oppressed, he transforms his belief in the revolution into poetry. It registers and makes immortal the long journey of a nation from oppression and humiliation to freedom and dignity. His poems are the standing ruins of time, which will inspire the new generation of young men and women in the Arab world and elsewhere while at the same time attesting to their triumph over dictatorship.

It is worth noting that the only poem Ḥijāzī writes in the classical form in this collection, or in the last two collections, for that matter, is his dedication to the Lebanese critic and poet Amīn Nakhla (1901–1976). In "Laka al-Khulūd: ilā Amīn Nakhla" (Eternity Is Yours: To Amin Nakhla), written in 1996, Ḥijāzī addresses Nakhla and celebrates his literary achievements on the twentieth anniversary of his passing. Knowing that Nakhla was very meticulous and insistent about writing poetry in the classical form, Ḥijāzī honors him by writing this dedicatory poem in the classical form, just as he would have preferred it. By this point, Ḥijāzī has been writing free verse for decades, but he selects the classical form not because it is better suited to the genre, as we have seen in his earlier elegies, but out of respect for a romantic critic-poet who defended the classical form and found the experiment of the modern poets "a renegade from Arab culture and language."[106] Ḥijāzī realizes that writing a poem in the classical form does not undermine his legacy as a free verse poet. To dedicate a poem to a poet who did not support the experiments of the Arab modern poets, for which Ḥijāzī has fought valiantly, and also to write it in the classical form is indeed a turning point in Ḥijāzī's poetics. Ḥijāzī identifies his stance on the prose form in poetry with Nakhla's stance on the free verse form. Ḥijāzī adapts Nakhla's stance on the old and the new in poetry; Nakhla insisted that "there is no particular merit in either; what decides the supremacy of the one or the other is its excellence."[107] This indeed was al-Bayātī's point of view: he accepted all forms and rejected choosing one over the others, advocating instead for excellence and innovation in poetry irrespective of form. Ḥijāzī, in contrast, refuses to accept the prose poem as a legitimate poetic form.

Ḥijāzī's poetry started as a direct expression of his personal thoughts and feelings, whether romantic or political, as in his first four collections, *Madīna bilā Qalb*, *Awrās*, *Marthiyat al-ʿUmr al-Jamīl*, and *Lam Yabqā illā al-Iʿtirāf*. In *Kā'ināt Mamlakat al-Layl* and *Ashjār al-Ismint*, Ḥijāzī moves beyond the initial stages of *iltizām* toward treating universal issues and criticizing political figures and dictatorships. In *Ṭalal al-Waqt*, he reaches a stage in which he employs advanced poetic and stylistic devices and concerns himself not only with pressing political issues but also metapoetic ones. In his dialogue with his predecessors, he invites other rising poets to familiarize themselves with the literary tradition of those who have preceded them.

Published in a critical time in the history of Arab politics, Ḥijāzī's collection represents a drastic change in his attitude toward his audience. His readers are no longer the defeated, deformed generation lamented in *Ashjār al-Ismint.* His audience is a generation of rebels, who not only said no to their oppressive regimes, but also inspired Ḥijāzī—and other poets—and empowered his voice. This generation is the mobilizing power in the streets and in poetry. By their actions they demanded a major change in the way the world and the poets view them. Thus, it is in this stage that poetry and the revolution inspire each other, becoming two sides of the same coin. Ḥijāzī's voice in this collection is empowering and empowered, inspiring and inspired. His people have brought poetry back to life and thrown their dictators in the garbage dump of history that al-Bayātī described.

Commenting on poetry in the 1970s, Jabra Ibrahim Jabra says, "Poets have never been less influential than recently. . . . When power is split between the military and technocrats, unless he is willing to remain an amorous entertainer, the poet will be simply exiled from the City."[108] Before the Arab Uprising, modern and contemporary Arab poets such as Ḥijāzī realized that their poetry had lost its influence on people. Society, politics, language, and ethics were declining as well, and poetry was forced into exile. After the revolution erupted, many Arab poets took part in their own way, by writing poetry to support their people. Governments in the Arab world realize the dangerous role of art in society. For example, the Syrian cartoonist Ali Farzat was kidnapped and beaten, and his fingers broken, after drawing a cartoon in opposition to Syrian president Bashar al-Assad, shortly after the Syrian revolution began in 2010. This explains why Arab artists and poets are determined to oppose oppressive regimes in their creative works. They know well that if they do so, their people will be more persistent in their quest for freedom.

Artists and poets believed this before the Arab Uprising, but they could only dream that their people would revolt. When the people did take to the streets and the death of thousands did not stop the demonstrations, the people knew this revolution was unlike any other. This revolution is the revolution of the people, and no matter how long it might take for actual reform to take place, what matters is the fact that Arabs have finally rebelled against a long history of oppression. This revolution will certainly send a message to the world: the Arab individual no longer accepts oppression, whether from government or from the outside.

In Ḥijāzī's transition from the poet of the regime in the 1950s and early 1960s to the poet of the people's revolution lies a rich body of poetry that establishes his legacy. Ḥijāzī is fortunate to have witnessed the Arab Uprising. Many of his contemporaries and friends from the 1960s generation have died. Poets such as al-Bayātī, Qabbānī, al-Ṣabūr, Dunqul, and Darwīsh would have taken a stand on the Arab Uprising and reflected that in their poetry. What distinguishes Ḥijāzī from other contemporary Arab poets responding to the Arab Uprising is his candid response and meditated stance. Ḥijāzī did not reach this position overnight; rather, it is the result of decades of engagement with social, political, and literary issues of concern to him and the Arab individual. It is worth noting that this turn in Ḥijāzī's poetry is highly political. It is as if he found in the revolution the perfect time to publish his collection. Its publication therefore announces his strong return to the poetry scene. He is a keen observer of the status quo in Egypt, and, while he published individual poems from time to time, his decision to not publish collections for twenty-two years is itself a poetic response to that status quo. Ḥijāzī continues to write poetry that expresses and shapes his stance on the revolution in Egypt and the current status quo in the Arab world.

In October 2013, Ḥijāzī published "The Sun and the Dark Ones," which criticizes the Muslim Brotherhood throughout the Arab world, especially in Egypt. Ḥijāzī has been attacking the Muslim Brotherhood in *Al-Ahrām Weekly* and *Al-Maṣrī al-Yawm* since the Egyptian revolution began in January 2011, warning of their arrival in power. What is worth mentioning in this context is the manner in which Ḥijāzī treats this issue, and the light he sheds on the history of oppression in Egypt.

. . .
كانوا يريدون لمصر أن تموت
مصر التي روضت الموت فصار في يديها فرسا مجنحا
سفينة ناشرة شراعها الأبيض بين خضرة وزرقة
تبحر بالموتى من الظل إلى الشمس ليحيوا من جديد
مصر التي حولت القبر إلى قصر مشيد
يريد منها هؤلاء أن تخاصم الحياة
أن تبيع للغزاة
أطفالها
أن تتوارى في الحجاب والنقاب
. . .
أواه يا مدينتي يا قاهرة
لو أفرخت في ليلك المؤامرة
أين تبيت الأغنيات الساهرات
أين تهاجر الليالي المقمرة
أين يغني الشعراء
للحب و الإخاء
والعدل والحقيقة؟
اقول لا!
لن تطفئوا شمسا علينا أبدا
ولن تهزوا جبلا!
لن تسكتوا يمامة
ولن تردوا للورود عطرها
إذا فشا في امسيات صيفنا واشتعلا!
لن تحبسوا قلبا
ولن تطاردوا على الشفاه القبلا
ولن تكون مصر أيها الظلاميون دولة لكم
ولن تكون منزلا![109]

. . .
They wanted death for Egypt
Egypt, which tamed death, so it became a winged horse
in her hands
A ship spreading its white sail between green and blue
Sailing with the dead from the shade to sun to resurrect again
Egypt, which turned the grave into a great palace

They want her to become an enemy of life
To sell its children
To the invaders
To hide behind the veil
. . .
O my city Cairo
If the conspiracy succeeds overnight
Where will the songs sleep?
Whither will the moonlit nights emigrate?
Where will poets sing
For love and brotherhood
And justice and truth?
I say No
You will not turn the sun off on us
You will not shake a mountain!
You will not silence a pigeon
And you will not return to the flowers their scent
If it suffuses and burns in the evenings of our summer!
You will not imprison a heart
And you will not go after kisses on the lips
And Egypt will not be a state for you, dark ones
And it will not be a home.

In this poem, Ḥijāzī portrays the Muslim Brotherhood as monstrous barbarians living in the dark and trying to assassinate Egypt. He criticizes them for wanting "death for Egypt," trying to make Egypt sell its children to the invaders, and forcing its women to hide behind the veil. Here the Muslim Brotherhood is a terrorist organization dragging Egypt and Egyptians backward, conspiring with tyrants to make Egypt a graveyard and its people corpses. However, Egypt defends itself and turns death into a winged horse. This horse becomes a ship sailing toward the sun, to enlighten its dead people and bring them back to life. Here we have an image of Egypt rescuing its citizens and turning its graveyard into a great palace that these terrorists will not be able to reach. In so warning his people against the Muslim Brotherhood, Ḥijāzī incites his people to foil the conspiracy by fighting the enemy from within and to join their fellow citizens in sailing from the shade to sun. He also warns of the Muslim Brotherhood's impact on art, on songs and poetry. If Egyptians fail to oust the Muslim Brotherhood completely from their lives, as an organization and culture, songs will be homeless and poets will not be able to pray for love, wisdom, and truth. At the end of the poem he affirms that Cairo will not become a haven for darkness and those who live in the dark; Cairo will always be a minaret for knowledge and freedom.

It is worth noting that Ḥijāzī seems to have written this poem in haste. Although some of it is good, most of it reads like an excerpt from a journal article. Perhaps this was the result of Ḥijāzī's reaction to the Muslim Brotherhood's rise to power in Egypt after the election of Mursī as president of Egypt in 2013. In a series of his recent articles published in *Al-Maṣrī al-Yawm*, we hear the poetic voice of a critic whose main concern is the future of Egypt. For Ḥijāzī, the *deterioration of culture in Egypt* is the catastrophe it has been dealing with for decades. Therefore, Ḥijāzī states, to attain democracy and rescue the revolution from those who try to kidnap it—the Muslim Brotherhood—the secular state and modern Egyptian culture have to be resurrected, and slogans from the terrorists, who live in the Dark Ages, need to be eliminated completely.[110]

Ḥijāzī states that the Muslim Brotherhood's thought has become enmeshed in Egyptian culture and education, which explains why it is hard for people to let go of their ideas, values, and propaganda.[111] Ḥijāzī, like his fellow poet al-Bayātī, is aware of the critical role culture plays in all aspects of a nation's formation, whether social, political, religious, economic, or literary. A country devoid of culture is one defeated and walking toward the death of civilization. Thus, Ḥijāzī writes a poem to attack the Muslim Brotherhood's extreme actions and to call for Egyptians to guard their freedom in religion, literature, and art so "poets can sing for love, brotherhood, justice, and truth."[112]

Ḥijāzī encourages his fellow citizens to learn from history by not making the same mistake he himself made when he considered the Free Officers Movement a revolution, when in reality it was a coup.[113] He affirms that from Nasser to Mubarak, only the names changed, not the regimes, and "every time a new president is announced, people continued to be subject to oppression."[114] Whether we agree with his politics or not, Ḥijāzī claims that his current stance vis-à-vis the status quo in Egypt is that of the guardian of the revolution, whose task is to educate people. He defines a revolution by its promises, potential, and achievements.

Therefore, a true revolution, in his words, is that "which destroys the present, or moves beyond it, to build a future."[115] For this reason, he considers the advancement of the Muslim Brotherhood to power in Egypt, through the election of Mursī as president, an "assassination of the sun," another title under which his poem appeared. The sun is the revolution of the Egyptian nation, which they rescued from assassination by revolting once again in 2013 against Mursī and his party. By ousting Mursī and his party, Ḥijāzī says, "Egypt has won its battle against ages of darkness, and has finally left the Middle Ages."[116] The process of rebuilding Egypt, a country in the making, inspires Ḥijāzī. It is true that he is inspired by political events now, as he was early in his life. Nonetheless, this inspiration, which brought him back to poetry, announces the rebirth of his voice as a critic-poet, whose concern for the Egyptian nation stems from a desire to guard its culture and civilization. Ḥijāzī's poetic and political stance represents a trend in modern Arabic literature. Poets and writers who find inspiration in key political events, who reinvent themselves without hesitating to criticize their own voices and poetry after reflecting on their old attitudes and works, belong to this trend.

However, it is worth noting that the overinvolvement of politics and journalism in poetry is having an alarming, if not dangerous, impact on modern Arabic poetry. Most poetry by young poets in the last few years has contributed to the development of neither form nor content in modern Arabic poetry. Furthermore, to have major poetic voices sound more like journalists than poets is a tragic misfortune. I am not talking here about the message of the poem, but about its language. This is one of the many challenges of writing the modern Arab poem: the topical poem is usually written in haste and in an emotional response to a political event. Such poetry "destroys more than it builds" and lacks basic poetic aesthetics, turning poetry into political commentary. It is worth noting that the four poems on the Egyptian revolution published in *Ṭalal al-Waqt* were consistent with Ḥijāzī's poetic standards, in contrast to his poem on the Muslim Brotherhood, which sounds like the propaganda poetry of the 1960s for which he has lately expressed distaste. The 1960s poetry of *iltizām* is a poetry of sentiment. It was considered propaganda poetry and was therefore reevaluated after the wake-up call of the 1967 defeat. Most contemporary topical poems in Arabic poetry, too, belong to this genre of sentimental works.

Ḥijāzī celebrated the overthrow of Mursī and has written articles in *Al-Ahrām Weekly* to offer advice to al-Sīsī. In an April 6, 2016, essay, he discusses his meeting, along with other Egyptian intellectuals and writers, with al-Sīsī to discuss the challenges facing Egypt.[117] Ḥijāzī reports to his readers that al-Sīsī is doing the right thing by meeting with the intellectuals of the country to discuss Egypt's current affairs. However, he reminds the Egyptians that what they witnessed in 2011 is only a reaction and not a revolution and that this is only the beginning.[118] Therefore, he maintains that to free Egypt from centuries of oppression, stagnation, and degredation in all aspects of society, al-Sīsī's government should provide "a true democratic regime and a new religious thought that responds to the needs and demands of our time."[119]

As we have seen, the first trend in modern Arab poetry, to which al-Bayātī, Qāsim Ḥaddād, and Saʿdī Yūsuf belong, is that of the poets who reevaluated their political stances and poetic positions after the 1967 defeat and looked for inspiration in sources more stable than politics, such as metapoetry. They continued to be committed to their causes, be they political or social, but this commitment was shaped by new perspectives, as well as new voices and innovative poetic langauges. The second trend, to which Ḥijāzī belongs, is that of the poets who reviewed their political stance after the 1967 defeat and became the poets of the people, and who refrained from publishing poetry collections or active engagement with the poetry scene until a major political event took place. The transformation in the career trajectories of the poets in this second category is understood in terms of the impact of politics on it. Before the 1967 defeat, poetry was the voice of political propaganda; slightly after the defeat, politics was a source of frustration; and finally, after the Arab Uprising, politics became a source of inspiration. Thus, politics transformed some poets from inactive participants in the poetic scene to active publishers of poetry, engaging in politics. The majority of their poetry continues to be politically inspired. The third category includes poets who write about conflicts that began before they were born and continue after they die. This category is different from the other two in its poets' treatment of issues that pertain to their personal life and experiences. Maḥmūd Darwīsh is a Palestinian poet who suffered displacement and exile throughout his life. The next chapter examines Darwīsh's treatment of the self and its other in the Israeli–Palestinian conflict. His poetry belongs to the literature of resistance.

CHAPTER 4

From Militant *Iltizām* to Humanist

Maḥmūd Darwīsh

Maḥmūd Darwīsh, the Palestinian national poet, was born in al-Berwe village in Galilee in 1941 and died in Houston, Texas, in 2008. He is often referred to as "the poet of resistance" due to his lifelong poetic battle in defense of his people and their resistance against the establishment of the State of Israel. He wrote more than thirty books of poetry and prose and received many international literary awards, including the Lotus Prize in 1969, the Lenin Prize in 1983, and the Moroccan Medal for Intellectual Merit. France named him a Knight of Arts and Belles Lettres in 1997, and in 2001 he won the Lannan Foundation's Prize for Cultural Freedom.

Unlike al-Bayātī and Ḥijāzī, Darwīsh did not write about the question of Palestine because it was a matter of Arab nationalism or commitment. For a rising poet like him it was a personal matter that meant life or death. What I argue here is not that Darwīsh was mainly inspired by political events or that he changed his subject matter after specific political changes in history, like his peer poets al-Bayātī and Ḥijāzī. Rather, I argue that for a poet of resistance and displacement, the subject matter does not change easily because it shapes a nation's life and existence. What changes is how he handles such a topic after fifty or sixty years of ongoing conflict and no resolution on the ground. His poetry witnesses a transition from a militant and anti-Israeli tone to inviting the other into a conversation in which self and other reconsider their dehumanization of each other. In the shift from his more extroverted political poetry to poetry that closely interrogates identity, the distinction between self and other begins to collapse. In his later work, Darwīsh moves toward a more introverted poetry, which attempts to bring issues that pertain to the humanity of the parties involved in the conflict to the center rather than to the margin of the conflict. This can happen if both self and other recognize each other's identity and understand the conflict in which they are trapped.

This trend is one of several seen among poets of ongoing, unresolved conflicts. In another trend, the poetry begins militant and violent and ends in the same way. In yet another, it begins humanistic, looking for resolution, and then ends violent and militant, such as that of the Jewish Romanian poet Paul Celan (1920–1970), who wrote in German about the sufferings of the Jews in Germany. Even after his death by suicide, his work influenced Darwīsh's poetry in the 1970s, especially in that both of them identified themselves and their nations as victims of the other, the German Nazi in Celan's case and the Zionist Israeli in Darwīsh's. Unlike Celan, whose suicide creates a metaphor for the violence on the ground, Darwīsh begins his career as a militant poet but becomes toward the end of his career and life more of a humanist and philosopher. In humanizing the one he called enemy all his life he sees an invitation for the enemy to see the human in himself. In so doing, they can stop dreading each other and instead look for ways to let the human side in each of them triumph. This resolution seems impossible, for neither militant nor peaceful talks have yet resulted in coexistence or recognition of the identity of both parties in the Israeli–Palestinian conflict. Therefore, while Darwīsh's decades-long, defensive, anti-Israeli poetic attempts failed to reach a resolution to the conflict, he leaves behind him a final poetic attempt aiming at a quality he knows will find listening ears one day: the human side of the self and its other.

When he was only six years old, Darwīsh fled with his family from his village to Lebanon. The next year, he returned with his family as an illegal resident and was given the status of a present-absent alien by the State of Israel. After the publication of his first collection of poetry, *ʿAṣāfīr bilā Ajniḥa* (Birds without Wings, 1960), he wrote extensively on Palestinian identity, resistance, love, death, hope, and exile. In 1960

Darwīsh began working in literary journalism in Haifa for *Al-Ittiḥād* and *Al-Jadīd*, newspapers published by the Israeli Communist Party, Rakkah.[1] Darwīsh was imprisoned several times by the Israeli authorities, in 1961, 1965, and 1967, because he did not have a travel permit when attempting to travel outside Israel.[2]

Darwīsh left for study in Moscow in 1970. In early February 1971, he moved to Cairo and announced his decision not to return to Palestine, a decision that would have a significant impact on his poetry. In a press conference in Cairo on February 11, 1971, he explained this decision:

> I insist that everyone understand that the dangerous step I took is based on serving the [Palestinian] cause from a more liberating and encouraging place. . . . I come from a place of siege and imprisonment to that of work. . . . I am getting closer to the point of paralysis as a citizen and a poet because of the great deal of oppression I am subject to [in my country]. . . . I am not the first citizen and poet who leaves his country to be closer to it.[3]

He lived in Arab capitals such as Cairo, Tunis, and Beirut before settling in Paris in 1983. He moved to Amman in 1995 until he was given a permit to visit his family in Ramallah in 1996.[4]

Darwīsh wrote on universal issues such as love, death, exile, and the struggle of humankind, dedicating his poetry to the Palestinian question, but he also responded to key events that took place in the Arab world. For example, he published *Ākhir al-Layl* (The End of the Night, 1967) in Beirut in response to the 1967 defeat, and he published "Qaṣīdat Beirut" (Ode to Beirut, 1982) after the Israeli invasion of Lebanon in 1982. In 1993 Darwīsh criticized and protested against the Oslo Declaration of Principles, resigned from the PLO executive committee, and published *Limādhā Tarakta al-Ḥiṣān Waḥīdan* (Why Did You Leave the Horse Alone, 1995). He published many poetry collections and poems during the first Palestinian *Intifāḍa* (Uprising) from 1987 to 1993 and the second in 2000. Among his most famous and celebrated poems in the Arab world is "Biṭāqat Huwiyya" (Identity Card), which was published in his second collection, *Awrāq al-Zaytūn* (Olive Leaves, 1964), in Haifa. In 1987, while in France, Darwīsh published *Ward Aqall* (Fewer Roses), which included his controversial poem "Ayyuhā al-Mārrūn bayna al-Kalimāt al-ʿĀbira" (O You Who Pass between the Fleeting Words).

The poems I explore in this chapter were published between the 1960s and 2009. They are selected both for their aesthetic value and for their political significance in identifying the shift in Darwīsh's poetry. The first section of this chapter investigates the representation of self and other and their identities in poems published between the 1960s and 2002. The poems I examine in the second section were published between 2003 and 2009 and reflect the shift in Darwīsh's treatment of the self and its male other. In these poems, Darwīsh does not attack the identity of the other; rather, he abandons his earlier tone and writes poetry on humanity and the mutual struggle and alienation of the self and its other.

It is worth noting that Darwīsh addresses the female other in his earlier poetry in his love poems to "Rita," the first Israeli woman with whom he falls in love, who becomes later a cultural icon in the Arab world.[5] For Darwīsh, the female other neither threatens his identity nor represents his enemy. He wrote several poems to Rita in the 1960s and 1970s, and he wrote to her one final time in "Rita's Winter," in his 1992 collection *Aḥada ʿAshara Kawkaban* (Eleven Planets).[6] In this poem, Rita complains of the long winter; she cries and begs her beloved to take her to a distant land, if there is any. Discovering that there is "no land for the two bodies in one body," the speaker advises Rita that they both should go their separate ways.[7] The speaker screams, "They have not killed us yet, O Rita, O Rita . . . this winter is heavy and cold."[8] Caught between the two abysses of their impossible love and their imminent departure, the speaker and Rita struggle in deciding whether to leave the land or each other. At the end of the poem, Rita "puts her small pistol on the poem's draft . . . / and leaves to the unknown barefoot, and it was time for me to leave."[9] A rifle was between the poet and Rita in "Rita and the Rifle, 1967." Likewise, in this poem a pistol is between Rita and her lover. Therefore, war stands in the way of "the longing of these two lovers across enemy lines" and continues to destroy "their love, firing at all they had before."[10] Rita announces that it is impossible for her and the speaker to be together on one land, so she leaves for the unknown, and he realizes it is time for him to leave too. Rita departs and says, "War is not my profession. I am myself, are you yourself?"[11] Rita does not return to

Darwīsh's poetry after this long, heavy, and cold winter. Nonetheless, Rita realizes that as long as she is in Palestine/Israel, she is part of the war/conflict, and therefore her humanity makes her sacrifice her love for her Palestinian other, the poet, and leave. Stating "I am myself" after refusing to be part of the war and deciding to leave, Rita affirms her identity outside the conflict by putting down her pistol, a symbol of war. Leaving unwillingly for the unknown, with a broken heart, Rita promises to "return when days and dreams change"; the speaker replies, "Love is like death, it is a promise that can neither be accomplished nor vanish."[12] Like the poet, Rita is a victim of the Israeli other. In Darwīsh's poetry, the Israeli other Rita is as human as the Palestinian self.

Although some might argue that Darwīsh has humanized the other in his earlier poetry by writing love poems to Rita, I argue that in Darwīsh's poetry, the enemy is the male other, represented by the State of Israel and its military, and not the female other. Thus, writing these poems to Rita does not negate Darwīsh's animosity toward the Zionist/Israeli male other. In his earlier works, Darwīsh treats the female other as another victim, next to himself and his people, in the Arab–Israeli conflict.

To examine the shift in Darwīsh's poetry from confrontational and anti-Israeli in tone to calling for mutual understanding and sharing a space between the self and its other, I focus on the following poems: "Biṭāqat Huwiyya" (Identity Card, 1964), "Jundī Yaḥlum bi-l-Zanābiq al-Bayḍā'" (A Soldier Dreaming of White Tulips, 1967), "Ayyuhā al-Mārrūn bayna al-Kalimāt al-'Ābira" (O You Who Pass between the Fleeting Words, 1987), "Ḥālat Ḥiṣār" (State of Siege, 2002), "Huwa Hādi' wa Anā Kadhālik" (He Is Quiet and So Am I, 2003), "Hiya fī al-Masā'" (She, in the Evening, 2003), "Maqha, wa-'Anta ma' al-Jarīda Jālis" (A Café, and You with the Newspaper, 2005), "'Anta Munthu alān, Ghairuk" (You, From Now On, Are Your Other, 2008), "'Aduw Mushtarak" (Common Enemy, 2008), and "Sīnāriū Jāhiz" (Ready Scenario, 2009).

Darwīsh was very popular in the Arab world for his early resistance poetry. However, he rebelled constantly against his premature popularity by writing poetry that makes the local tragedy a universal one.[13] Although Darwīsh wrote on topics other than politics, he is known and celebrated for his political poetry. Darwīsh's earlier poems, such as "Jawāz Safar" (The Passport) and "Biṭāqat Huwiyya," were a result of his long, unhappy record of pain and exile.[14] His poetry of resistance in the 1960s and 1970s drew the public's attention to him as the national Palestinian poet of resistance. Darwīsh's struggle against the constraints, harassments, and regulations of the State of Israel throughout his life sharpened his political stance and enabled him to use his poetry to express his resistance to Israel. Through sophisticated language and poetry, Darwīsh documents his childhood memories, weeps for the ruins of his demolished village, and yearns for times and places that create their own kingdom in his poetry. His earlier poetry is militant and charged with emotion and anger; his later poetry is sad, nostalgic, and universal. By studying examples of Darwīsh's most celebrated poems and comparing them to some of his late poems, we can examine the trajectory of his poetry through its treatment of the self and the other.

ARAB NATIONALISM AND PALESTINIAN IDENTITY

"Biṭāqat Huwiyya" is one of the most celebrated poems in the Arab world. Schoolchildren across the Arab world used to recite it as early as elementary school. The poem tells the story of an Arab farmer who had to show his identity card to an Israeli officer:

بطاقة هوية

سجل
أنا عربي
ورقم بطاقتي خمسون ألفْ
وأطفالي ثمانيةٌ
وتاسعهم سيأتي بعد صيف
فهل تغضبْ؟

سجل
أنا عربي
وأعمل مع رفاق الكدح في محجرْ
وأطفالي ثمانيةٌ
أسل لهم رغيف الخبزِ

والأثواب والدفترْ
من الصخرِ
ولا أتوسل الصدقات من بابكْ
ولا أصغرْ
أمام بلاطِ أعتابك
فهل تغضبْ؟

سجل
أنا عربي
اسمٌ بلا لقبِ
صبورٌ في بلادٍ كل ما فيها
يعيش بفورة الغضبِ
جذوري
قبل ميلاد الزمان رستْ
وقبل تفتح الحقبِ
وقبل السرْوِ والزيتونْ
وقبل ترعرع العشبِ
أبي من أسرة المحراث
لا من سادةٍ نُجُبِ
وجدي كان فلاحاً
بلا حسبٍ ولا نسبِ
وبيتي كوخ ناطورٍ
من الأعواد والقصبِ
فهل ترضيك منزلتي
انا اسمٌ بلا لقبِ

سجل
أنا عربي
ولون الشعر فحْميٌّ
ولون العين بنيٌّ
وميزاتي:
على رأسي عقالٌ فوق كوفيهْ
وكفي صلبة كالصخرِ
تخمش من يلامسها
وأطيب ما أحب من الطعام
الزيت والزعتر

وعنواني:
أنا من قريةٍ عزْلاءَ... منسيهْ
شوارعها بلا أسماءْ
وكل رجالها في الحقل والمحجرْ
يحبون الشيوعيه!
فهل تغضبْ؟

سجل
أنا عربي
سلَبْتَ كروم أجدادي
وأرضاً كنت أفلحها
أنا وجميع أولادي
ولم تترك لنا ولكل أحفادي
سوى هذي الصخورِ...
فهل ستأخذها حكومتكم كما قيلا!؟

إذن
سجل برأس الصفحة الأولى:
أنا لا أكره الناسَ
ولا أسطو على أحدٍ
ولكني إذا ما جعتُ
آكل لحم مغتصبي
حذار حذار من جوعي
ومن غضبي.[15]

Identity Card

Write down!
I am an Arab
And my identity card number is fifty thousand
I have eight children
And the ninth will come after a summer
Will you be angry?

Write down!
I am an Arab

Employed with fellow workers at a quarry
I have eight children
I get them bread
Garments and books
From the rocks.
I do not beg charity at your doors
Nor do I belittle myself
At the steps of your chamber
So will you be angry?

Write down!
I am an Arab
I have a name without a title
Patient in a country
Where people are enraged
My roots
Were entrenched before the birth of time
And before the opening of the eras
Before the pines and the olive trees
And before the grass grew
My father descends from the family of the plow
Not from a privileged class
And my grandfather was a farmer
Neither well-bred nor well-born!
And my house is like a watchman's hut
Made of branches and cane
Are you satisfied with my status?
I have a name without a title!

Write down!
I am an Arab
Color of Hair: jet-black
Color of Eyes: brown
My distinguishing features:
On my head the *ʿiqāl* cords over a *kūffiyya*
And my hand is as tough as the rock

Scratching who touches it
And the most delicious food I love is
Olive oil and thyme
My address:
I am from a village, remote, forgotten
Its streets are without names
And all its men are in the fields and quarry
Love communism[16]
Will you be angry?

Write down!
I am an Arab
You have stolen the orchards of my ancestors
And the land which I cultivated
Along with my children
And you left nothing for us and for all of my grandchildren
Except for these rocks.
So will the State take them as it has been said?!

Therefore!
Write down on the top of the first page:
I do not hate people
Nor do I encroach
But if I become hungry
The usurper's flesh will be my food
Beware . . .
Beware . . .
Of my hunger
And my anger![17]

In this six-stanza poem Darwīsh defines Arab identity in what seems to be a response to an Israeli officer who stops the speaker for traveling in Israel without an identity card. Here Darwīsh expresses his anger and frustration with the Israeli occupation and his pride in his Arab roots. He also sends a direct message to the State of Israel and criticizes it for stealing the land of his ancestors. Every stanza in this poem deals with a specific theme that asserts the identity of Palestinians and Arabs and their objection to the occupation of Palestine. In the first and fourth stanzas, the speaker asks the Israeli officer to write down his identity card number, the color of his hair and eyes, his distinguishing features, and his address. These details appear on the identity card the speaker is supposed to carry, and he repeats them to the officer. However, he adds key information to this list: his hand is as tough as the rock, rough to the touch; he is from a remote, forgotten village whose streets had no names; and he has many children. He is not a beggar. He is from the laboring class, of peasant origin, and, above all, native to the land. These sociopolitical elements are inserted throughout the poem to augment what are supposed to be the "simple" or "basic" facts of the identity card. Both of these stanzas end with "will you be angry?" in a threatening tone, as if the speaker is provoking the addressee's anger.

Asserting his Arabism and strong connection to his village by repeating "I am an Arab" in every stanza except the last, the speaker speaks for every Arab. The speaker does not accept the fact that the Israeli state has the right to define and challenge the identity of Arabs in Palestine. Darwīsh challenges the Israeli state and its authority by giving the Israeli officer not only the ID facts the Israeli government demands, but also the facts that enable the Arab speaker to take control of defining his identity, an identity that will anger the Israeli authority. Stanzas 2 and 3 give more details about the vocation, the family, and the status of the speaker.

In stanzas 3 and 4, the speaker expresses his pride in being a hardworking Arab man who works with his fellow laborers at a quarry to feed his children and live a dignified life. The significance of mentioning that he works at a quarry in the third stanza lies in the symbol of the rocks with which he gets his children bread (lines 10–13). The speaker maintains that these rocks—the land itself—are his source of livelihood and thus symbolize life. Therefore, when he mentions in the fifth stanza that he heard the state will take these rocks, he means that the state is planning to take his land and destroy his last source of income, and thus kill his children. The speaker also makes it clear to the Israeli officer that despite his poverty, he will never grovel before his chamber nor beg for charity at his door. Darwīsh sends the Israelis a message: regardless of how poor or challenged Palestinians become under your occupation, they will never accept your charity and never surrender.

Another key element in the fourth stanza is the speaker's focus on the land, the roots, and the enraged people. The speaker maintains that he has no title, his father comes from a poor family, his grandfather is a farmer, neither well-bred, nor well-born, and his house is made of branches of cane. Establishing that he comes from a poor, unprivileged class, the speaker sheds some light on a matter more important for him than his social status: his patience and his roots. The speaker says in lines 21–22 that he is "patient in a country / where people are enraged" and in lines 23–27 that his roots "were entrenched before the birth of time / and before the opening of eras / before the pines and olive trees / and before the grass grew." Clarifying the issue of the Palestinian's roots in Palestine is very important for a poet such as Darwīsh. In the Israeli–Palestinian conflict, roots in Palestine/Israel determine the right of inheritance and existence. Both nationalities claim that their roots in the country go back centuries. Thus, it is vital to bring up the issue of roots to assert one's right to own the land.

In this stanza, the speaker maintains that his roots were entrenched before the birth of time and before the grass grew, which challenges and defies the claims of any other nationality. The last two stanzas reflect the speaker's assessment of the situation under occupation. The fifth and sixth stanzas are the most direct stanzas in this poem. In the fifth, the speaker accuses the Israelis of stealing the orchards of his ancestors and the land that he cultivated with his children. Furthermore, he accuses them of stealing everything from them and leaving only "these rocks," which are his last remaining source of income. When the speaker hears that the state will also take them, he warns the Israeli officer, in the sixth and last stanza, against angering him or making him starve. The speaker mentions in the third stanza that he is patient, but in the sixth stanza he makes it clear that although he neither hates people nor encroaches on the property of others, he will eat his usurper's flesh if he becomes hungry enough. The speaker asks the Israeli officer to write this bold statement at the top of the first page, which signifies its importance in the poem. Then he says, in the last four lines, "Beware . . . / beware . . . / of my hunger / and my anger." His hunger and anger can only be placated by taking revenge on his usurper.

Darwīsh's images, which construct the Palestinian memory, strike the reader throughout the poem. Images of hardworking men cutting rock at a quarry to feed their children after their land was stolen by the Israelis provoke simultaneous feelings of anger and pride. These men refuse to humiliate themselves and beg for charity at the doors of the Israeli government; rather, they resist the occupation and insist on cultivating their land or working in stone quarries. Their *ʿiqāl* and *kūffiyya* and their dark features unify them, along with their hands, which are as tough as the rocks they cut. This image of these men, who come from poor, obscure families, is intensified by their pride and their love for their land. Darwīsh knew well the significance of pride and dignity for any citizen of an oppressive state. Darwīsh's image of his Arab speaker eating the flesh of his usurper speaks of his anger about the exploitation he and his people endure under the regulations and constraints of the State of Israel. This image suggests not only a threat to the Israelis, but also a reminder to the Arabs of their role and responsibility as a nation in the Arab–Israeli conflict. This poem was published in 1964, in the midst of Nasser's Arab nationalist movement. Provoking the sense of Arab nationalism in in this way contributed to Darwīsh's commitment to drawing the Arabs' attention to the Palestinian question. In this poem, Darwīsh not only stirs his fellow Arab citizens to his cause, but also makes a political statement to the Israeli other and government, and to the world.

Darwīsh raises his voice, as the voice of the nation, and claims his right to live in his country by asserting his Arab identity and his right to his land. In lines 23–27 he maintains that his roots "were entrenched before the birth of time / and before the opening of the eras / before the pines and the olive trees / and before the grass grew." By asserting that his Arab ancestors were the first to inhabit Palestine, he denies the Israelis' right to his land. The image of the Arab speaker in this poem, a quarry worker, is juxtaposed with that of the Israeli other, an officer who represents the Israeli government, which stole the speaker's land, threatened his livelihood, and challenged his identity. In this poem, Darwīsh is direct, emotional, and confrontational. This poem evoked a sense of pride in Arabs in general and Palestinians in particular. It affirmed their roots in Palestine and their right to live and work there. It expressed and shaped the Palestinians' frustration with the State of Israel and its practices against them. "Identity Card" was written to "assert an Arab identity denied by Israel and the West."[18] It is the poet's way of objecting to the Israeli government's practices in Palestine and its failure to acknowledge the Palestinians' identity.

Writing in this confrontational tone, Darwīsh reached millions of Arabs and provoked their sense of nationalism. He continued publishing poetry of this sort through the 1960s, and like his peers al-Bayātī and Ḥijāzī, he had to react to the 1967 defeat in poetry. Like most poets of the 1960s generation, al-Bayātī and Ḥijāzī were shocked by the defeat, which in their poetry translated into pessimism and self-doubt. However, Darwīsh reacted differently to this key political event: he "did not cry after June 5. He did not say everything ended and we have nothing left but tears. On the contrary, he felt stronger and that the defeat sparked a great storm which will uproot obstacles ahead."[19] This was also the reaction of the poets of resistance in Palestine, whose "works became clearly present in Arabic literary life after the 1967 defeat."[20] In his book on Darwīsh as poet of the Occupied Land, which was first published in 1969 with a second edition in 1971, the prominent Egyptian critic Rajā' al-Naqqāsh says, "They refused to let feelings of pessimism and defeat control them. On the contrary, Darwīsh's poetry after the 1967 defeat reveals a great faith in the fact that the struggle continues and victory will eventually be achieved. Each verse he wrote after the defeat affirms that the most miserable people are the strongest and most persistent people. Also, he affirms that the Arab citizen who is subject to the harshest form of persecution inside the Israeli walls is at the same time the strongest. Among other Arab citizens, this Arab citizen insists most on resistance and steadfastness."[21] This book drew attention to the poetic voices from inside the Occupied Territories, especially after the 1967 defeat. These voices, such as those of Darwīsh, Samīḥ al-Qāsim, and Tawfīq Zeyād, were celebrated for their optimism despite the great disappointment the defeat had brought not only to Arab society, but also to the Arab psyche. This psychological defeat left its stamp on modern Arabic literature, and with their resistance poetry the poets of the Occupied Territories thus "represent a new psychological phenomenon in contemporary Arabic literature."[22] Placing utmost faith in the persecuted Palestinian Arab *inside* the Occupied Territories and promising victory over the State of Israel, Darwīsh's poetry evoked feelings of pride and steadfastness among Palestinians and Arabs after the 1967 defeat, when it was needed most.

FRIENDSHIP WITH THE ENEMY?

In 1967, Darwīsh published "Jundī Yaḥlum bi-al-Zanābiq al-Bayḍā'" (A Soldier Dreams of White Tulips) in his collection *Ākhir al-Layl* (The End of the Night). Where "Biṭāqat Huwiyya" celebrates what it means to be an Arab, in "Jundī Yaḥlum bi-al-Zanābiq al-Bayḍā'" Darwīsh celebrates everything about being a Palestinian who is compassionate about his land and people. As he criticizes the Israeli enemy in "Biṭāqat Huwiyya," he criticizes that enemy and all that he represents in "Jundī Yaḥlum bi-al-Zanābiq al-Bayḍā'." Here, the identity of Arabs or Palestinians has to be contrasted with that of the Israelis in order for it to be defined. The two identities clash; each of them becomes the opposite of the other.

جندي يحلم بالزنابق البيضاء

يحلم بالزنابق البيضاء
بغصن زيتون
بصدرها المورق في المساء
يحلم_ قال لي_ بطائر
بزهر ليمون
ولم يفلسف حلمه لم يفهم الأشياء
إلا كما يحسّها.. يشمّها
يفهم_ قال لي_ إنّ الوطن
أن أحتسي قهوة أمي
أن أعود في المساء
سألته: و الأرض؟
قال: لا أعرفها
و لا أحس أنها جلدي و نبضي
مثلما يقال في القصائد
و فجأة، رأيتها
كما أرى الحانوت..و الشارع.. و الجرائد
سألته: تحبها
أجاب: حبي نزهة قصيرة
أو كأس خمر.. أو مغامرة
من أجلها تموت ؟
كلا!
و كل ما يربطني بالأرض من أواصر

مقالة نارية.. محاضرة
قد علّموني أن أحب حبّها
و لم أحس أن قلبها قلبي،
و لم أشم العشب، و الجذور، و الغصون
و كيف كان حبّها
يلسع كالشموس ..كالحنين؟
أجابني مواجها:
وسيلتي للحب بندقية
وعودة الأعياد من خرائب قديمة
و صمت تمثال قديم
ضائع الزمان و الهوية!
حدّثني عن لحظة الوداع
و كيف كانت أمّة
تبكي بصمت عندما ساقوه
إلى مكان ما من الجبهة
و كان صوت أمه الملتاع
يحفر تحت جلده أمنية جديدة:
لو يكبر الحمام في وزارة الدفاع
لو يكبر الحمام!

دخّن، ثم قال لي..
كأنه يهرب من مستنقع الدماء:
حلمت بالزنابق البيضاء
بغصن زيتون
بطائر يعانق الصباح
فوق غصن ليمون
وما رأيت؟
رأيت ما صنعت
زنابقا حمراء
فجرتها في الرمل.. في الصدور.. في البطون
و كم قتلت ؟
يصعب أن أعدّهم
لكنني نلت وساماً واحداً
سألته، معذبا نفسي، إذن
صف لي قتيلا واحدا
أصلح من جلسته، وداعب الجريدة المطويّة
و قال لي كأنه يسمعني أغنية:

25

30

35

40

45

50

كخيمة هوى على الحصى
و عانق الكوكب المحطمة
كان على جبينه الواسع تاج من دم
وصدره بدون أوسمة
لأنه لم يحسن القتال
يبدو أنه مزارع أو عامل أو بائع جوال
كخيمة هوى على الحصى ..و مات
كانت ذراعاه
ممدودتين مثل جدولين يابسين
و عندما فتّشت في جيوبه
عن اسمه، وجدت صورتين
واحدةً ..لزوجته
واحدةً.. لطفله
سألته: حزنت؟
أجابني مقاطعاً: يا صاحبي محمود
الحزن طير أبيض
لا يقرب الميدان. و الجنود
يرتكبون الإثم حين يحزنون
كنت هناك آلة تنفث ناراً وردى
وتجعل الفضاء طيراً أسودا

حدثّني عن حبه الأول،
فيما بعد
عن شوارع بعيدة،
و عن ردود الفعل بعد الحرب
عن بطولة المذياع و الجريدة
و عندما خبأ في منديله سعلته
سألته: أنلتقي؟
أجاب: في مدينة بعيدة
حين ملأت كأسه الرابع
قلت مازحاً: ترحل... والوطن ؟
أجاب: دعني ..
إنني أحلم بالزنابق البيضاء
بشارع مغرّد و منزل مضاء
أريد قلبا طيبا، لا حشو بندقية
أريد يوما مشمسا، لا لحظة انتصار
مجنونةً.. فاشيّة

أريد طفلاً باسماً يضحك للنهار،
لا قطعةً في الآلة الحربية
جئت لأحيا مطلع الشموس
لا مغربها
وإنني أرفض أن أموت
أن أحارب النساء و الصغار
كي أحرس الكروم والآبار
لأثرياء النفط والمصانع الحربية

ودعني، لأنه.. يبحث عن زنابق بيضاء
عن طائر يستقبل الصباح
فوق غصن زيتون
لأنه لا يفهم الأشياء
إلاّ كما يحسّها.. يشمّها
يفهم_ قال لي_ إن الوطن
أن أحتسي قهوة أمي
أن أعود، آمناً مع، المساء.[23]

A Soldier Dreams of White Tulips[24]

He dreams of white tulips, an olive branch, her breast in evening blossom.
He dreams of a bird, he tells me, of lemon flowers.
He does not intellectualize about his dream. He understands things as he
senses and smells them.
Homeland for him, he tells me, is to drink my mother's coffee, to return
at nightfall.
And the land? I don't know the land, he said.
I don't feel it in my flesh and blood, as they say in the poems.
Suddenly I saw the land as one sees a grocery store, a street, newspapers.
I asked him, but don't you love the land? My love is a picnic, he said, a glass
of wine, a love affair.

—Would you die for the land?
—No!
All my attachment to the land is no more than a story or a
fiery speech!
They taught me to love it, but I never felt it in my heart.
I never knew its roots and branches, or the scent of its grass.
—And what about its love? Did it burn like suns and desire?
He looked straight at me and said: I love it through my gun.
And through unearthing feasts in the garbage of the past
and a deaf-mute idol whose time and identity are lost.
He told me about the moment of departure, how his mother
silently wept when they led him to the front,
how her anguished voice gave birth to a new hope in his flesh
that doves might flock through the Ministry of War.
He drew on his cigarette. He said, as if fleeing from a swamp
of blood,
I dreamt of white tulips, an olive branch, a bird embracing
the dawn in a
lemon tree.
—And what did you see?
—I saw what I did:
Red Tulips.
I blasted them in the sand . . . in their chests . . . in their bellies.
—How many did you kill?
—It's impossible to tell, but I received one medal.
Pained, I asked him to tell me about one of the dead.
He shifted in his seat, fiddled with the folded newspaper,
then said, as if breaking into song:
He collapsed like a tent on stones, embracing shattered planets.
His high forehead was crowned with blood. His chest was
empty of medals.
He was not a well-trained fighter, but seemed instead to be
a peasant, a
worker or a peddler.
Like a tent he collapsed and died, his arms stretched out
like dry creek beds.

When I searched his pockets for a name, I found two
photographs, one of his
wife, the other of his daughter.
Did you feel sad? I asked.
Cutting me off, he said, Mahmoud, my friend,
sadness is a white bird that does not come near a battlefield.
Soldiers commit a sin when they feel sad.
I was there like a machine spitting hellfire and death,
turning space into a black bird.
He told me about his first love, and later, about distant streets,
about reactions to the war in the heroic radio and the press.
As he hid a cough in his handkerchief I asked him:
Shall we meet again?
Yes, but in a city far away.
When I filled his fourth glass, I asked jokingly:
Are you off? What about the homeland?
Give me a break, he replied.
I dream of white tulips, streets of song, a house of light.
I need a kind heart, not a bullet.
I need a bright day, not a mad, fascist moment of triumph.
I need a child to cherish a day of laughter, not a weapon of war.
I came to live for rising suns, not to witness their setting
And I refuse to die
I refuse to kill women and children
To protect the vines and wells
Of the oil and war factories wealthy owners
He said good-bye and went looking for white tulips,
a bird welcoming the dawn on an olive branch.
He understands things only as he senses and smells them.
Homeland for him, he said, is to drink my mother's coffee,
to return safely,
At nightfall.[25]

This poem takes the form of a dialogue between a Palestinian speaker and an Israeli soldier. Darwīsh writes in the free verse form, which enables him to record a very natural dialogue between the self and the other.

In this poem, Darwīsh celebrates his love for Palestine and criticizes the other, his enemy. Although he humanizes the Israeli soldier, he does so only after the soldier regrets his wrongdoings and decides to leave "the homeland." Darwīsh sends a message to the other, the Israeli soldier, to the State of Israel, and to his fellow Palestinian citizens fighting for their land. In this poem, as in "Biṭāqat Huwiyya," the representation of the Israeli enemy is juxtaposed with that of the Palestinian peasant, who cultivates his land, loves his country, and dies in its defense.

Darwīsh here juxtaposes the self with its enemy by contrasting their definitions of homeland, their connections to the land, and their perspectives on love, sadness, heroism, and death. Darwīsh wrote the poem about one of his Israeli friends, whom he knew from the Communist Party, who grew "tired of his country [and] disillusioned by politics" and who "was preparing to leave."[26] For writing this poem Darwīsh was equally criticized by Israelis and Arabs. On one hand, the secretary general of the Israeli Communist Party wondered if in writing such a poem, Darwīsh wants the Israelis to leave the country and become peace lovers.[27] On the other hand, many Arabs criticized Darwīsh for humanizing the Israeli soldier, who is portrayed as a friend.[28] Neither the Israelis nor the Arabs were happy with Darwīsh's representation of the other. The Israeli politicians attacked Darwīsh for representing them as cruel and lacking in humanity, while Arabs attacked him for sympathizing with an Israeli soldier who killed Arabs. However, what the Arab audience missed is that Darwīsh humanizes the Israeli other only after that other regrets his wrongdoings and criticizes the practices of the Israeli government.

Lines 1–4 introduce the Israeli soldier with whom the speaker will be talking throughout the poem. This soldier is like any man: he dreams of white tulips, an olive branch, his beloved's breast in the evening, a bird, and lemon flowers. This soldier, Darwīsh continues, does not intellectualize things; rather, he understands life as he senses and smells it. Thus, it is as if Darwīsh is preparing to tell the reader that what he will read next is neither intellectualized nor fake. This soldier will answer Darwīsh's questions about life as he understands and senses it. In this way Darwīsh establishes credibility for the Israeli soldier's answers. The significance of this lies in Darwīsh's attempt to make his poem transparent. This poem speaks of the real experiences of an Israeli soldier who is tired of the politics of his country and decides to leave, looking for another home. This poem humanizes the Israeli soldier because he admits his wrongdoings and ends his engagement with the Israeli army. Some might argue that Darwīsh is thus asking the Israelis to leave so that peace can spread in the region. Others might argue that Darwīsh humanizes the other only when the other becomes closer to Darwīsh by rejecting his past identity as a soldier and embracing a more humanitarian one. This poem invites the reader to examine both what it means to be an Israeli soldier and what it means to be a Palestinian.

This encounter establishes Darwīsh's early stance on the identity of the self and the other. This poem, like "Biṭāqat Huwiyya," highlights the identity of the Palestinian by contrasting it with that of the Israeli other. The Israeli–Palestinian conflict can only be solved if the Israeli other quits the scene and departs. When the Israeli soldier regrets killing Palestinians and decides to leave the country, only then does Darwīsh see him as a human being looking for peace, love, and a normal life. Man in Darwīsh's works is "either the oppressed or the oppressor. He is either subject to exploitation and aggression, or a manufacturer of this exploitation and aggression."[29] This explains why the self becomes the opposite of its other in Darwīsh's earlier, anti-Israeli works. The Palestinian is the oppressed while the Israeli is the oppressor, and the Palestinian is subject to exploitation and aggression at the hands of the Israeli. Therefore, when the Palestinian self, the farmer, talks to the Israeli other, the soldier, he speaks from the perspective of a victim whose homeland and land were taken from him by force.

In lines 5–16 Darwīsh asks the Israeli soldier about homeland and land. To the question of what the homeland means to him, the soldier responds, "to drink my mother's coffee, to return at nightfall." This soldier's definition of homeland, like Darwīsh's own, is not restricted to geography. Just as Darwīsh yearns for his mother's coffee and a place to return to at night, the Israeli soldier does too. The Israeli soldier's mother in lines 21–24 hopes for peace at the moment of his departure, so her son can return to her safe and sound. Likewise, the speaker's mother and all the mothers of the Palestinians hope their sons will return home safe and sound in a country where those who leave might never return home. The humanization of the Israeli soldier and his mother stems from Darwīsh's stance on peace and war, and the right to live in Palestine/Israel. In lines 7–16 Darwīsh asks the soldier what the land means to him. The soldier answers by saying that he neither knows the land nor feels it in his flesh and blood. Asked whether he loves the land and would die for it, the soldier says that love is a picnic, a glass of wine, and a love affair, and he would not die for the land. This love is a pleasure outing, not a permanent, serious enterprise. In lines 14–16 the soldier explains this kind of love by saying that he is not attached to the land, which might be read as an accusation of those Israelis who express their love for the land in fiery speeches "in the heroic radio and the press." The soldier admits that although he was taught to love the land, he never felt it in his heart. This statement is key here because it brings to mind its great contrast with how Darwīsh expresses the Palestinians' feelings toward their land. For Darwīsh, while the Israeli neither knows the land's "roots and branches, or the scent of its grass," nor feels its love in his heart, the Palestinian does. The Israeli is the Palestinian's opposite. The image of the Palestinian farmer—who plows his land every day and knows its roots and smallest details by heart, and who is willing to die for his land without the slightest hesitation—is not explicitly mentioned in the poem, but it is present. Whenever we see images of the Israeli soldier, we see counter-images of the Palestinian farmer. Darwīsh creates these images to maintain the Palestinians' legitimacy and the Israelis' illegitimacy in Palestine/Israel.

Lines 18–20 affirm Darwīsh's previous statement on legitimacy in Palestine/Israel. The image of the Israeli soldier looking straight at the poet and admitting that he loves the land through his gun makes the poem even more anti-Israeli in tone. It is as if Darwīsh is saying that the Israelis' love of what they call their land is only by force or violence, which suggests violation or rape. He says he loves the land "by unearthing feasts in the garbage of the past / and through a deaf-mute idol whose time and identity are lost." This image of the Israelis unearthing feasts in the garbage of the past is a metaphor for their right to the State of Israel; they must dig through the past to legitimize their existence and violence in Israel/Palestine, presumably using the Hebrew Bible and archaeological remains to legitimize and build the State of Israel. Darwīsh perceives the Israeli state as a loved and worshipped deaf-mute idol with neither age nor identity. In this poem, the Israeli state not only does not belong to time, but also has no legitimate identity. The Palestinian identity does not seem to need supporting evidence, whereas the Israeli identity is in constant need of evidence to support its historical narrative. Thus, for Darwīsh, this intrusive state can have an identity only if it destroys the identity of the other, the Palestinian, and makes up a new identity by digging in the past. This alludes to a political reality in which one nation's identity is erased so a new one can flourish. For Darwīsh, the State of Israel will continue to destroy the Palestinian identity and memory to build and legitimize the Israeli identity. Therefore, coexistence of Palestinians and Israelis in the same place is not an option, at least not in this poem or at this stage in Darwīsh's poetry.

In lines 42–49 the Israeli soldier recalls one of his battle encounters with a Palestinian man. Images of the slain victim flash back to the Israeli soldier's memory and pain him and Darwīsh. The soldier sympathizes with his victim when he tries to learn about his identity. Assuming that he is a well-trained fighter like him, the Israeli soldier is shocked to discover that he was "a peasant, a worker or a peddler." The image of this Palestinian, whose "high forehead was crowned with blood" and whose "chest was empty of medals," lying dead in the middle of the battlefield evokes emotions of agony, sadness, love, and pride at the same time. This Palestinian is not a soldier. He came neither to occupy the land of another people nor to collect medals or hear his name "in the heroic radio and press." He is a simple peasant or worker who died defending his right to live on his land, which he knows well. Becoming more intrigued by the identity of his enemy, the Israeli soldier comes closer to inspect his corpse. What is revealed to him is how mistaken he was about his enemy's identity. He searches his victim's pocket for a name, only to find photographs of the man's wife and daughter. What is important here is not the fact that the soldier could not know his victim's name, but rather that his victim has universal human family relationships and people to return to. Like the speaker in "Biṭāqat Huwiyya," the Palestinian victim here has no name, no social status, and nothing to brag about. Rather, he has love and pride for his land and a yearning to protect and return to his family. This deepens the soldier's pain, and when asked by the speaker if he felt sad after seeing the photographs of the family of the man he has just killed, the soldier responds with something that takes the reader aback: "Sadness is a white bird that does not come near a battlefield / Soldiers commit a sin when they feel sad. / I was there like a machine spitting hellfire and death, / turning space into a black bird." According to the poem, the Israeli soldier is taught not only to love a land he does not know, but also to kill and never feel sorry. He is turned into a machine "spitting hellfire and death" and "turning space into a black bird." The images of this war machine turning everything into death and hellfire, making the space a bloody black bird, are the soldier's confession of his heinous acts as a member of the Israeli army. This confession contradicts Israel's narrative of being the only democracy in the Middle East and undermines its legitimacy because it is founded on the blood and remnants of the crushed other.

In lines 50–71 the soldier remembers his first love and dreams of white tulips, a symbol of peace and friendship, and "a kind heart, not a bullet." The soldier dreams of everything that he lacks because of his military status. He needs a kind heart, not a bullet; a song, not the heroic radio speeches about war; and "a bright day, not a mad, fascist moment of triumph." The Israeli soldier needs what the Palestinian has: "a child to cherish a day of laughter" and to "live for rising suns." To make the dream perfect, he wants to be liberated from what defines him as an Israeli soldier: "a weapon of war," and witnessing the setting of suns. In the last lines of this poem, the Israeli soldier negates what defines him as an Israeli soldier and looks for what would define him as a human being. When he leaves Darwīsh, he is looking for white tulips, for peace, and for a life he understands "as he sees and smells" and not as he is taught and indoctrinated by the State of Israel. Darwīsh ends the poem with the reiteration of what a homeland means for this Israeli soldier: to drink his mother's coffee and to return home at nightfall. Home for him is not Israel or Palestine; rather, it is family and safety, a place where one's happiness is not based on the misery, destruction, and negation of the other. Thus, Darwīsh in this poem sees the Israeli's home and safety outside the borders of Palestine. The speaker's country is reduced to a war zone if the Israeli decides to stay, and it becomes a haven of peace and friendship if he leaves. The soldier's decision to leave opens a door into a new, normal life where he can live without committing crimes. This poem sees no hope of peace between Israelis and Palestinians if the Israelis choose to live in Israel/Palestine and fight the Palestinians. Darwīsh encourages Israeli soldiers to follow the steps of his friend, who realizes that he was turned into a war weapon, killing innocent people to satisfy the blind ambition of the Israeli politicians.

The dialogue between this speaker and the Israeli soldier suggests a dialogue between the Arabs and their enemy, the male Israeli soldier, who regrets his crimes and decides to leave. In this poem, Darwīsh portrays Israeli soldiers as war machines rewarded by the Israeli state for killing Palestinian civilians, though they may retain "the pacific streak that is repressed in them by military logic."[30] The soldiers trained as war machines must repress their pacific streak, but they may recover it if they renounce the war on the Palestinians. Darwīsh only sees this "pacific streak" in the Israeli other when he is liberated from that military logic. Thus, Darwīsh remains traditional in his depiction of the other in this poem: the other is humanized when he listens to Darwīsh and leaves the Israeli military to look for a homeland where "his feelings to the land" are not "artificially induced."[31]

This dialogue brings the two men together at the end of the poem, when the Israeli soldier regrets his past and declares a new beginning. Thus, Darwīsh seems to suggest that negotiations and dialogue between the Israelis and the Palestinians will take place only after the Israelis renounce their crimes and abandon their criminal practices against the Palestinians. Darwīsh sees the Israeli other as a friend and a fellow human being, with whom he shares dreams and aspirations, but only after he acknowledges the Palestinians' right to their land and voices his decision to look for another homeland. Thus, the other in this poem, as in the previous one, is the enemy who can be seen as a friend only outside the war zone. It is worth noting that this poem was published in 1967. Thus, Darwīsh takes the national catastrophe and defeat of the 1967 war to emphasize the animosity of the Israeli state for the Arab nations.

THE IDENTITY OF THE ISRAELI OTHER

Published in Paris "three months after the beginning of the Palestinian Intifada on December 9, 1987," in *Al-Yawm al-Sābi'*, "Ayyuhā al-Mārrūn bayna al-Kalimāt al-ʿĀbira" (O You Who Pass between the Fleeting Words) is an example of Darwīsh's representation of the other as an enemy whose existence threatens the existence and identity of the self.[32] The images in "Ayyuhā al-Mārrūn" disturbed certain Israeli Jews because of their powerful expression of Palestinian identity and the attachment of the Palestinian to his land.[33] Although this poem expresses and defines Palestinian identity in a provocative way, what really angered the Israelis was not only Darwīsh's negation of their identity, but also his call for them to leave the land to its natives. When Shefi Gabbi's translation of "Ayyuhā al-Mārrūn" into Hebrew was published in the newspaper *Ma'ariv* in 1988, Gabbi wrote that Darwīsh "advises the Israelis to pack their bags and return to the Diaspora along with the coffins of their dead, since the Palestinians reject even any traces of the Jews."[34] Darwīsh does not name the Israelis in the poem, yet he identifies them as those "who pass between the fleeting words." In this four-stanza poem, Darwīsh employs powerful imagery to express his frustration and give shape to his rejection of the Israeli identity and confiscation of his land. He questions the history and legitimacy of the Israelis and addresses them directly with his confrontational tone and repetitive use of the imperative. It is worth noting that this poem appears in the first edition of *Ward Aqall* (Fewer Roses), the Haifa edition, but appears to have been dropped from all the other editions.

أيها المارّون بين الكلمات العابرة

-1-
أيها المارّون بين الكلمات العابرة
احملوا أسماءكم، وانصرفوا
واسرقوا ما شئتم من زرقة البحر ورمل الذاكره
وخذوا ما شئتم من صور، كي تعرفوا
أنكم لن تعرفوا
كيف يبني حجر من أرضنا سقف السماء

-2-
أيها المارّون بين الكلمات العابرة
منكم السيف ومنا دمنا

منكم الفولاذ والنار ومنا لحمنا
منكم دبابة أخرى ومنا حجر
منكم قنبلة الغاز ومنا المطر
وعلينا ما عليكم من سماء وهواء
فخذوا حصتكم من دمنا وانصرفوا
وادخلوا حفل عشاء راقص.. وانصرفوا
وعلينا، نحن، أن نحرس ورد الشهداء
وعلينا،نحن، أن نحيا كما نحن نشاء!

-3-

أيها المارّون بين الكلمات العابرة
كالغبار المر، مروا أينما شئتم ولكن
لا تمروا بيننا كالحشرات الطائرة
فلنا في أرضنا ما نعمل
ولنا قمح نربيه ونسقيه ندى أجسادنا
ولنا ما ليس يرضيكم هنا:
حجر.. او حجل
فخذوا الماضي، إذا شئتم، إلى سوق التحف
وأعيدوا الهيكل العظمى للهدهد، إن شئتم،
على صحن خزف.
فلنا ما ليس يرضيكم : لنا المستقبل
ولنا في أرضنا ما نعمل

-4-

أيها المارّون بين الكلمات العابرة
كدسوا أوهامكم في حفرة مهجورة ، وانصرفوا
وأعيدوا عقرب الوقت إلى شرعية العجل المقدس
أو الى توقيت موسيقى مسدس!
فلنا ما ليس يرضيكم هنا ، فانصرفوا
ولنا ما ليس فيكم، وطن ينزف شعبا ينزف
وطنا يصلح للنسيان او للذاكرة
أيها المارّون بين الكلمات العابرة
آن أن تنصرفوا
وتقيموا أينما شئتم، ولكن لا تموتوا بيننا
فلنا في أرضنا ما نعمل
ولنا الماضي هنا
ولنا صوت الحياة الاول

ولنا الحاضر، والحاضر، والمستقبل
ولنا الدنيا هنا... والآخرة
فاخرجوا من أرضنا
من برنا.. من بحرنا
من قمحنا.. من ملحنا.. من جرحنا
من كل شيء ، واخرجوا
من ذكريات الذاكرة
أيها المارّون بين الكلمات العابرة .[35]

O You Who Pass between the Fleeting Words

1
O you who pass between the fleeting words
Carry your names, and be gone
Steal what you will from the blueness of the sea and
the sand of memory
Take what pictures you will, so that you understand
That which you never will:
How a stone from our land builds the ceiling of our sky.

2
O you who pass between fleeting words
From you the sword—from us the blood,
From you steel and fire—from us our flesh
From you yet another tank—from us stones,
From you tear gas—from us rain
Above us, as above you, are sky and air
So take your share of our blood—and be gone
Go to a dancing party—and be gone
As for us, we have to water the martyrs' flowers
As for us, we have to live as we will.

3
O you who pass between fleeting words
As bitter dust, go where you wish, but
Do not pass between us like flying insects
For we have work to do in our land:

We have wheat to grow which we water with our bodies' dew
We have that which does not please you here:
Stones and partridges
So take the past, if you wish, to the antiquities market
And return the hoopoe's skeleton, if you wish,
On a pottery platter
We have that which does not please you: we have the future
And we have things to do in our land.

4
O you who pass between fleeting words
Pile your illusions in a deserted pit, and be gone
Return the hand of time to the law of the golden calf
Or to the time of the revolver's music!
For we have that which does not please you here, so be gone
And we have what you lack: a bleeding homeland
    of a bleeding people
A homeland fit for oblivion or memory
O you who pass between fleeting words
It is time for you to be gone
Live wherever you like, but do not die among us
For we have work to do in our land
We have the past here
We have the first cry of life
We have the present, the present and the future
We have this world here, and the hereafter
So leave our country,
Our land, our sea,
Our wheat, our salt, our wounds
Leave everything and leave
The memories of memory
O you who pass between the fleeting words.[36]

In the first line, the speaker makes it clear to the Israelis that this poem voices his and his people's wish to be left alone in their country by the Israelis' permanent departure. In the first stanza, Darwīsh gives the

Israelis permission to steal what they "will from the blueness of the sea and the sand of memory." In this image, the Israelis are portrayed as intruders who take not only the physical land of the Palestinians, but also the blueness of their sea and the sand of their memories. He sees them as insignificant and incapable of erasing the Palestinian psyche. Therefore, despite the Israelis' efforts to claim the Palestinian land and register it under their names, the Palestinian identity will remain intact. Darwīsh tells the Israelis that it does not matter how many pictures they take to prove their legitimacy in Palestine to others. He explains that the Israelis will never understand how a stone from the land the Palestinians know by heart is capable of building the ceiling of their sky. The sky and the land are connected through a stone—a stone of resistance that becomes the horizon of their dreams and aspirations. The Israelis' photos of buildings and excavations have no effect on or value to Darwīsh when compared to the effect of that stone. Though deemed worthless, the stone symbolizes the Palestinians' sense of belonging and perseverance.

In the second stanza, Darwīsh juxtaposes the other with its counterpart, the self. The sword represents the other; the blood, the self. The relationship between sword and blood is like the relationship between killer and victim. The sword sheds blood; thus, in this image, the Israelis are the violent intruders who shed the blood of the natives. Also, the Israelis' weapon is the sword, while all that the Palestinians have to defend themselves with is their blood. In lines 8–10 the Israelis bring fire, steel, another tank, and tear gas to the battlefield, while the Palestinians have only their flesh, their stones, and rain. The image of the Palestinians defending themselves with stones and their bare chests as the Israelis march toward them with their tanks, steel, fire, and tear gas indicates the asymmetrical nature of the Israeli–Palestinian conflict. The Palestinians are fighting an unequal battle in which the Israelis use advanced weapons of war. This image recalls the iconic war between intruders and natives, in which the intruders always have better equipment and weapons and the natives have only themselves. When Darwīsh says that the Israelis have tear gas while the Palestinians have rain, he indicates that nature sympathizes with the natives of the land and washes their tears with rain. The Palestinians have the (eternal) forces of nature, such as rocks, blood, and rain, whereas the Israelis have war matériel.

In lines 11–15 Darwīsh asks the Israelis to take their share of their blood and be gone. He asks them to leave and do what they want somewhere else, so the Palestinians can also live and do what they want. He asks them to do what they like to do—go to dancing parties to celebrate after shedding the blood of the Palestinians—so that the Palestinians can water their martyrs' flowers. In line 12, Darwīsh tells the Israelis to put an end to their unnecessary violence in Palestine/Israel and leave with their bloodstained hands. He tells them in line 11 that they share the same sky and air, but it is each side's decision to make of this land a garden or a graveyard. The Palestinians, for Darwīsh, plant flowers in their land and water them with the blood of their martyrs, whereas the Israelis dance on the misery of the Palestinians and bring destruction and death to the land. Darwīsh sees the Palestinians and Israelis as two opposites: if one represents life, the other represents death. The continued Israeli presence can only come at the expense of the Palestinians. Darwīsh sees no right for the Israelis to exist in Palestine, and he criticizes their barbaric and violent treatment of the Palestinians.

In the third stanza, the Israelis are likened to bitter dust and flying insects that prevent the Palestinians from working in their land. This reflects Darwīsh's annoyance with their presence, which he sees as insignificant when compared to that of the Palestinians. The image of the Israelis as flying pests is juxtaposed with the image of the Palestinian farmers growing wheat, which they water with their blood and their bodies' dew. The Palestinians work so hard that their sweat waters their plants, an indication of the relationship between the Palestinian and his land. In lines 21–27 Darwīsh reminds the Israelis of two things: the insignificance of what they do in someone else's land and how ephemeral their presence is. Darwīsh tells the Israelis that while they are busy manipulating the past to legitimize their presence and identity, they lack what the Palestinians have: the future. For Darwīsh, the Palestinians own the future, which does not please the Israelis. When the Israelis are busy manipulating the past, the Palestinians are busy cultivating their land—they do not need to do anything other than live their lives as they have been doing for years. According to Darwīsh, the Israelis need to do one thing: "Go where you wish / for we have work to do in our land." In this poem, the self conceives the other as a threat to its existence, memory, and identity; while the self is represented in a peaceful manner, the other is portrayed as a machine of war and destruction. Thus, the prospect for peace and reconciliation between these two opposites seems far-fetched.

In the last stanza Darwīsh compares the assets of the Palestinians to those of the Israelis. He tells the Israelis that the Palestinians have a bleeding homeland of a bleeding people with a past, present, and future to live for. This future can only arrive if the Israelis realize that they should pile their illusions in a deserted pit and leave, for despite their attempts to manipulate history, this country will never be theirs. He asks the Israelis to understand that they may go anywhere they want, but they should not die among the Palestinians and make Palestine a graveyard. He asks the Israelis to leave their country, land, sea, and wheat, and even their salt and wounds.

In this poem, the Israelis have caused the Palestinians profound pain that has stained their memory, both individual and collective. Darwīsh asks the Israelis to leave the Palestinians' wounds alone so that they may heal. The Israelis have become like a disease that contaminates the Palestinian land. The Palestinian land is united with the Palestinian body, both of which need to be purified, like the wheat and salt, of the remnants of the Israelis' presence. In the last line, Darwīsh maintains that the Israelis have even intruded on the Palestinian memories of memory. Poetry recalls memories, and the Israeli government's monitoring of Darwīsh's poems is an attempt to intrude on that which guards the Palestinian memory. For Darwīsh, Palestinians can live in peace, guard their memories, and live for the future, as they did in the past, only in the absence of the Israelis. Darwīsh here makes a clear statement on the Israeli–Palestinian conflict: the existence of one can only be at the expense of the other, and there is no place for two peoples in one land. There is room for one people only, and the only legitimate inhabitants are the Palestinians.

In this poem Darwīsh asks the Israelis repeatedly to leave his country, seeing no room for negotiation with them. They use their weapons and regulations to defend their right to exist, while he uses his poetry to defend his identity and people. For Darwīsh, the Israeli other only "passes" between words, words that themselves pass and become a memory. The Israeli presence is only passing and will not continue for long, unlike the presence of the Palestinian, who will continue to water the land he loves with his blood and sweat. Thus, Darwīsh concludes, "It is time for you to be gone."

From the Israeli side, Mike Evans argues, "That dream, 'to be a free people in our land, the land of Zion and Jerusalem,' finally became a reality, after two thousand years of suffering, when Israel regained her independence and then restored her sovereignty over the City of Peace."[37] However, in this poem, Darwīsh negates the Israeli narrative by affirming that the Israelis established their state at the expense of the Palestinians, on whose land they intruded. These two nations have the same dream: "to be a free people in our land." Nevertheless, each negates the identity and legitimacy of the other. What is interesting about this poem is the fact that Darwīsh had packed his belongings and left Palestine/Israel in 1970, long before the publication of this poem in 1987. It is as if Darwīsh felt that the Israelis were supposed to be the ones packing and leaving Palestine/Israel for good, not him. This is Darwīsh's most controversial and ardently anti-Israeli poem. It is Darwīsh's "weapon" during the first Palestinian *Intifāḍa* in 1987, which gave rise to bold political and poetic statements.

Palestinian writers have portrayed Zionists in negative images in their literature, and Darwīsh's "Ayyuhā al-Mārrūn" is a striking example of this.[38] Amy Elad-Bouskila maintains, "The Israelis that Palestinians encounter most frequently are soldiers, followed by policemen, secret servicemen and Jewish settlers in the occupied territories. . . . The negative image of Israelis appears in two main areas: the inhuman behavior of soldiers and the soldiers' coarse attitudes toward Palestinians and the values they hold dear. This dehumanization of the Israeli soldier is derived first and foremost from his daily humiliation of Palestinians."[39] This is one reason that Darwīsh considered the other male his enemy, whom he felt the urgent call to resist and fight in his poetry. Seeing the Jewish settlers live comfortably on his land while his people are expelled and humiliated, and experiencing this daily humiliation firsthand, Darwīsh depicts the dehumanization of the Palestinian self by the Israeli other and condemns the latter to leave. The negative images of the Israeli other in Darwīsh's poetry are based on the bitter reality of the Israeli–Palestinian conflict from the perspective of the Palestinian. For Darwīsh, the Israeli other—whether the settler or the soldier—is the source of misery for the self. Thus, he asks the Israelis to end the conflict by leaving his people and country alone. Yet, instead of seeing the enemy leave, Darwīsh was forced to leave his country in order to write freely against the oppression and lack of freedom of expression he was subject to in his homeland.

UNDER SIEGE

Poems such as "Ayyuhā al-Mārrūn" still deny the right of the other to exist and negate his identity only to confirm the identity of the self. *Ḥālat Ḥiṣār* (State of Siege), a work more recent than those discussed above, continues that negation. It is a book-length metapoetic epic written and published during the siege of Ramallah in 2002. The voice of the speaker in this poem overlaps with that of the poet. Darwīsh maintains that he wrote this poem in an attempt to challenge the expectations of his readers and to liberate himself from questions that have besieged him and his poetry.[40] Darwīsh says that in this poem, which he refers to as the Ramallah text, "there is a larger space for the other. In the search for the common, it is necessary to accept the other on the condition that the other accepts me as well. . . . The search for normal life in this country has to include a solution for the other. This is a paradox, and unlike any other in history—the victim has also to find a solution for its oppressor."[41]

Although Darwīsh mentions that there is a larger space for the other in *Ḥālat Ḥiṣār*, the other is still portrayed as an intruder in his space and is again asked to leave. The other continues to be his oppressor, and yet the poet realizes the need to take the other into consideration when looking for solutions for the conflict. For Darwīsh, it is absurd that the Palestinian victim must look for a solution to accommodate his Israeli oppressor. The answer is to search for "normal life in this country." If life is to be normal in Palestine/Israel under the current circumstance, the Palestinians and Israelis have to look for an inclusive solution. Darwīsh writes *Ḥālat Ḥiṣār* to negotiate between the celebrated identity of the self and the denied identity of the other. He sees coexistence with the other as a forced solution to the conflict. This poem questions the Israeli and Palestinian identities by recalling memories from the Israelis' past. On one hand, Darwīsh tries to convince his Arab reader that to coexist with the Israeli in Palestine is to accept the presence of and to find a solution for his oppressor and enemy. On the other hand, Darwīsh humanizes the enemy and accepts coexistence with him only from the perspective of a native who has no option but to befriend his intruder if he is to stay in his own country. It is worth noting that at this time, the two-state solution had already been discussed, and the poem thus reflects Darwīsh's stance on this political solution. He asks the Israelis to leave the Occupied Territories, not Israel.[42] Although Darwīsh "stressed later that he was referring to the Israeli occupation of the West Bank and Gaza and not to all of historic Palestine," this did not change how Israeli readers heard his poem.[43] Darwīsh maintains, "Poems can't establish a state. But they can establish a metaphorical homeland in the minds of the people. I think my poems have built some houses in this landscape."[44] Poems such as this establish a Palestinian home, one that people can visit and belong to. Darwīsh wrote his poetry with a goal in his mind: "to prevent those who 'colonized the land' from 'colonizing memory as well.'"[45]

This poem juxtaposes the Israelis' perceptions and definitions of key terms such as *peace*, *war*, *identity*, *humanity*, and *freedom* with those of the Palestinians. Such terms define the Israeli–Palestinian conflict and offer a solution for the oppressor from the perspective of the victim. This solution might entail coexistence with the enemy, but it also recognizes that the Palestinians have no choice but to accept this solution. Thus, coexistence with the other in this poem is not by choice, but by force. Darwīsh's poem is similar to the earlier "Ayyuhā al-Mārrūn" in its rejection of coexistence with the Israeli other. Although Darwīsh sees many similarities between himself and his enemy, he asks still asks the other to leave the West Bank (now part of Israel).

أيها الواقفون على العتبات ادخلوا
واشربوا معنا القهوة العربية!
[قد تشعرون بانكم بشر مثلنا]

أيها الواقفون على عتبات البيوت
اخرجوا من صباحاتنا
نطمئن الى اننا بشر مثلكم.[46]

You, standing at our thresholds, come in,
Sip some Arab coffee with us!
You may feel you're as human as we are.

You! at the thresholds of our houses,
Vacate our mornings,
So we may be certain we're as human as you are.[47]

The speaker invites the other to sip some Arab coffee with them so he may feel he is as human as they are. Darwīsh invites the other to take a closer look at his double by trying his coffee. For Darwīsh, the Israeli soldier will realize that he is as human as the Palestinians when he stops watching them for a moment and does what they do: sip Arab coffee. Only then will the Israeli realize that he is besieging people who are only living their lives. However, Darwīsh does not mention going into an Israeli house and doing what they do to feel as human as they are. On the contrary, he asks the Israelis to vacate his mornings so he may be certain that he is as human as the Israelis are. In so doing, Darwīsh portrays the existence of the Israelis in the same place with the Palestinians as an obstacle. He perceives that the humanity of the Palestinians is validated only when the Israelis vacate the country so the Palestinians can become as human as the Israelis. He invites the other to his house to show him that the Palestinians are just as human as he is, so he may leave them to live their lives and be the humans they are. Darwīsh still cannot let go of his anti-Israeli tone in his dialogue with the other; this poem was written under siege and is still addressed to an enemy. He still presents the existence of the other as a threat to the existence of the self. It is worth noting how the poet turns the tables: the Israeli discovers not that the Palestinians are human like him, but that he is human like them.

In another stanza, Darwīsh accuses the Israelis of creating their identity at the expense of the identity of the Palestinians.

[إلى قاتل :] لو تأملت وجه الضحية
وفكرت، كنت تذكرت أمك في غرفة
الغاز، كنت تحررت من حكمة البندقية
وغيرت رأيك : ما هكذا تستعاد الهوية![48]

[To a killer:] if you had looked into the face of your victim
And thought carefully, you might have remembered your mother
in the Gas Chamber,
And freed yourself from the rifle's prejudice
And changed your mind.
Come now, this is no way to restore an identity![49]

The other, in this poem, is a killer, who, had he looked into the face of his victim and thought carefully, might have remembered his mother in the gas chamber. Darwīsh recalls memories from the Jewish Holocaust to compare what happened to the Jews during the Holocaust to what is happening to the Palestinians now. The Israeli soldier may only find his freedom, according to Darwīsh, when he frees himself from his rifle. Thus, Darwīsh speaks to his other as to one who was once a victim and who is now a killer. Darwīsh accuses the Israelis of restoring their lost identity by creating another Holocaust in Israel/Palestine. This identity, according to the poem, is neither valid nor legitimate. However, Muhammad Siddiq argues that in this section Darwīsh humanizes the Israeli other: "Significantly, the Israeli 'killer' is not cast here in the traditional abstract guise of a faceless enemy that remains invisible behind or inside distant, conspicuously indifferent war machines. Rather, he is a distinct individual, with intimate family ties and memories, and, above all, a conscience that may be momentarily atrophied but perhaps not irrevocably lost. . . . It gets the point across vividly and forcefully without antagonizing the intended target of the imaginative exercise: the Israeli 'other.'"[50]

Humanizing the Israeli other in this section highlights the cruelty and violence of the Israeli other. By mentioning that the killer had a mother who died in the gas chambers of the Holocaust, Darwīsh provokes the Israeli other not to do unto Palestinians what was done unto his mother. Although Siddiq argues that the other is no longer a weapon or a war machine, this humanization of the killer only makes his crime more hideous. Associating such crimes with the Israeli other as an individual makes it less likely that the Palestinian victim will forgive him or forget his crimes. Thus, this humanization complicates the conflict and makes it more dramatic.

In another stanza, Darwīsh presents an image of the Israeli soldiers and the Palestinian martyrs:

هدوءاً، هدوءاً، فإن الجنود يريدون
في هذه الساعة الاستماع إلي الأغنيات
التي استمع الشهداء إليها، وظلت كرائحة
البن في دمهم... طازجة.[51]

Be quiet—quiet! The soldiers are trying to listen to the same songs
The martyrs listened to
And which remained circulating in their blood
Like the smell of freshly ground coffee beans.[52]

This scene takes place on the battlefield where the Israeli soldiers have just killed some Palestinian men. The Israeli soldiers are trying to listen to the same songs the Palestinian martyrs were listening to before they were killed. These songs continue to circulate in the blood of the martyrs like the smell of freshly ground coffee beans, leaving the soldiers unable to understand them or what they symbolize. The soldier Darwīsh calls a killer in the previous stanza is the same soldier he accuses of restoring his identity at the expense of the Palestinian identity. Here, this soldier tries to listen to the same songs the martyrs were listening to, not to understand the other or learn about his identity, but to steal his identity and memory. The freshly ground coffee beans here are the same Arab coffee beans Darwīsh invited the Israeli to try in order to realize that he is as human as the Palestinians are. Ironically, the smell here is coming from the corpses of the Palestinian victims. In this scene, Darwīsh raises rhetorical questions such as: How can the Israeli realize that he and the Palestinian are equally human when one is a killer and the other is a victim? How can these two coexist under the umbrella of peace when neither is willing to accept the other? Peace for Darwīsh is not chosen but compelled.

سيشتد هذا الحصار
ليقنعنا
باختيار عبودية لا تضر
ولكن بحرية كاملة.[53]

This siege will grow even harsher
To convince us
That we should choose some harmless slavery
As if by our own free will.[54]

The Israeli siege will only grow harsher, so harmless slavery may seem and feel like peace. Accepting the status quo might seem to be a freely made choice, but for Darwīsh it is not. The choice cannot be free when the conflicting forces are not equal because, as Darwīsh says, "there can be no peace between master and slave."[55] Peace becomes a forced reality "when the stronger apologizes to the weaker, / who are weaker only in weaponry / though theirs is the endless horizon."[56] Darwīsh sees no possibility for real freedom or peace with the other because the dynamics of power are unbalanced. Thus, he looks for another way to fight the enemy, a way that enables him to look at the situation from a comical perspective.

الكتابة جرو صغير يعض العدم
الكتابة تجرح من دون دم.[57]

Writing is a puppy snapping at nothingness,
Writing wounds with no blood.[58]

At this stage, writing becomes a comic tool. Mighty as he seems, the enemy is reduced to nothingness in Darwīsh's poetry when writing becomes a snapping puppy. Darwīsh knows well that his one and only way to hurt, anger, and possibly even wound the enemy is by writing his poetry. Darwīsh writes to defend his people and reveal what might not please his enemy. Darwīsh celebrates that which he has and his enemy does not.

نفعل ما يفعل السجناء،
وما يفعل العاطلون عن العمل:
نربي الأمل.[59]

We do as prisoners
And the unemployed do:
We nurse hope.[60]

Although under siege, like prisoners and the unemployed, his people have something that does not please their enemy: hope. They own the future, and they work on their land to nurse hope. Darwīsh provides his people "a psychical compensation that alleviates the pain from the actual conditions of repression. Love and hope become far greater weapons of resistance that do not allow the psyche to be broken."[61] He writes to lift the Palestinian spirit and guard its psyche from infiltrating defeat, which he sees as his enemy's ultimate goal. Darwīsh's definition of his enemy is encapsulated in these two lines:

كلما وجدت واقعا لا يلائمها
عدلته بجرافة.[62]

To confront an undesirable reality they simply
"adjust" it with bulldozers.[63]

For Darwīsh, what sets the self apart from the other is the other's constant desire to change reality according to what pleases him. His tool is the bulldozer. He demolishes villages, like that of Darwīsh's family, and edits history to establish his identity on the remnants of other people's identity. For Darwīsh, his people's reaction to such actions is to nurse hope, cultivate the land, and pose a question to the Israelis:

ألهذا أخَذتَ حياتي لتصنع منها حياتك؟[64]

Is this why you took my life to make from it yours?[65]

Darwīsh sees in the other's refusal to recognize his identity and right of existence in his land an invitation to deny his identity, as long as it is established at the expense of the Palestinians' identity. Thus, he cannot conceive of these two identities coexisting in the same place. Each of them negates the other and reveals a long history of conflict and animosity toward the other. Darwīsh poses a question to his Israeli other: Can you not have your life without ruining mine? Rejecting such an imposed, unjustified reality, Darwīsh sends his enemy a message of defiance:

واقفون هنا. قاعدون هنا. دائمون هنا.
خالدون هنا. ولنا هدف واحد واحد: أن نكون.[66]

Standing here. Sitting here. Remaining here forever.
We have only one goal: to be![67]

Darwīsh uses the pronoun *we* to establish a collective, unified stance against the enemy's efforts to demolish the Palestinian identity. In these two lines, Darwīsh maintains that whether standing or sitting, to stay in Palestine is indeed steadfastness. By keeping this one goal in mind and insisting on not leaving the land, Darwīsh maintains, Palestinians will succeed in protecting their identity and remaining in existence forever. *State of Siege* gives shape to the feelings of loss and oppression from personal and universal perspectives. Torn between wanting to continue fighting the enemy and see him gone, and realizing the urgency of finding a solution, which includes treating the conflict from a new perspective, Darwīsh writes this epic poem to consider solutions as well as to process emotions. We see here the seeds of Darwīsh's further treatment of the relationship between self and other and the conflict, and its future implications. This relationship evolves in his next collection, published one year later.

THE SELF AND ITS OTHERS

In *Lā Taʿtadhir ʿammā Faʿalt* (Do Not Apologize for What You Did, 2003), Darwīsh protests against the mutual dehumanization of himself and his enemy. He questions his relationship with the enemy as his double and calls for a recognition and understanding of the conflict with the other. In so doing, the poet calls neither for peace nor for war. He questions the way the self and the other perceive each other. By understanding the worries of the other, the self might be able to negotiate and communicate with him. In his late poems "Huwa Hādi' wa-Anā Kadhālik" (He Is Quiet and So Am I) and "Hiya fī al-Masā'" (She, in the Evening), Darwīsh neither urges his fellow Palestinians to fight the enemy nor strips the enemy of his identity. On the contrary, he invites his reader, whether a Palestinian, an Israeli, or a peace activist from either side, to look at the conflict between the self and the other from a new perspective.

Before and during the 1967 Arab–Israeli war, the term *iltizām* "became increasingly militant and anti-Israeli in tone," which explains the militant tone in Darwīsh's early works.[68] Darwīsh played a vital role in creating readers committed to Arab nationalism in general and the Palestinian question in particular, and in shaping the national identity of Palestinians and Arabs alike. The ongoing Israeli–Palestinian conflict widened the gap between the two peoples and made it impossible for them to attain peace or mutual understanding. Neither the Israelis nor the Palestinians made substantial efforts to recognize one another or understand their conflict. As summarized by Herbert C. Kelman, because "the resistance on each side to recognizing the nationhood of the other is rooted in the view that their respective national identities are inherently incompatible" and "the fulfillment of one can be achieved only at the expense of the other," each nation will continue to delegitimize the identity and existence of the other in order to prove its own identity and right to exist.[69] This explains Darwīsh's efforts to maintain the Palestinian identity and guard it against what he called the Israelis' intention to "falsify and deny the humanity of the other," which he resisted by writing poems that are "an adamant refusal to accept the language of the occupier and the terms under which the land is defined."[70] The poems discussed above are examples of Darwīsh's attempts to create and maintain the Palestinian identity and voice his refusal to accept the language of the other. Darwīsh also does not see why Palestinians must recognize the State of Israel, the oppressive state that is constantly trying to demolish their sovereignty. However, he understands that, given the complicated circumstances and the imbalance of power in the Israeli–Palestinian conflict, if Palestinians want to live a "normal" life they will have to consider coexisting with the Israelis; the two-state solution. This solution remains imperfect, and Palestinians will not be as free as they would like to be, but it seems more realistic.

Critics such as Edward Said have suggested that neither Palestinian nor Israeli politicians were seriously willing to speak about the peace process, as Said stresses that "the peace process must be demystified and spoken about truthfully and plainly."[71] Because Israeli politicians Yitzhak Rabin and Shimon Peres, among others, and Palestinian politicians such as Yāsir ʿArafāt "did not conceptualize the impact of a two-state solution implicit in the agreement . . . and the full consequence of mutual recognition," the Israeli–Palestinian conflict remains unresolved.[72] Therefore, the lack of mutual recognition hinders serious attempts by the self and the other to question each other's identity.

Homi Bhabha maintains that "to exist is to be called into being in relation to an Otherness."[73] Darwīsh translates the urgency of an awareness about the relationship between the self and its otherness as an exercise of existence in *Lā Taʿtadhir ʿAmmā Faʿalt*. In "Huwa Hādiʾ wa-Anā Kadhālik" and "Hiya fī al-Masāʾ" he poses questions not only about his own people's identity, but also about the identity of the other. These questions challenge the perceptions of the self and the other of their mutual conflict and their self-enclosed identities.

In "Huwa Hādiʾ wa-Anā Kadhālik," the poet presents an image of two men; the only difference between them lies in what they drink. The reader is to understand from this detail that the coffee drinker is Palestinian and the tea drinker is Israeli.

هو هادئ وأنا كذلك

هو هادئ وأنا كذلك
يحتسي شايا بليمون
وأشرب قهوة
هذا هو الشيء المغاير بيننا
هو يرتدي مثلي قميصا واسعا ومخططا
وأنا أطالع مثله صحف المساء
هو لا يراني حين أنظر خلسة
أنا لا أراه حين ينظر خلسة
هو هادئ وأنا كذلك
يسأل الجرسون شينا
أسأل الجرسون شينا
قطة سوداء تعبر بيننا
فأجس فروة ليلها
ويجس فروة ليلها
أنا لا أقول له السماء اليوم صافية
وأكثر زرقة
هو لا يقول لي السماء اليوم صافية

Line numbers in margin: 5, 10, 15

هو المرئي والرائي
أنا المرئي والرائي
أحرك رِجلي اليسرى
يحرك رجلَه اليمنى
أدندن لحن أغنية
يدندن لحن أغنية مشابهة
أفكر هل هو المراة أبصر فيه نفسي؟
ثم أنظر نحو عينيه
ولكن لا أراه
فأترك المقهى على عجل
أفكر ربما هو قاتل أو ربما
هو عابر قد ظن أني قاتل
هو خائف وأنا كذلك.[74]

He Is Quiet and So Am I

He is quiet and so am I.
He sips tea with lemon,
While I drink coffee.
That's the difference between us.
Like me, he wears a wide, striped shirt,
and like him, I read the evening paper.
He doesn't see my secret glance.
I don't see his secret glance.
He's quiet and so am I.
He asks the waiter something.
I ask the waiter something . . .
A black cat walks between us.
I feel the midnight of its fur
and he feels the midnight of its fur . . .
I don't say to him: The sky today
is clear and blue.
He doesn't say to me: The sky today is clear.
He's watched and the one watching
and I'm watched and the one watching.
I move my left foot.
He moves his right foot.

I hum the melody of a song
and he hums the melody of a similar song.
I wonder: Is he the mirror in which I see myself?
And turn to look toward his eyes . . .
But I don't see him.
I hurry from the café.
I think: Maybe he's a killer . . .
or maybe a passerby who thinks I am a killer.
He's afraid . . . and so am I.[75]

The poem brings two men together by listing their similarities and posing a question to the poet, the other, and the reader. The two men wear the same kind of shirt, wide and striped, read the same newspaper, order the same thing, pet the same cat that walks between them, mirror the movements of their feet, and sing similar songs. Thus, these two men are one another's double, yet neither of them tells the other that "the sky is clear today" or "sees the other when he looks in his eyes." The speaker asks, "Is he the mirror in which I see myself?" in an attempt to break the barrier between himself and the other; he is asking whether they are at once the same and the opposite of each other, like a reflection in a mirror. Although almost identical in appearance and behavior, these two men fail to communicate with each other. They fail to recognize that not only do they dress, read, order, touch, sing, and look in the same way, but they also think the same, which is key in this context. They go their separate ways at the end of the evening without the slightest effort to communicate with each other or break the deadly silence in the room. On the contrary, they leave full of fear and suspicion: "I think: Maybe he is a killer . . . / or maybe a passerby who thinks I am a killer / He's afraid . . . and so am I." The poem questions this kind of behavior, and yet the speaker leaves the room, like his double, with many questions on his mind. The last four lines in this poem encapsulate the Israeli–Palestinian conflict and raise questions: Who exactly is the enemy? What are the dimensions of this psychological conflict between these two enemies, who are at once identical and opposite?

Kelman argues, "As long as the other's identity is seen as a threat to one's own identity and must therefore be rejected, there is no space for developing a transcendent identity shared with the other."[76] Darwīsh's recognition that the lack of communication between the self and the other is a threat to the identity of both is part of his understanding of their mutual conflict and shared fears. Kelman claims that "to assert one's own identity requires negating the identity of the other," which we witnessed in Darwīsh's earlier works. Darwīsh focuses on the human qualities of his enemy and then questions his own and his enemy's perception of one another. After decades of "a state of siege" by the Israeli other, Darwīsh presents the conflict from a psychological perspective, one that is key in the understanding of the conflict.

Commenting on the psychological conflict between the Palestinians and the Israelis, Julia DiGangi says,

> Although the battles over resources and politics exacerbate the situation, on the deepest psychological level, the Israeli–Palestinian conflict is a struggle for existence and identity. Both the Israelis' and Palestinians' perception that the other side is attacking their core identity creates a host of other psychological problems, including insecurity, anxiety and hostility. These conditions inhibit the establishment of an empathic response, by preventing each side from seeing the other's point of view and ultimately resolving the conflict.[77]

Among the psychological problems apparent in the poem are "insecurity, anxiety and hostility," from which the two men both suffer: "Maybe he is a killer" and "he is afraid and so am I." These psychological problems hinder any attempt at communication between the self and the other and prevent each side from cooperating to resolve the conflict. By addressing these psychological problems, the poem questions the mutual denial of the other. Also, through humanizing the enemy, Darwīsh invites the enemy to humanize him and look beyond their mutual fear and denial. Here, Darwīsh does not humanize the enemy or seek coexistence with the condition that the other humanizes him or recognizes his existence, as in *State of Siege*. In this poem, Darwīsh invites himself and his other to consider a new way of looking at the conflict, by demanding that the self look at the other in the same way the self demands that the other look at it.

This psychological conflict between the two men in the poem creates a hostile atmosphere that discourages communication. These two men realize that they are one another's double, but because of their anxiety and mutual fear, neither makes any effort to break the silence. They leave the café with the same thoughts they entered with: the other is the enemy, whom I should fear. Realizing that the other stands for the self means that the other considers the self its enemy in the same manner; for the same reasons, the self considers the other its enemy, regardless of whether the other has the right to or not. Treating the conflict from a purely psychological perspective is what makes this poem unique. Darwīsh does not argue with the other about his wrongdoings or "stolen" identity. Instead, he is trying to bring the psychological aspects of the conflict to the center.

The poem questions the identity of the self in its relation to the other and his identity: "I wonder: Is he the mirror in which I see myself?" and "I turn to look toward his eyes . . . / but I don't see him." The self's inability to see the other indicates the speaker's acknowledgment of the lack of communication between the two people. Neither is able to see the other person's point of view. In this poem, the speaker hopes the self and the other will start a conversation about how they feel and how they dehumanize each other, and eventually start looking for a solution. Unlike the solution he has offered to his enemy in the previous poems—to leave the country to its natives—in this poem the speaker invites his male other to make a serious effort to understand the conflict. Only then will the self and the other be able to look beyond the politics that have governed their mutual conflict and search for the common ground required to live a normal life. It is worth noting that Darwīsh's poetry after *State of Siege* seems to have lost its traditional "resistance mode." His language no longer seeks to incite or provoke, but rather to think and meditate. In part, this is due to the failure to achieve any political victory on the ground. Darwīsh admits that the Palestinians have been militarily defeated, and therefore his poetry needs not to preach but instead to reexamine itself and raise hope through "an aesthetic force and presence."[78] This explains why *State of Siege* represents the borderline between Darwīsh's militant works and his humanist and philosophical later works. In the four collections published after *State of Siege*—*Lā Taʿtadhir ʿammā Faʿalt* (Do Not Apologize for What You Did, 2003),

Kazahr al-Lawz aw Ab'ad (Almond Blossoms and Beyond, 2005), *Athar al-Farasha* (The Butterfly Effect, 2008), and *Lā Urīdu li-Hāthī al-Qaṣīda ʿan Tantahī* (I Do Not Want for This Poem to End, 2009)—Darwīsh turns into a philosopher who poses more questions than he answers, on issues such as the distance between the self and the other, the value of life and death, and the universal anguish of man. His voice is that of an exhausted, disappointed, and wandering poet.

THE PHILOSOPHER AND HUMANIST POET

Published in the same collection as "Huwa Hādi' wa-Anā Kadhālik" in 2003, "Hiya fī al-Masā'" (She, in the Evening) offers the reader another example of the vitality of communication between the self and the other. This poem is about a lonely woman having dinner in a restaurant in the evening.

هي في المساء

هي في المساء وحيدة،
وأنا وحيد مثلها
بيني وبين شموعها في المطعم الشتويّ
طاولتان فارغتان [لا شيء يعكِّرُ صمْتنا]
هي لا تراني، إذ أراها
حين تقطف وردة من صدرها
وأنا كذلك لا أراها، إذ تراني
حين أرشف من نبيذي قُبلَة
هي لا تُفتِّت خبزها
وأنا كذلك لا أريق الماء
فوق الشرشف الورقيّ
[لا شيء يكدّر صفونا]
هي وحْدها، وأَنا أمام جمالها
وحدي. لماذا لا توحِدنا الهشاشة؟
قلت في نفسي
لماذا لا أَذوق نبيذها؟
هي لا تراني، إذ أراها

حين ترفع ساقها عن ساقها
وأنا كذلك لا أراها، إذ تراني
حين أخلع معطفي
لا شيء يزعجها معي
لا شيء يزعجني، فنحن الآن
منسجمان في النسيان
كان عشاؤنا، كُل على حدة، شهيّاً
كان صوت الليل أزرق
لم أكن وحدي، ولا هي وحدها
كنا معاً نصغي إلى البلور
[لا شيء يكسر ليلنا]
هي لا تقول
الحب يُولد كائناً حيّا
ويُمْسي فكرة
وأنا كذلك لا أقول
الحب أمسى فكرة
لكنه يبدو كذلك.[79]

She, in the Evening

She's alone in the evening
and I am alone like her . . .
Between her candles and me in the winter restaurant
are two vacant tables (nothing disturbs our silence).
She doesn't see me, when I see her
picking a rose from her chest,
and I also don't see her, when she sees me
sipping from my wine a kiss . . .
She doesn't crumble her bread
and I also don't spill the water
on the paper tablecloth
(nothing disturbs our peace of mind).
She's alone, and I am in front of her beauty
alone. Why doesn't delicacy unite us?
I said to myself, why don't I taste her wine?
She doesn't see me, when I see her

uncrossing her legs . . .
And I also don't see her, when she sees me
taking off my coat . . .
Nothing bothers her when she's with me,
nothing bothers me, because we are now
harmonious in forgetfulness . . .
Our dinner was, separately, delicious.
The night sound was blue.
I wasn't alone, and neither was she alone.
We were together, listening to the crystal
(nothing fractures our night).
She doesn't say:
Love is born a living creature
and it becomes an idea,
and I also don't say:
Love became an idea
But it seems like it.[80]

This woman shares many characteristics with the speaker in nearly the same way the man does in the previous poem. She does not see him when he looks at her, and he does not see her when she looks at him. Each of them is aware of the other's presence, but neither acknowledges the other. In addition, each enjoys dinner alone, which explains how they are similar: "nothing disturbs our silence," "nothing fractures our night," "nothing disturbs our peace of mind," and "nothing bothers her when she's with me, / nothing bothers me, because we are now / harmonious in forgetfulness." Although they do not know or talk to each other, their presence in the same place at the same time, though each at a separate table, creates an atmosphere different from the one we witness in the first poem. This atmosphere makes their dinner "delicious" and brings them together: "I wasn't alone, and neither was she alone / we were together, listening to the crystal / (nothing fractures our night)."

Bhabha argues that the "exchange of looks between native and settler . . . structures their psychic relation in the paranoid fantasy of boundless possession and its familiar language of reversal: when their glances meet he ascertains bitterly, always on the defensive, 'They want to take our place.'"[81] The man and the woman watch each other secretly, like the speaker and his double in the previous poem, but the nature of exchanged glances in this poem is different. The "she" in this poem suggests a different type of other from the other in the first poem. The self and the other in the first poem are paranoid, with a mutual defensive attitude toward each other. Each is scared of the other and perceives him to be a killer. By contrast, the two characters in the second poem do not pose a threat to each other. On the contrary, their awareness of their presence together creates a positive atmosphere that makes their night go more smoothly and decreases the impact of their loneliness. Darwīsh writes "Hiya fī al-Masā'" to challenge the kind of behavior we see in "Huwa Hādi' wa-Anā Kadhālik," the passive-aggressive behavior that has its roots in the past.

Perhaps there is something inherited about the exchange of looks between the Palestinian self and the Israeli other in Darwīsh's works. This is suggested in the story Jeremy Bowen tells of an Israeli intelligence officer, Shmarya Guttman. This officer had watched hundreds of Palestinians expelled from the towns of Ramle and Lydda in 1948, recounting, "A multitude of inhabitants walked after one another. Women walked burdened with packages and sacks on their heads. Mothers dragged children after them . . . warning shots were heard. . . . Occasionally, you encountered a piercing look from one of the youngsters . . . and the look said: 'We have not yet surrendered. We shall return to fight you.'"[82]

The look exchanged between the Palestinian youngster and the Israeli officer in this excerpt is the same kind of look exchanged between the speaker and his double in the café. On one hand, the Palestinian's look reveals anger, resistance, and a pledge to "return to fight." Perhaps Darwīsh was among these children, and the look the Israeli officer saw some sixty years before the poem was written is the very same "piercing look" the Israeli sees in the speaker's eyes in the café. On the other hand, and from a Palestinian perspective, the Israeli's looks convey bloodshed and violence for the Palestinian. Thus, these looks create tension, fear, and suspicion between the two and recall painful memories that make communication between them impossible. By comparison, in the second poem, the characters' willingness to look beyond their painful memories is what makes a difference in their attitudes toward each other. In this poem, neither the self nor the other casts blame or accusations. Instead, they spend the evening peacefully and succeed in creating a common ground and a positive atmosphere that brings peace to both. The tone in which the speaker addresses the other in the second poem is different from that of the first poem. Although he calls for communication and recognition of the other in both poems, he takes a step further in the second and succeeds in bridging the gap between himself and the other. In this poem's closing lines, the speaker and the woman enjoy their evening without sensing the slightest threat from each other.

These two poems focus on the distance between the self and the other in order to shrink or eliminate the gap between them. Bhabha maintains that "it is not the colonialist Self or the Colonized Other, but the disturbing distance in between that constitutes the figure of colonial otherness."[83] When the two men leave the café, the distance between them widens because they do not try to communicate with each other or eliminate the hostile atmosphere between them. In contrast, when the speaker and the woman leave the restaurant, they have enjoyed an unacknowledged romantic encounter. It is worth noting that in the second poem, unlike the first, we do not actually see the two characters leave the restaurant. This suggests that in the first poem, the characters' mutual fear and misunderstanding leads to the urge not to be in the same space with the other because each threatens the existence of the other. The second poem, however, ends with the poet and the woman enjoying their dinner because they are willing to live in the present and indulge in the moment that brings two strangers together. It is significant that in the first poem we have two men and in the second a man and a woman. The question of gender or sex, same in the first poem and different in the second, maps onto the differences in perspective we find in the two poems. Darwīsh has personified the kind of mutually negating, "bad" politics he is protesting against as a male–male relation, and the kind of open, "good" politics or ethics he is advocating as a male–female relation. Here we see a traditional kind of cultural machismo at work, in which male–male relations are conceived as rivalries while male–female relations are imagined as potential romances.

These two poems assert that the self has to recognize and understand the urgency of interacting with its double if it demands and aspires to be recognized by the other. Unlike "Ayyuhā al-Mārrūn" and *Ḥālat Ḥiṣār*, they imply that the mutual recognition, the willingness to look beyond the violent past, whose memories imprisoned both parties, and a change of attitudes toward one another are preconditions for any attempt to resolve the fundamental issues in a conflict between self and other. As Kelman observes, the Israeli–Palestinian conflict "is dominated by a multivictim dynamic in which each side perceives the other as the direct source of its insecurity. . . . As long as these fundamental issues remain unsolved, they will be the ultimate obstacles to lasting peace in the region."[84] "Huwa Hādi' wa-Anā Kadhālik" and "Hiya fī al-Masā'" warn that this conflict is doomed to continue indefinitely if the two sides continue to deny each other's existence and identity. They register a cry of protest against this state of affairs, against this status quo. The political as well as literary value of this protest in these two late poems is remarkable. In an interview with Darwīsh on July 18, 2005, in Ramallah, Darwīsh responded to Najat Rahman's question of his position and role as a poet in the Arab world, saying, "The self and the enemy are entangled and embroiled, trapped in a land with too much history and too many prophets. Perhaps the time I write has the chance, the potential for peace. Self and other are always interlinked. I can also be myself's other."[85] Unlike "Ayyuhā al-Mārrūn" and *Ḥālat Ḥiṣār*, in "Huwa Hādi' wa-Anā Kadhālik" and "Hiya fī al-Masā'" the speaker recognizes that being trapped with the other in one land requires the self and the other to look for peace. These two poems humanize the other and do not advise him to leave the land or quit the scene. Furthermore, the solutions these late poems suggest to the other are the same solutions they suggest to the self: to understand mutual fears and communicate. These poems address the other as another human being trapped in the same complex situation as the self. They invite the other to search with the self for a solution for their situation. Patrick Sylvain notes, "Darwish's poetic corpus can be viewed as a discourse that articulates a Palestinian consciousness of history and a social project for the region that is based on respect for humanity and self."[86]

In the last two collections published while he was alive, *Almond Blossoms and Beyond* and *The Butterfly Effect*, Darwīsh further explores the self–other relationship. For example, in "Fakkir bi-Ghayrik" (Think of Others), in *Almond Blossoms and Beyond*, Darwīsh asks the self to "as you wage your wars / think of others / (do not forget those who seek peace)."[87] In another poem, "I Do Not Know the Stranger," Darwīsh's humanistic compassion extends to everybody because whether one is "a writer, a worker, a refugee, a thief, or a murderer / what is the difference? / the dead are all equal in the face of death."[88] In "Maqha, wa-ʿAnta maʿ al-Jarīda Jālis" (A Café, and You with the Newspaper) Darwīsh tells himself:

. . .
فاصنع بنفسك ما تشاء، اخلع
قميصك أو حذاءك إن أردت، فأنت
منسي وحر في خيالك، ليس لاسمك
أو لوجهك ههنا عمل ضروري. تكون
كما تكون.... فلا صديق ولا عدو
هنا يراقب ذكرياتك.
. . .
والتمس عذرا لمن طلب اغتيالك
ذات يوم لا لشيء... بل لأنك لم
تمت يوم ارتطمت بنجمة... وكتبت
أولى الأغنيات بحبرها....
مقهى، وأنت مع الجريدة جالس
في الركن منسي، فلا أحد يهين
مزاجك الصافي،
ولا أحد يفكر باغتيالك
كم أنت منسي وحر في خيالك![89]

. . .
Do what you will with yourself
Take off your shirt or shoes, if you want
Because you are forgotten and free in your imagination.
There is no pressing work for your face or your name here.
You are as you are—no friend, no enemy
To study your memories.
. . .
Seek forgiveness for the man who sought
To assassinate you one day, for no reason,
or because you did not die that day

you bumped into a star and wrote
those early songs with its ink.
A café, and you with a newspaper, sitting.
in the corner, forgotten. No one to insult
your peaceful state of mind and no one to think of murdering you.
How forgotten you are, and how free in your imagination![90]

Here, the speaker is in disguise, hidden from others, friends and enemies. Sitting in a café where no one seems to recognize his name or face, the speaker enjoys being able to do what he wants, without feeling he is being watched by others. Only when he is liberated from the gaze of others, and the implicit responsibility it burdens him with as a poet, is he able to exercise this freedom in his imagination by writing a poem like this one. His memories are not watched by a friend or an enemy; he is not judged as Darwīsh the poet. Thus, when he is liberated from his name and its associations, from others who recognize his face or watch his memories, he is able to seek forgiveness even for the one who wanted to assassinate him one day: the enemy. Here, Darwīsh wants to forget and be forgotten, if only for a while. It is liberating for him to forget and be forgotten because this will enable him to enjoy a safe zone in his imagination, where he fears no assassination attempts, and more importantly, he asks himself to forgive the one who wanted to see him murdered.

This is a metapoetic poem in which Darwīsh treats the anxieties of poetic creativity as well as the alienation of the poet in his society. Alienation here is not physical but rather psychological, in that the poet needs to escape from the public to freely exercise his freedom of speech. Darwīsh escapes by writing a poem such as this one, in which he is able to express his feelings as a poet and also as a human being. Watched by others, he seeks to be forgotten so that he may be what he wants to be, far from the judgment of others. Escaping from reality into the realm of imagination, Darwīsh is able to say what he wants to say by writing this poem. Therefore, his poetry becomes his arena of peace and freedom where he does not fear being murdered and is free to forgive everyone. This is utopia for Darwīsh: forgiveness, forgetfulness, and freedom, which come only in his imagination, whose fruit is this poem. It is worth noting that *Almond Blossoms and Beyond* is divided into eight sections titled, in order: You, He, I, She, Exile (1), Exile (2), Exile (3), and Exile

(4). In one reading of these titles in order, the "You" is a double of the "I" in the same manner that the "He" is a double of the "She." Also, the four sections on exile may imply that the you, he, I, and she are all exiles. The treatment of the self–other relation continues in *The Butterfly Effect* and his last collection, *I Do Not Want for This Poem to End.*

In *The Butterfly Effect*, written mainly in the prose form and as poetic texts, Darwīsh further explores the relationship between self and other and the emergence of one hybrid identity in the self–other psyche in poems such as "Wa-mā ʿAnā ʿIllā Huwa" (I Am No One but Him,)[91] "ʿAnta Munthu alān, Ghairuk" (You, From Now On, Are Your Other),[92] "ʿAduw Mushtarak" (Common Enemy),[93] and "Gharībān"(Two Strangers).[94] In "Common Enemy," he calls for people to reconsider their association with war, because after all, death is the common enemy.

. . .
المحاربون من الجانبين يقولون كلاما متشابها
بحضرة من يحبون. اما القتلى من الجانبين،
فلا يدركون الا متاخرين، ان لهم عدوا
مشتركا هو: الموت. فما معنى
ذلك، ما معنى ذلك؟[95]

. . .
Fighters from both sides say similar things in
The presence of those whom they love, whereas the dead
    from both sides
Realize, but late, that they have a common enemy:
It is death. What does that mean?
What does that mean?[96]

In this prose poem, the speaker warns the Palestinians and the Israelis that they are engaged in an infinite war that consumes them both. Death is their enemy, but they realize this only after they are killed by one another. Both sides have people they love and care for, and by the same token, both sides suffer immensely from this conflict. Therefore, the speaker urges them to pause for a minute and defeat death, their common enemy. This can only happen if both parties stop killing each other. Darwīsh here does not ask his fellow Palestinians to surrender or to be defeated; on the contrary, he asks them to resist, each in his own way, and to be aware of the consequences of being part of the Israeli–Palestinian conflict by shedding more blood for no reason. Darwīsh affirms, "Defeat can be turned into a source of energy, a way of confronting the fact of one's existence. Such deep awareness can compel one to keep working, striving, and expressing oneself: 'I renew myself by acknowledging defeat, and I resist through poetry and language because this area is not defeatable.' "[97] Announcing the defeat of Palestinians, including himself, and acknowledging that he can still play a role in the conflict by resisting through continuing to write poetry, Darwīsh confronts his own existence and invites others to do the same. He chooses to employ his energy in an undefeatable arena, poetry. Darwīsh has always been a poet who resisted by writing poetry, but at this stage, his poetry no longer calls for political influence on the ground. It sends a universal call for humanity and self-renewal in creative outlets far from war and death. Despite the obvious defeats of Palestinians on the ground, Darwīsh refuses to surrender, and he guards his fellow Palestinians' steadfastness wherever they may be. However, he does not incite them to fight and die. He invites them to look for other ways to resist, by acknowledging that this decades-long war with the other will never be an equal one, and death will continue to harvest souls from both sides. Therefore, Darwīsh calls for peace.

Darwīsh's latest poetry transforms his means of resistance from military action to a peaceful form. At this stage, the enemy, while continuing to be the enemy, is seen as a human being too. Darwīsh's latest poetry calls for steadfastness. Each citizen should resist in his or her own way, yet with a new awareness of the human dimension of the conflict. Darwīsh is a poet, and thus he resists through his aesthetics, which "is not defeatable." In Darwīsh's works after the militant *iltizām* stage, the persona is no longer the heroic fighter or martyr but rather "a normal human being." He calls for guarding culture and language through poetry by urging "Palestinians to begin writing as if there was no occupation and to prepare themselves for their future."[98] Darwīsh states, "The hero is tired of maneuvering between being a hero and a victim. . . . He wants to become a normal human being. This transformation has taken place in numerous literary traditions. . . . The poet is now aware that he is not a savior or rescuer, not a messiah or a prophet."[99]

This human being has feelings and aspirations, and a life worth living, exactly like his or her enemy. This human being has seen enough bloodshed to question the human value behind this conflict, which has resulted in a great number of deaths on both sides, mostly on the Palestinian side, and has the potential to burden and destroy generations to come. Therefore, to pause and be able to see the human side of the enemy, and to refrain from calling for armed resistance—to invite the enemy to participate in a serious conversation in which both consider the humanity of the other—is indeed a transformative force behind Darwīsh's voice. In Darwīsh's last three collections, we hear the voice of a poet calling everybody, the self and the other, to value life instead of wasting it in fighting. Darwīsh succeeded in transforming the personal and national into the universal. Because he has come to consider commenting on political issues "an outdated concept of poetry,"[100] he outlines a new vision in his latest works, refraining from commenting on political events, unlike Ḥijāzī, who continues to use his poetry to comment on politics. Darwīsh does not abandon politics in its entirety, but issues of political value no longer constitute the majority of his works. Also, he treats political issues in his poetry rather than commenting on them. He engages with philosophical and universal subject matter and experiments with language. Darwīsh was always a metapoet, and yet the space he creates for poetic experimentation in his latest works welcomes new venues for innovation, in form and content. He further experiments with the prose poem and poetic texts and treats a variety of universal subjects, including exile, death, love, alienation, the self and its others, poetry, and the philosophy of existence. Darwīsh's latest poetry also raises questions about some aspects of modern Arab culture. It is worth noting that his latest poems do not waste an opportunity to criticize the current culture, religious and political, of the Arab world. In "'Anta Munthu alān, Ghairuk" (You, From Now On, Are Your Other), published in *The Butterfly Effect*, the speaker wonders if the killer is a victim of religious dogma in Arab society.

1 هل علينا أن نسقط من علو شاهق،
ونرى دمنا على أيدينا ... لندرك أننا لسنا
ملائكة... كما كنا نظن؟
[. . .]

من يدخل الجنة أولا؟ من مات برصاص 57
العدو، أم من مات برصاص الأخ؟ بعض
الفقهاء يقول: "رب عدو لك ولدته امك"!

حار الفقهاء أمام النائمين في قبور متجاورة: 60
هل هم شهداء حرية؟ أم ضحايا متناحرة في
عبث المسرحية؟ حارالفقهاء واتفقوا على
أمر واحد هو: أن الله اعلم.

القاتل قتيل أيضا!
[. . .]
أنت، منذ الان، غيرك![101] 74

Did we have to fall from a high place 1
To see our blood on our hands . . . to realize that
We are not angels, as we thought?
[. . .]

Who enters heaven first? He who died by the bullets 57
Of the enemy or by the bullets of the brother?
Some Muslim jurists say: "Your mother might give birth to
your enemy!"

The Muslim jurists were confused by those sleeping in
neighboring graves. 60
Are they freedom martyrs?
Or suicidal victims in the absurdity of a play?
The Muslim jurists were confused and agreed on one thing,
which is: God knows!

The killer is a victim too!
[. . .]
You, from now on, are your other! 74

In this prose poem, the speaker attacks the strife in Gaza between Hamas and the PLO, "which led to the expulsion of the latter from the area."[102] Darwīsh's speaker addresses his people with deep disappointment right from the first line in the poem. Assuming the role of the critic-poet, Darwīsh tells his people how disappointed he is in them, in the hope that they might correct this flaw. Seeing the blood of their own people on their hands, they realize they are not the angels they thought they were. This blood is not the result of a battle against their enemy; rather, it is the blood of their kinsmen, whom they fought in Gaza. Misguided and deluded by religious dogma, the brother kills his brother, ironically thinking he will go to heaven. Encouraged by this blind religious dogma, the killer believes that his brother might also be his enemy. This is a play on a saying in Arabic, "Someone might be your brother even if your mother didn't give birth to him." This is to say that whether they belong to Hamas or the PLO, they are killing each other in the name of Islam. This is the worst and most dangerous stage of the status quo in Palestine and the Arab world. In her 2014 collection of poems in the form of letters, *Dear Darwish*, the Israeli poet Morani Kornberg-Weiss addresses Darwīsh and attempts to engage in a conversation with him through his poetry. Commenting on the notion of both the Israelis and the Palestinians "having blood" on their hands, it is rather interesting that Kornberg-Weiss tells Darwīsh at the beginning of her book that "so many Israelis walk around with blood on their hands, hands soaked in red . . . blood trying to wash itself but it's a blood so ordinary you cannot even see it."[103] Kornberg-Weiss maintains that everyone recalls "images of Palestinians who have blood on their hands," but nobody thinks of the blood on the Israelis' hands, which "marks one difference between Israelis and Palestinians."[104] Kornberg-Weiss hopes the two nations will realize that they both have blood on their hands and need to stop fighting. It is also interesting that Kornberg-Weiss draws attention to that which Darwīsh called for: the State of Israel should be held to account for its crimes.

This poem applies also to the horrifying acts of killing by ISIS. It is as if Darwīsh were writing this poem about ISIS and their culture of death. Claiming they are serving the Islamic nation and reclaiming the caliphate in Syria and Iraq, ISIS calls its killers martyrs. Here, the killer becoming a victim is an ironic response to those killers who are praised as martyrs and victims of the war on Islam. It is also a statement on the brainwashing of young Muslim men who are indoctrinated to believe they are fighting the enemy, when in fact they are fighting their own kinsmen. In such a war, the killer and the killed are both victims of a tyranny, like that in Egypt when Egyptian soldiers shot their fellow demonstrators in 2011. The scene in the Arab world five years after the eruption of the Arab Uprising is indeed an absurd play, in which the common folk lose their lives for no noble reason. Whether in Egypt, Syria, or Iraq, we see people killing one another as if they have become each other's enemy, in absolute faith that they are "freedom martyrs." Fighting one another, Hamas and the PLO have contributed to dividing Palestinians and weakening the Palestinian resistance. Darwīsh rejects the status quo and affirms in the last line of his poem that "You, from now on, are your other!" The self, which is no longer as pure and "clean from crimes" as an angel, has transitioned into the other it rejects, with full consent.

Aesthetically, this poem, like many others in his late collections, is not an example of Darwīsh's best artistic work. This is due to the function of topical poems, which are "written out of emotion," and "meant to affect change immediately."[105] His topical poems are similar to Ḥijāzī's 2013 poem "The Sun and the Dark Ones," which is intended to drive change in Egyptian society against the culture of the Muslim Brotherhood and does not rise to a high aesthetic level. Interestingly, both Darwīsh and Ḥijāzī have written such poems to attack those speaking in the name of Islam, which many consider the vile modern enemy. Darwīsh judged that they encourage bloodshed among Palestinians; Ḥijāzī accused them of dragging Egypt backward into the Dark Ages. The difference between the two is that Darwīsh is aware of the place of poems of this sort in his works; he refused to include many topical poems, such as his elegy to Muḥammad al-Durra, the Palestinian boy who was killed by the Israeli army "in the fall of 2000, a few days after al-Aqsa Intifada ignited,"[106] in his published collections. Ḥijāzī, however, relies on political and other events to inspire his poetry because the Arab Uprising and other key events enable him to say things he could not say before. Furthermore, Darwīsh admits that such poems have a political function more than a poetic one, while Ḥijāzī does not seem to distinguish between the two.

Finally, in a rather interesting poem in his final collection, *Lā Urīdu li-Hāthī al-Qaṣīda ʿan Tantahī* (I Do Not Want for This Poem to End), published in 2009, one year after his death, Darwīsh offers a poetic scenario of a dialogue between two men, one Israeli and the other Palestinian. As one would expect from Darwīsh's late poems, the self and the other engage in a dialogue in one of the last poems he wrote before his death. In "Sīnāriū Jāhiz" (Ready Scenario), the self and the other explore the dynamics of their conflict and ridicule their immature attitudes from their common end: death. Darwīsh writes:

سيناريو جاهز

لنفترض الآن أنّا سقطنا،
أنا والعدو،
سقطنا من الجو
في حفرة...
فماذا سيحدث؟

سيناريو جاهز
في البداية ننتظر الحظ...
قد يعثر المنقذون علينا هنا
و يمدون حبل النجاة لنا
فيقول: أنا أولا
وأقول: أنا أولا
ويشتمني ثم أشتمه
دون جدوى،
فلم يصل الحبل بعد...

يقول السيناريو:
سأهمس في السر:
تلك تسمى أنانية المتفائل
دون التساؤل عما يقول عدوي

أنا وهو
شريكان في شرك واحد
وشريكان في لعبة الاحتمالات
ننتظر الحبل... حبل النجاة
لنمضي على حدة
وعلى حافة الحفرة الهاوية
إلى ما تبقى لنا من حياة
وحرب...
اذا ما استطعنا النجاة!

أنا وهو،
خائفان معا
ولا نتبادل أي حديث
عن الخوف... أو غيره
فنحن عدوان...

ماذا سيحدث لو أن افعى
أطلت علينا هنا
من مشاهد هذا السيناريو
وفحت لتبتلع الخائفين معا
أنا وهو؟

يقول السيناريو،
أنا وهو
سنكون شريكين في قتل افعى
لننجو معا
أو على حدة...

ولكننا لن نقول عبارة شكر وتهنئة
على ما فعلنا معا
لأن الغريزة، لا نحن،
كانت تدافع عن نفسها وحدها
والغريزة ليس لها أيديولوجيا...

ولم نتحاور،
تذكرت فقه الحوارات
في العبث المشترك
عندما قال لي سابقا:
كل ما صار لي هو لي
وما هو لك
هو لي
ولك!

ومع الوقت، والوقت رمل ورغوة صابونة
كسر الصمت ما بيننا والملل
قال لي: ما العمل؟

قلت: لا شيء... نستنزف الاحتمالات
قال: من أين يأتي الامل؟
قلت: يأتي من الجو
قال: ألم تنس أني دفنتك في حفرة
مثل هذي؟
فقلت له: كدت أنسى لأن غدا خلبا
شدني من يدي... ومضى متعبا
قال لي: هل تفاوضني الآن؟
قلت: على أي شيء تفاوضني الآن
في هذه الحفرة القبر؟
قال: على حصتي وعلى حصتك
من سدانا ومن قبرنا المشترك
قلت: ما الفائدة؟
هرب الوقت منا
وشذ المصير عن القاعدة
ههنا قاتل وقتيل ينامان في حفرة واحدة
وعلى شاعر آخر أن يتابع هذا السيناريو
إلى آخره![107]

Ready Scenario

Let us now say that we fell
I and the enemy
We fell from the sky
Into a pit . . .
So, what will happen?

Ready scenario:
At the beginning we wait for luck
The rescuers might find us
And extend the cord of deliverance to us
So he says: I am first
And I say: I am first
And he insults me, then I insult him
To no avail
The cord has not reached us yet

The scenario says:
I will whisper secretly
That is called the selfishness of the optimist
Without wondering about what my enemy says

Me and him
Two partners in one trap
And two partners in the game of possibilities
Waiting for the cord . . . the cord of deliverance
So we go our separate ways
And on the edge of the pit—the abyss
To what is left for us of life
And war . . .
If we could survive

Me and him
Both are scared
But we do not exchange any words
About fear . . . or anything else
Because we are enemies . . .

What is going to happen if a snake
Appears to us here
From the scenes of this scenario
And hisses to swallow the two scared men together
Me and him?

The scenario says:
Me and him
Will be partners in killing the snake
To survive together
Or alone . . .

But we will not say the words of thanks or congratulations
For what we did together
Because instinct, not us,
Was defending itself only
And instinct does not have an ideology

And we did not talk
I remembered the rules of dialogue
In the joint tampering
When he told me previously:
All that has become mine is mine
And what is yours
Is mine
And yours!

And with time, and time is the sand and the foam of soup
Silence broke what is between us and boredom
He said: What do we do?
I said: Nothing . . . we exhaust the possibilities
He said: Where does hope come from?
I said: From the sky
He said: Have you forgotten that I buried you in a pit
Like this?
I said: I was about to forget because tomorrow was made
to look beautiful
Tomorrow pulled me from my hand and, feeling tired, it left
He told me: Do you want to negotiate with me now?
I said: About what are you negotiating with me now
In this pit, the grave?
He said: About my share and your share
From our nothingness and from our joint grave
I said: What is the use?
Time escaped from us
And fate became the exception to the rule
Here are a murderer and a murdered sleeping in one pit
And another poet has to follow this scenario
To its end!

This free verse poem captures the Israeli–Palestinian conflict from the poet's perspective. The Israeli enemy and the Palestinian self, trapped in the same pit, are both scared. However, they "do not exchange any words / about fear . . . or anything else / because we are enemies." The speaker understands the urgent need to initiate a dialogue with the other, but also realizes that the state of animosity between the two stops them from discussing their fear, or anything else. Waiting in vain for luck, the rescuers, and the cord of deliverance, both wish to be rescued first. They insult each other. However, the speaker whispers to himself that wanting to be rescued first without thinking of his enemy is selfish. He and his enemy are both selfish because each wants to be rescued first, without the other person in the picture. This reflects the speaker's understanding of the conflict: neither the Israeli nor the Palestinian is looking for a solution that takes both parties into consideration. Furthermore, the speaker realizes that the self and the other have to start talking about their fear of each other, which Darwīsh addressed in "He is Quiet and So Am I." They are two partners in one trap, and their fate after being rescued is also subject to "the game of possibilities." They either live or die, and with these two possibilities comes more life or more death. This statement suggests that if the self lives, one would expect the other to die, and vice versa.

A hissing snake is introduced to the scenario. Seeing the snake about to eat them both, they realize they are one in the face of death. Therefore, the partners in one trap and the game of possibilities become partners in killing the snake in order to survive. Put in a life-threatening situation, the instinct to survive makes them forget they are enemies, so they unite to kill the snake. The snake is death itself, which both the self and the other will eventually face, together or alone. Interestingly, even after defeating the snake together, these partners refuse to talk. They refuse to thank each other or express any feelings of gratitude for what they have done together, because it was survival instinct alone that made them cooperate against a common enemy, death. Once this threat is over and both feel safe again, even if only momentarily, they return to their state of war. The survival instinct, which "does not have an ideology," is the urge to kill whatever or whoever threatens one's life. Therefore, the hostile relationship between the self and the other is likely to continue indefinitely, so long as each thinks his life is threatened by the other.

Wondering why they have not talked for a very long time, the self remembers a past conversation with the other. In this conversation, the other insisted on enjoying its share alone and taking from the self's share as well: "All that has become mine is mine / and what is yours / is mine / and yours!" Having to share its part of the land with the enemy, which enjoys its part and wants to share or gradually take over the self's part, the self rejects this oppression and concludes that a dialogue with the other will not be useful. Therefore, when the other, in the last stanza, invites the self to a dialogue by asking "Do you want to negotiate with me now? . . . on my share and your share? . . . of our nothingness and from our joint grave," the self answers, "What is the use? / time escaped from us." Although it is surprising to hear the other offering to negotiate both shares with the self, it is less surprising that the self rejects this offer. This offer came too late: negotiation over a wasteland is a waste of time. Threatened by the other's attempt to take over its share, the self perceives negotiation as fruitless. Ending the poem with an image of the two partners sharing the grave as murderer and murdered, the speaker affirms that their death is imminent in this pit, which they have turned into a grave by choice. The self and the other need to stop war immediately and start talking before it is too late. If this conflict continues, neither the Israelis nor the Palestinians will live in peace.

This poem is Darwīsh's final statement on the Israeli–Palestinian conflict. He is the speaker-observer analyzing the conflict poetically. The poem notes four times that both partners failed at talking: "But we do not exchange any words," "But we will not say the words of thanks or congratulations," "But we do not exchange any words," "And we did not talk." Thus Darwīsh notes and protests the absence of *serious* talks between the Israelis and the Palestinians. This is not to say that Darwīsh's poem is pessimistic; rather, he is offering a candid evaluation of the status quo. He warns that death will come to both sides of the conflict if neither attempts seriously to solve it. In this poem, the sky, from which the speaker and the enemy fell into the pit, is the same sky that brings hope. Therefore, Darwīsh answers his enemy's question of where hope comes from with "from the sky." The memory of the place—the sky in this context—is highlighted in this poem as a continuing source of hope/rain despite its associations with war.

Based on his memories of unjust past negotiations with the other, the speaker judges that any future negotiations will be futile. The speaker struggles with his memory, especially when the enemy chooses to remind him of something he did in the past: "Have you forgotten that I buried you in a pit / like this?" Taken aback by the question, the speaker replies, "I was about to forget." It is as if the other refuses to let the speaker's memory heal from his past wrongdoings and keeps reminding him of them despite the speaker's willingness to forget. This conversation is a window into the role of memory in the Israeli–Palestinian conflict. Representing the Palestinian side of the conflict, the speaker maintains that it is possible to focus less on old memories with the enemy other, however painful they are, and to make new, better future memories. However, he warns against wasting time waiting for the impossible to happen or for the conflict to solve itself. Knowing he will die before seeing the actual end of this scenario, Darwīsh hopes another poet will "follow this scenario / to its end."

Conclusion

The Poets and Their Vocation in the Modern World

The Iraqi ʿAbd al-Wahhāb al-Bayātī, the Egyptian Aḥmad ʿAbd al-Muʿṭī Ḥijāzī, and the Palestinian Maḥmūd Darwīsh represent three representative directions in modern Arab poetry: the metapoet, the recommitted poet, and the humanist poet. The poetry of each has evolved from the *iltizām* of the 1960s to its current form. Major twentieth-century Arab political and social events and movements, such as Nasserism, the 1967 Arab–Israeli war, the Israeli–Palestinian conflict, and in Ḥijāzī's case, the Arab Uprising, have influenced their poetry. These three writers also represent three different directions in modern Arabic poetry: experimenting with new subject matter and language, as in the case of al-Bayātī and Darwīsh; changing poetic voices, as in the case of Ḥijāzī; and inventing new representations of the self and its other, as in the works of Darwīsh. Although these directions by no means include all newly evolving directions in modern Arabic poetry and literature, they represent a wide range of Arab poets of the twentieth century.

Al-Bayātī's late works witness a great transition toward metapoetry—poetry about the art of poetry itself. Ḥijāzī resurfaces as a recommitted poet who finds inspiration in the people's revolution in Egypt. Darwīsh moves from earlier, more extroverted political poetry to poetry that closely interrogates identity, in which the distinction between self and other begins to collapse.

Arabic poetry of the 1950s and 1960s is shaped by the political dynamics of Arab society during the Nasserist era, when Arabs and their poets saw in Nasser a nationalist hero and in his regime a promise of nationalism and social equity. However, after failing to bring about Arab nationalism and then being defeated by the Israeli army in the 1967 war, Nasser belonged to a bygone era, and poets such as al-Bayātī and Ḥijāzī began exploring new subjects. The poetry of the late 1960s and beyond mirrors the Arab public's great sense of defeat and disappointment. Modern Arab poets tried to incite the Arab public to revolt against and break free from their dictatorships, but poetry did not seem to move the crowds, and most poets gradually lost faith in their people. Therefore, they began searching for other opportunities to explore and innovate in their poetry, outside the restrictions and limitations of commitment to *iltizām*. Although some of these poets did treat issues of sociopolitical commitment in their later works, they did not do so out of a mere sense of duty. On the contrary, their exploration of other subjects and poetic language enabled them to revisit issues of commitment from a more candid and mature perspective.

After writing many poems on sociopolitical issues, Nasser, and Arab nationalism, Al-Bayātī dedicated himself to metapoetry. After the 1967 June war, Nasser gradually disappears from al-Bayātī's poetry; other themes and subjects occupy the poet instead, encouraging him to further experiment with free verse poetry. His late poems focus on issues that pertain to metapoetry and especially the role of the modern Arab poet in culture and literature. Al-Bayātī realizes that it is the duty of the Arab poet to preserve language and maintain excellence in Arabic literature. Thus, he advocates for abandoning "poor" and "paid for" literature. Al-Bayātī's poetry transforms from political to metapoetic and from sentimental to meditative. Haunted by forces of change, he becomes a Sufi rebel who finds deliverance in the strangest of places: arenas of terror. The poet becomes a terrorist against the absurd in the Arab world. He carries the pains of humankind and calls for love, justice, and, more important, resistance against mediocre and poor literature. Al-Bayātī's commitment shifts from political causes to literary ones. His innovations in language and treatment of universal subjects contribute vastly to the literary canon and represent a direction in modern Arabic poetry. Among the other poets who belong to this movement from *iltizām* to metapoetry is the Iraqi poet Saʿdī Yūsuf.

Ḥijāzī wrote poetry from the 1950s to the 1980s because he believed his people would listen to his words and revolt against the status quo.

After writing many collections on Nasser and Arab nationalism and then facing the humiliating defeat of 1967, Ḥijāzī realized that he had to introduce new topics and move beyond his pro-Nasserist phase. He began writing against Sadat's and Mubarak's regimes, but once he realized that his people were unable and unwilling to oppose dictatorship, he kept a low profile and published few poems and no poetry collections after 1989. However, following the eruption of the Egyptian revolution in 2011, he published a new collection, maintaining that the revolution he was calling for had finally resurrected not only his people, but also his poetry. Ḥijāzī's voice in his late works is that of the orator-critic more than a poet. He represents another direction in modern Arabic poetry in which commitment resurfaces in the poet's works after decades of writing. However, this commitment is different from that of the 1960s. Ḥijāzī's works undergo a transformation from writing on *iltizām* to writing against oppression and authoritarianism from a mature perspective. Ḥijāzī's voice is no longer that of a regime—rather, it is the voice of the people. This voice is critical of the status quo—and even of the people—rather than celebratory.

The Arab public has always been responsive to and heavily influenced by Darwīsh's anti-Israeli poetry. In his late poetry, however, Darwīsh gradually moves beyond his armed-resistance stance and adopts a revolutionary approach toward the other and his identity. From this unique new perspective on the relationship of self and other, he not only addresses the other as his double but also invites him to examine their mutual conflict and fears. Darwīsh's ability to see and treat the other as another human being who—though still the enemy—has fears and dreams, like the self, signals a new stage in the development of his poetics. He invites the Israeli other to a conversation in which both sides of the conflict have to realize each other's humanity and recognize each other's identity.

The career trajectories of these three prominent, committed modern Arab poets of the twentieth century suggest three kinds of transformation. In their later works, each develops a unique poetic voice that distinguishes his later poetry from his earlier works. All three shape their own identities by treating a variety of topics and issues throughout their poetic careers. They experiment with free verse and encourage innovation in poetic forms (with the exception of Ḥijāzī, who attacks the prose poem) to enrich their poetry and shape their poetic legacy. Although al-Bayātī, Ḥijāzī, and Darwīsh shape unique poetic identities and create individual voices, all three share nearly the same view of the Arab public. They all believe, and use their poetry to emphasize, that the Arab public must play an active and influential role in their society. It is time for Arab citizens to rise and change the image of their nation, not only in the eyes of the world, but also in the eyes of Arabs themselves. Although some Arab countries have revolted against their dictators and ousted them, the majority of Arabs have not yet been able to leave the shelter of their regimes. Even countries that revolted against their regimes still have a long way to go before they are capable of governing themselves. Arabs need to realize that being unable to accept and negotiate with opposing points of view will hold them back. Democracy is not the offspring of a revolution; rather, it is the result of a long process that entails rebuilding the state after the revolution. Before demanding that the people revolt, modern Arabic poetry demands that its audience be aware of their responsibilities and critical of their role in society. These Arab poets question their own poetry and its role in society as well. They encourage readers to be critical of poetry and literature. They also invite readers to contribute to the development of modern Arabic poetry and preserve it from stagnation and decline. Contributing to the social, political, cultural, literary, and other scenes, poets in modern Arab society remain true to their vocation.

That vocation continues to be one of the most controversial topics in modern Arabic poetry. Although some scholars argue that the poet's role is that of the savior of culture and language, others make a strong case for the role of the poet as an artist. While these two ideas do not necessarily conflict with each other, the heavy burden of expressing and shaping the feelings and aspirations of one's society remains relevant in literary circles in the Arab world. Nowadays, as some Arab nations revolt against their dictatorships, we are witnessing the rise of new poetry that corresponds to this political and potential change in the social fabric of Arab society. For example, as millions of Syrians, Egyptians, Tunisians, and Libyans take part in the political struggle and its consequences after the Arab Uprising, many Arab poets are assuming new roles in response. Some, such as Ḥijāzī, resumed publishing poetry collections right after witnessing the Arab public's break from the stereotype of a defeated nation. Ḥijāzī published poetry to support both his fellow Egyptian citizens and Arabs in general, those who challenged their regimes and demonstrated in the streets. Since Ḥijāzī had addressed this audience in his past collections as a defeated and good-for-nothing nation, his decision to address it now as a "heart of the city" reinforces the significant role the audience plays in poetry and society. For Ḥijāzī and poets like him, the audience that plays an active role in politics and society is the same audience that plays a constructive role in poetry. This very audience inspires the poet to innovate in his poetry and engage the reader with it. Thus, one role of the poet in the modern Arab world is to recommit to society, culture, and poetry. In expressing the aspirations of a nation in the making, the modern Arab poet responds to the demands and necessities of his time. Although poetry does not have to be politically or socially engaged, it does have to speak to its age. Therefore, it remains an issue of controversy whether modern Arabic poetry should shift its attention in a more artistic direction rather than toward the social or political. In retrospect, the problem is not with poetry treating social or political issues, but instead with turning poetry into a tool to indoctrinate people or promote political and social dogmas. To avoid this, poets should not devote themselves completely to writing topical poems, making their poetry a political manifesto devoid of aesthetics. the Egyptian poet Imān Mirsāl (b. 1966) is a good example of a rising poet whose poetry speaks to its age, without compromising its artistic and aesthetic values.

THE ARAB UPRISING AND POETRY

With the outbreak of the Arab Uprising, and perhaps earlier, many began writing what they call revolutionary poetry. The problem with this kind of poetry is that in their focus on the political, many writers compromise aesthetic value. This is why so many poems written during and after the Arab Uprising do not conform to what makes poetry poetry. These days, many young Arab writers write more than they read. This creates a gap in their writings because, in their excitement to take part in the remaking of their societies through literature, they tend to lose focus and write sentimental prose instead of poetry. It is also worth noting that many contemporary young Arab poets write in prose and say that they prefer the free verse or prose poem form because it frees them from the strict prosodic rules of the classical poem. However, many of these poets do not understand free verse or prose poetry. They write their prose and then call it prose poetry or free verse. This is a serious issue in modern Arabic poetry. While many poets of the 1960s generation, including al-Sayyāb, Qabbānī, Adūnīs, al-Bayātī, and Ḥijāzī, learned their poetic tradition well before they experimented with free verse and considered it a better fit for their subject matter, it remains a challenge not to jump on the bandwagon of the new poetry without properly comprehending its underpinnings.

OLD AND NEW NOTIONS OF "COMMITMENT"

The emerging culture of the Arab Uprising encouraged an active public engagement in politics and poetry. Arab poets writing about the Arab Uprising have contributed to the changing notions of commitment in modern Arabic poetry. In the 1950s and early 1960s Arab poets wrote about Arab nationalism, supported Nasserism, and drew the public's attention to the Palestinian question. Such poetry was later criticized for promoting political ideology instead of criticizing Arab regimes and societies and helping to educate and create a better Arab nation. Nowadays, "commitment" is acquiring new meanings. It is no longer tied to a specific ideology or regime. It is tied to the people and the vocation of the poet in the modern world. Poetry is the voice of the multitude: the silenced and unheard. This multitude includes not only the public, but also the emerging generation of poets who struggle in their quest to write and engage the Arab audience in their poetry. Since the Arab Uprising, Arab poets have faced many challenges in their commitment to poetry and the spirit of the time. Writing metapoetic verse is also a form of commitment. When poetry is alienated and poets are called terrorists, metapoetry becomes the poet's means of maintaining aesthetics and the artistic value of the work.

Modern Arab poets such as Darwīsh, al-Bayātī, Ḥijāzī, and Adūnīs, who experiment with and write about the relationship between poetry, language, and audience, contribute to the development of modern Arabic poetry. To preserve poetic identity through language, the modern Arab poet tries to engage the reader in the process of writing. The relationship between audience and poet has always played a vital role in the reception of Arabic poetry. The pre-Islamic Arab poet composed his poetry and recited it to engage his audience in the political, social, and literary aspects of their Bedouin life. After Islam, a religious aspect was introduced to poetry. In the late nineteenth and early twentieth centuries, the Arab poet thrived on voicing the Arab public's disappointment with and opposition to the imperial and colonial powers. After the establishment of the state of Israel in 1948, modern Arab poets wrote enthusiastically in support of the rise of Arab nationalism, which was supposed to bring back the golden days of Arabs and liberate Palestine. Thus, Arab poets have always tried to use poetry to reflect their audience's demands and dreams. Political defeats, however, produced a poetry of paralysis and consequently a paralyzed nation. In this phase, the audience as much as the poet is stuck, unable to deal with present challenges because it identifies with its past more than its present or future. It is easier to dream than to act. Therefore, most of the poetry published between 1948 and 1967 was dreamy and pompous. The poet–reader relationship was passive because Arabic poetry was prescriptive: the poet instructed his reader to believe in this or do that. After the 1967 defeat, this relationship had to change. The reader was no longer interested in hearing nationalist poetry, nor was the poet interested in writing for a defeated generation.

Although some poets continued writing to instill confidence and defiance in the Arab public, even after the 1967 defeat or the peace treaties with Israel, they lost their poetic inspiration after trying for decades to treat social ills and political failures in their societies. It is for such reasons that al-Bayātī and Darwīsh, among others, shifted their focus and looked for ways to make their poetry universal. The modern Arab poet needs to belong and contribute to the universal literary canon. Poets and readers cannot be isolated in the narrow sphere of Arab social and political realities. If modernity means speaking to the spirit of the age, universality means making a valuable contribution to the timeless literary tradition at large. Therefore, the new generation of Arab writers urgently needs an understanding of what makes poetry poetic, modern, and universal. This takes us to some of the challenges modern Arabic poetry faces in the present time, especially in the aftermath of the Arab Uprising.

CHALLENGES OF WRITING MODERN ARABIC POETRY

In closing, I would like to comment on the danger of poets' use of poetry to hastily and emotionally comment on current political events, at the expense of literary aesthetics. For example, the prominent Iraqi poet Saʿdī Yūsuf, who has written on romantic, social, political, and metapoetic issues, claimed in 2004 that poetry should not be political, criticizing Qabbānī's poetry for just that.[1] However, his own poetry is ardently political, especially in later poems published on his personal website. In September 2013, he published a poem to oppose U.S. President Barack Obama's proposed military intervention in Syria. Although written in the form of a prose poem, it does not read like poetry. Yūsuf's choice of diction and expressions is poor and inadequate, and racist as well. This poem is an example of the pitfalls awaiting poets who are eager to dash off topical poems to comment on politics.

Here is the poem:

لكأن أبراهام لنكولن لم يكن، حتى مع فيلم سبيلبرج
كأن تحرير الزنوج كان خطأ تاريخيا
كأن والت ويتمان لم يكتب "أوراق العشب"
وإلا كيف يتقدم زنجيان، أسيادهم البيض، في قتل غير البيض (نحن العرب مثلا)؟
كولن باول، الكاذب الاكبر، الزنجي المحرر، كان وراء استباحة العراق في 2003
باراك اوباما، المتشدق الأكبر، الزنجي المحرر مع امرأته ميشيل (حمالة الحطب) يريد
أن يستبيح سوريا، ويسبي نساءها، ويجعل أعزة أهلها أذلة، كما فعل سلفه الأسود
كولن باول، في العراق
اللعنة
العمى[2]
لا أريد أن أستعيد المتنبي
أريد أن أقول إن الانتقال من العبودية إلى الحرية ليس سهلا
ميونيخ. 09.07.2013[3]

As if Abraham Lincoln did not exist, even with Spielberg's film
As if freeing the Negroes was a historic mistake
As if Walt Whitman did not write *Leaves of Grass*.
Otherwise, how could two Negroes surpass their white masters
in killing the nonwhites (We, Arabs, for example)?

Colin Powell, the biggest liar, the freed Negro,
was behind assaulting Iraq in 2003.
Barack Obama, the greatest loudmouth, the freed Negro,
with his wife Michelle (the wood carrier)
wants to assault Syria, rape its women, degrade its noble people,
as did his black predecessor, Colin Powell, in Iraq.
Damn
Blindness
I do not want to recall al-Mutanabbī
I want to say that the transition from slavery to freedom is not easy.
—Munich 09.07.2013

The speaker wonders why two key African American political figures—Colin Powell, a retired general in the United States Army and former secretary of state, and Barack Obama, the ex-president of the United States—"surpass their white masters in killing the nonwhites." Calling them freed Negroes, Yūsuf condemns Powell for assaulting Iraq and Obama for wanting to assault Syria. Race has nothing to do with such military interventions, so Yūsuf has erred by choosing to write such a poem in such a manner. It is unfortunate that a great poet such as Yūsuf expressed his opposition to the prospect of U.S. intervention in Syria, and compared it to the invasion of Iraq, by using racial slurs. Such poor choices, driven by immediate sentiments, have "opened the door for accusing Yūsuf of being racist," stirring—and rightfully so—a great backlash against the poet, whose work in the 2000s has been criticized for "lacking a strong presence like that of his poetry in the 1980s and 1990s."[4]

In an interview following the publication of this poem, Yūsuf wondered if it was he who was the racist or Obama, who is sending his "missiles, warships, marines and spies to kill us Arabs."[5] He defends his poem in a post on his website, saying, "I did not say that freeing the Negroes was a historic error; I said that the way to liberation is not easy. Why does Obama act as a slave to the white politicians?"[6] In the poem above, he employs "as if" as a provocative hypothetical: Abraham Lincoln *did* exist, Whitman *did* write *Leaves of Grass*, and freeing African Americans was not a mistake. Yet, Yūsuf seems to imply, those events might as well not have happened because these two African American men are still doing what their white masters tell them, and worse, they surpass them in killing people who, like them, are not white. In the same post, Yūsuf states that with the U.S. invasion of Iraq from March 20 to May 1, 2003, an Iraqi fascism ended and an American fascism immediately began, which explains, in his words, why he decided not to return to Iraq after the deposition of Saddam Hussein.[7] He says the Americans turned his country into an American colony and surrendered it to the Kurds; therefore, "Iraq is no longer constitutionally part of the Arab world."[8]

Using poetry as a platform for his political commentary on the status quo in Syria, Yūsuf maintains that "the fate of Syria is in the hands of its people, whose first task is to defeat the Gulf, the Saudis and foreign mercenaries."[9] In so saying, Yūsuf is engaging politically not only as an Arab citizen, but also as an Arab poet. He offers the Syrians his ultimate support and faith in their ability to liberate themselves from Assad's dictatorship by imposing his political view on the situation: Syrians will win if they "defeat the Gulf, the Saudis and foreign mercenaries." As an Arab citizen, Yūsuf is entitled to freedom of speech, including his views on politics. However, as a public figure, he ought to filter racism and bigotry from his work and not allow such language to replace a language of love and humanity, even in an emotionally charged topical poem. Witnessing rapid political changes on the ground in the Arab world and, more important, key changes close to home, modern Arab poets face a challenge: they can either react hastily and emotionally, with little art, or practice vigilance over what they say and how they say it.

Poets need not compromise their poetics for their politics—an ominous tendency evident in recent poetry by major voices, including Yūsuf and Ḥijāzī. Where Yūsuf was alarmed by Obama's intention to intervene in Syria, Ḥijāzī was and still is alarmed by the Muslim Brotherhood's intervention in Egypt's politics and culture. Both poets fell victim to their own unfortunate choices: Yūsuf exposed his racism and made it immortal, and Ḥijāzī, despite his goodwill in guarding Egyptian culture, allowed his poetry to sound more like a journal article, while, ironically, his journal articles have become more poetic. If these poets, among many others, continue writing poetry of this quality, it will be a challenge to maintain the high standards poets such as Darwīsh, al-Bayātī, and Qabbānī embodied and called for in their work.

Furthermore, the development of modern Arabic poetry and its contribution to the literary canon are at stake. Remarkably, Darwīsh was aware of the hazards of the topical poem; while he wrote some, he refrained from including most of them in his collections because they were written for a temporary function, mainly immediate political influence, and so do not add to the aesthetics of his poetics. Many modern Arab poets continue to write topical poems from the perspective of commitment to their society, unaware of the damage they cause to the literary canon in the Arab world and to their legacies as modern Arab poets, especially in the case of Yūsuf, whose hurried recent writings harm his legacy and fail to contribute to modern Arabic poetry. It is an attack on modern Arabic poetry, not just a reflection of the poet per se.

Thus, among the major challenges of writing modern Arabic poetry are young poets and readers' lack of grounding in the literary tradition, and the earlier generation's tendency to write topical political poems at the expense of quality. The combination is alarming because if the older generation continues to write such poetry, and the younger generation fails to recognize or write poetry, modern Arabic poetry is reduced to the archives—a sobering threat to the literary canon of the Arab world. It is worth noting that the modern Arab poet also engages with a challenged audience, for there is a gap between the Arab reader and the poet. The Arab audience needs a "mental" revolution, as Adūnīs calls it; therefore, the Arab poet is responsible for destroying all that keeps this reader in backwardness, that is, all that is between him and change.[10] Adūnīs maintains that "real Arabic art is war of values, system of language and thought. This war involves two movements: destroying the current infrastructure of art and culture, and creating a new one."[11] This is what al-Bayātī and Darwīsh called for in their late poetry. Rebuilding or establishing a new culture is the first phase in reviving the Arab poetic project. Poets need to address the cultural ills in society, starting with reading and writing, especially in the case of the young generation, which, as al-Bayātī said, has no values to fight for and is thus walking blindly toward the unknown. To provoke change in society, the poet needs to start with readers, encouraging them to think beyond the traditional channels in which they have been indoctrinated. Poets need not write what readers ask for; rather, they should write what readers need to hear. Poets need to create an audience capable of thinking independently, but before that, the poets themselves need to be able to think and write freely. However, Adūnīs affirms, "before and after the 1967 defeat, Arabic literature has been subjected to two powers: that of the tradition and of the regime, which in turn resulted in the suffocation of Arabic literature and culture. . . . If the Arab writer wants to move freely between Arab capitals, he should not raise any questions; he should not say anything. . . . Therefore, useless Arab books fill the Arab libraries."[12]

Much contemporary poetry these days is written, not spoken. When poetry was oral, the audience played a critical role and meter and rhyme mattered. Being exposed to a new poem by reading it in print has resulted in confusion for the reader, whose ear is no longer used to the music of poetry. Because the audience no longer plays a critical role in poetry, the relationship between poet and reader is confused, with the reader now a passive recipient. Darwīsh maintains that there is a crisis between the poet and the reader in the Arab world because the reader feels entitled to help define poetry.[13] Some poets underestimate their readers, Darwīsh warns, while others offer them some concessions by writing what they want to read or reading what they want to hear.[14] He asserts that only confidence between the two gives the poet the freedom to innovate.[15] Another problem poetry faces is the emphasis on quantity over quality in the Arab world, which has resulted from the spread of subsidy publishers and self-publishers. We are in dire need of readers who want to continue to develop their poetic taste and poets their poetic tools.[16] Carrying historical or documentary value does not suffice to make great poetry. Poetic aesthetics is not to be compromised, for it is what distinguishes poetry from other forms of writing. Modern Arabic poetry needs the collaborative, serious work of poets, readers, and critics to maintain its past glory and refine new realms of innovation.

Appendix

Interview with Aḥmad ʻAbd al-Muʻṭī Ḥijāzī

JANUARY 2012

Q: Why did you use both the free and Amudi verse in some of your poems, such as "From the Song of Songs," and "Elegy to al-Malki"?

A: It depends on the occasion of writing the poem. For example, al-Mālkī, who was a Nasserite officer, was watching a match between the Syrian and Egyptian teams in Damascus Stadium in 1945 when people assassinated him—I mean his political enemies. Every year the Syrians remember him by inviting an Arab poet to participate in the anniversary, and I was invited in 1959. Therefore, I do not write the poem to publish it, but to read it for thousands of people. A poem read on such an occasion needs to be close to people by using strong music. Amudi verse is the poetry people read and love. Therefore, I mixed the Amudi verse and the new verse.

Q: How did Eliot's poetry influence you?

A: I started writing free verse in 1955. Ṣalāḥ ʻAbd al-Ṣabūr did so one year before me, and ʻAbd al-Raḥmān al-Sharqāwī did so approximately ten years before both of us. There were attempts to write free verse starting in 1930 and 1931, before me and before ʻAbd al-Ṣabūr, Nāzik al-Malā'ika, al-Sayyāb, and al-Bayātī. We were all influenced by the French and English free verse. However, this influence was only successful after there were reasons for its success in Egypt.

Q: And what are these reasons?

A: Language changed, and we needed a lively language and not a language of old poetry. We needed music that fits this language, which we use in newspapers, and in which we read.

Q: Was this change based on a realistic change?

A: Exactly. Language changed, and the new language is the one used in journalism and officially. Life changed, and people needed a language that describes their life and not poetry telling them about old poets' tales.

Q: You were influenced by Eliot, but we see your employment of myths in the later part of your works. Why?

A: Using mythology requires pedantry, which I hate. Mythology should be used only when needed. For example, I used it in my poem "The Fire Stealer," and in "Mid Time." When the subject of the poem is realistic, then forcing the use of mythology is false. I love Greek and Egyptian myths, and I use them in the right place in my poetry.

Q: What is the impact of the fall of Nasserism, and of your travel to France, on your poetry?

A: My travel meant my maturity. I was able to follow the news in Egypt while keeping a distance. The 1967 defeat and the fall of Nasserism meant the death of a phase in my life and my poetry. I discovered that Nasserism was not a revolution. It was an army coup in 1952. Nasser's slogans were lies, and nothing was achieved. When I traveled to France, I got to know a new society that thinks and behaves in a different way. Staying there for seventeen years gave me the chance to see Egypt from distance; I mean the real Egypt. When one is inside the country, he is busy with what is happening around him, so when he leaves, he can think clearly and is able to connect the events.

Q: Do you believe that the role of poetry is to serve the revolution? Do you believe poetry should be politicized? For example, we notice that you officially returned to writing poetry during the January 25 revolution. It is obvious that you link between the idea of writing poetry and the revolution, or the spirit of the revolution.

A: It is not the revolution, but the substantial changes in life that awaken man and revive his consciousness and existence, and provide him with new material to write about.

Q: We notice in your poetry a transformation from writing about Nasser to writing about the nation, meaning from the regime revolution to the people's revolution. What do you think of this?

A: Of course. It is no longer about an individual. It is the movement of the audience, life, and society. It is the objective changes that are not related to one person.

Q: Is this maturity in poetry or in thought?

A: It is a maturity whose main source is discovering that placing hopes on one person is wrong and that objective reasons are the ones leading to change and indeed making it. It is no longer a matter of emotions or slogans.

Q: In regard to you considering the prose poem lacking, there are critics who consider free verse lacking too. What do you say?

A: Of course, some people disagree with the lack of political factor in writing poetry. There is a difference between someone who draws an image and uses a yellow color, and another telling him, "No, use the blue color" and between someone else who does not use any color. Music is a must in poetry. Poetry is lacking when it does not have any music.

Q: Did you leave Egypt in 1973 or 1974?

A: 1974.

Q: Because of al-Sadat?

A: Yes. Journalism rejected me because I opposed al-Sadat. I was not alone. Other writers did too. I was then a writer in *Rose al-Yūsuf*, and my salary was 100 pounds. Al-Sadat forced retirement on me from February 1, 1973, to September 28, 1973.

Q: In your first four collections, you wrote about your love and longing for the countryside and you criticized the city, especially Cairo. However, when you traveled to Paris, you stopped writing about Cairo and started writing about Paris. Why did Cairo become, in Paris, like the countryside was in Cairo?

A: When I was away from Cairo, I missed it because it no longer became a city causing me stress. It became the capital of the country I long for and the homeland I dream to return to. My attitude from Cairo is completely different. Therefore, I expressed it in a poem: "Song for Cairo," in the collection *Cement Trees*.

Q: And what is the second reason?

A: It is related to Paris. My relationship to Paris was not a relation of shock. I did not hate it. The French received me kindly, appointed me in the University of Paris, and translated my poetry. They celebrated me. But my attitude from Paris was different and somehow complicated. Paris is not just a city but a symbol of a civilization of cement. I was critical of this fake and manufactured civilization. Therefore, I called the collection *Cement Trees*. It is a civilization of cement and iron. It is a civilization far from natural civilization, which is the opposite of the countryside. While writing about the civilization of cement, I was indirectly praising nature or the countryside.

Q: How did the free verse succeed? How did the Amudi verse fail in expressing specific subjects?

A: Free verse is not only free poetic patterns. It is also the language and its vocabulary and expressions. Old poetic patterns bring with them old language and, thus, old subject matters.

Q: Is poetry associated with a specific environment?

A: Yes. Poetic patterns are linked to vocabulary in the dictionary, and the dictionary is linked to subject matters; therefore, free verse liberated us from old poetic patterns and subject matters.

Q: Which collection is the closest to your heart?

A: Closest to my heart? All my poetry is close to my heart. But there are some poems that I like more than others. For example, "The Path to the Lady," "Until We Meet," "Lemon Basket," "Letter to an Unknown City," and "Death of a Boy" in the first collection. And in the second collection, the poem "Awrās." In the third collection, my poem about Lumumba and "No One," and "Silence and Blood."

Q: Your collection *Nothing Remains but Confession* has no poem with this title. Why?

A: No, there is an indication in the collection. There is a poem, "Do Not Ask Christ," in the third collection, and it inspired this title.

Q: There is an indication that this collection is a message from you to Arabs to express your gratitude to Nasser. Is this true?

A: No. No. The indication is that I confess to feeling guilty because Lumumba was killed, and we are responsible for his death because we did not support him like we should have.

Q: I have a question about *Poetry Is My Companion.* If you were to rewrite it, would you change anything?

A: No. I would leave it as it is, but I might add to it.

Q: What would you add to it?

A: Experience. *Poetry Is My Companion* is a book that includes my essays and confessions about poetry until the date of its publication in the 1990s. It has been twenty years since then, and these years have offered experience worthy of adding to the book.

Q: What do you think of writing about poetry, challenges of writing poetry, the poet and metapoetry?

A: Metapoetry is the essence of poetry, not the minutes of it. Poetry points at metapoetry and its main ideas, which continue to be relevant to poetry.

NOTES

CHAPTER 1 The Politics and Poetics of the Modern Arab World

1. Quoted in James P. Jankowski, *Nasser's Egypt, Arab Nationalism, and the United Arab Republic* (Boulder, CO: Lynne Rienner, 2002), 30.

2. Ibid., 183.

3. Ibid., 32.

4. James L. Gelvin, *The Modern Middle East: A History* (New York: Oxford University Press, 2008), 199.

5. Ibid., 201.

6. Youssef M. Choueiri, *Arab Nationalism—A History: Nation and State in the Arab World* (Oxford: Blackwell, 2000), 21.

7. Michael B. Oren, "The Revelations of 1967: New Research on the Six Day War and Its Lessons for the Contemporary Middle East," *Israel Studies* 10, no. 2 (2005): 2.

8. Jankowski, *Nasser's Egypt*, 183.

9. Albert Habib Hourani, *A History of the Arab Peoples* (Cambridge, MA: Belknap Press of Harvard University Press, 1991), 417.

10. Ibid.

11. Ibid., 412.

12. Ibid., 416–17.

13. Tareq Y. Ismael and Rifaʿat El-Saʿid, *The Communist Movement in Egypt, 1920–1988* (Syracuse, NY: Syracuse University Press, 1990), 114.

14. Ibid., 114–15.

15. Tareq Y. Ismael, *The Communist Movement in the Arab World* (London: Routledge Curzon, 2005), 2.

16. Ibid., 3.

17. Ibid., 3.

18. Ibid., 118.

19. Joseph Andoni Massad, *Desiring Arabs* (Chicago: University of Chicago Press, 2007), 18.

20. Ibid.

21. Ibid.

22. Muhsin Jassim Al-Musawi, "Engaging Tradition in Modern Arab Poetics," *Journal of Arabic Literature* 33, no. 2 (2002): 177.

23. Saddik Gohar, "The Integration of Western Modernism in Postcolonial Arabic Literature: A Study of Abdul-Wahhab al-Bayati's Third World Poetics," *Third World Quarterly* 29, no. 2 (2008): 378.

24. Salma Khadra Jayyusi, *Modern Arabic Poetry: An Anthology* (New York: Columbia University Press, 1987), 14.

25. Ibid., 13; Salma Khadra Jayyusi, *Trends and Movements in Modern Arabic Poetry* (Leiden: Brill, 1977), 13–14.

26. Jayyusi, *Modern Arabic Poetry*, 76.

27. Suzanne Bernard, *Le Poème en prose du Baudelaire jusqu'à nos jours*, trans. Rawiya Sadeq (Cairo: Dār Sharqiyyāt, 1998), 33.

28. Mohammed Mustafa Badawi, "Commitment in Contemporary Arabic Literature," in *Critical Perspectives on Modern Arabic Literature*, ed. Issa J. Boullata (Washington, DC: Three Continents, 1980), 33.

29. Ibid.

30. Jean-Paul Sartre, *What Is Literature?* (New York: Philosophical Library, 1949), 77.

31. Mohammed Mustafa Badawi, *A Critical Introduction to Modern Arabic Poetry* (New York: Cambridge University Press, 1975), 217.

32. Ṣalāḥ ʿAbd al-Ṣabūr, *Wa-tabqā al-Kalima: Dirāsāt Naqdiya* (Beirut: Dār al-Adab, 1970), 107.

33. Mona Mikhail, "Iltizam: Commitment and Arabic Poetry," *World Literature Today* 53, no. 4 (1979), 598.

34. Quoted in ibid., 598.

35. Badawi, "Commitment," 44.

36. Ibid.

37. Ibid.

38. Ibid., 33.

39. Jabra Ibrahim Jabra, "The Rebels, the Committed, and Others: Transitions in Arabic Poetry Today," in *Critical Perspectives on Modern Arabic Literature*, ed. Issa J. Boullata (Washington, DC: Three Continents, 1980), 192.

40. Verena Klemm, "Different Notions of Commitment (Iltizām) and Committed Literature (al-Adab al-Multazim) in the Literary Circles of the Mashriq," *Arabic and Middle Eastern Literature* 3, no. 1 (2000): 55.

41. Jabra, "Rebels," 23.

42. Ibid.

43. Klemm, "Different Notions," 56.

44. Ibid.

45. Ibid., 57.

46. Ibid.
47. Ibid.
48. Ibid.
49. Badawi, "Commitment," 36.
50. Klemm, "Different Notions," 58.
51. Ibid.
52. Badawi, "Commitment," 42.
53. Dorothy Baker, *Mythic Masks in Self-Reflexive Poetry: A Study of Pan and Orpheus* (Chapel Hill: University of North Carolina Press, 1986), 3.
54. Rene Wellek, *Discriminations* (New Haven, CT: Yale University Press, 1971), 261–63.
55. Aida Azouqa, "Metapoetry between East and West: ʿAbd al-Wahhāb al-Bayātī and the Western Composers of Metapoetry—A Study in Analogies," *Journal of Arabic Literature* 39 (2008): 38.
56. Ibid., 39.
57. Klemm, "Different Notions," 58.
58. Azouqa, "Metapoetry," 39.
59. Ibid.
60. Ami Elad-Bouskila, *Modern Palestinian Literature and Culture* (London: F. Cass, 1999), 28.
61. Ibid., 141.
62. Ibid.
63. Rebecca L Torstrick, *The Limits of Coexistence: Identity Politics in Israel* (Ann Arbor: University of Michigan Press, 2000), 320.
64. Haim Bresheeth, "Self and Other in Zionism: Palestine and Israel in Recent Hebrew Literature," in *Palestine: Profile of an Occupation*, ed. Khamsin Collective (London: Zed Books, 1989), 148.
65. Ibid., 149.
66. Ammiel Alcalay, *Memories of Our Future: Selected Essays, 1982–1999* (San Francisco: City Lights, 1999), 100.
67. Bresheeth, "Self and Other," 150.
68. Badawi, "Critical Introduction," 210.
69. Badawi, "Commitment," 44.

CHAPTER 2 From *Iltizām* to Metapoetry

1. Khalīl Shukrallāh Rizk, "The Poetry of ʿAbd al-Wahhāb al-Bayātī: Thematic and Stylistic Study" (Ph.D. dissertation, Indiana University, 1981), 5–6.
2. Ibid., 7.
3. Mounah A. Khouri and Hamid Algar, *An Anthology of Modern Arabic Poetry* (Berkeley: University of California Press, 1975), 241.

4. Klemm, "Different Notions," 58.

5. Badawi, *Critical Introduction*, 211.

6. Issa J. Boullata, "Abd al-Wahhab al-Bayati," *Contemporary World Writers*, 2nd ed. (London: St. James Press, 1993), 47–50.

7. ʿAbd al-Wahhāb al-Bayātī, *Al-Aʿmāl al-Shiʿriyya* (The Complete Poetic-Works), 2 vols. (Beirut: al-Mu'assasa al-ʿArabiyya lil-Dirāsāt wa-al-Nashr, 1995), 1:197.

8. Hussein N. Kadhim, *The Poetics of Anti-Colonialism in the Arabic Qaṣīdah* (Leiden: Brill, 2004), 198.

9. Nazeer El-Azma, "The Tammūzī Movement and the Influence of T. S. Eliot on Badr Shākir al-Sayyāb," *Journal of the American Oriental Society* 88, no. 4 (1968): 671.

10. Ibid., 678.

11. Al-Bayātī, *Al-Aʿmāl al- Shiʿriyya*, 1:215.

12. Ibid., 2:7–8.

13. Ibid., 2:42–49.

14. Gohar, "Integration of Western Modernism," 8.

15. Badr Shākir al-Sayyāb, *Dīwān* (Collected Poems), 2 vols. (Beirut: Dār al-ʿAwda, 2005), 2:297–317.

16. Saadi A. Simawe, "The Lives of the Sufi Masters in Abd al-Wahhāb al-Bayātī's Poetry," *Journal of Arabic Literature* 32, no. 2 (2001): 124.

17. Aida Azouqa, "Defamiliarization in the Poetry of ʿAbd al-Wahhāb al-Bayātī and T. S. Eliot: A Comparative Study," *Journal of Arabic Literature* 32, no. 2 (2001): 171.

18. Al-Bayātī, *Al-Aʿmāl al-Shiʿriyya*, 2:73–74.

19. ʿAbd al-Wahhāb Al-Bayātī, *Love, Death, and Exile: Poems Translated from Arabic*, trans. Bassam Frangieh (Washington, DC: Georgetown University Press, 2004), 7–8.

20. Salih J. Altoma, "Postwar Iraqi Literature: Agonies of Rebirth," *Books Abroad* 46, no. 2 (1972): 215–16.

21. Al-Bayātī, *Al-Aʿmāl al-Shiʿriyya*, 2:77–78.

22. Ibid., 2:73–74.

23. Al-Bayātī, *Love, Death, and Exile*, 21–27 (with emendation).

24. Kadhim, *Poetics of Anti-Colonialism*, 184.

25. Muhsin Jassim Al-Musawi, *Arabic Poetry: Trajectories of Modernity and Tradition* (London: Routledge, 2006), 230.

26. Bassam Frangieh, "Modern Arabic Poetry: Vision and Reality," in *Tradition, Modernity, and Postmodernity in Arabic Literature: Essays in Honor of Professor Issa J. Boullata*, ed. Kamal Abdel-Malek and Wael B. Hallaq (Leiden: Brill, 2000), 228.

27. Suzanne Pinckney Stetkevych, *The Mute Immortals Speak: Pre-Islamic Poetry and the Poetics of Ritual* (Ithaca, NY: Cornell University Press, 2011), 78.

28. Klemm, "Different Notions," 53.

29. Ibid.

30. Badawi, *Critical Introduction*, 212.

31. Al-Bayātī, *Al-Aʿmāl al-Shiʿriyya*, 2:109–12.

32. Ibid., 2:117.

33. Ibid., 2:118.

34. Ibid., 2:231, 234.

35. Ibid., 2:254.

36. Ibid., 2:260.

37. Ibid., 2:294–97.

38. Al-Musawi, *Arabic Poetry*, 215.

39. Rabindranath Tagore, *The English Writings of Rabindranath Tagore* (New Delhi: Atlantic & Distributors, 2007), 104.

40. Ibid., 94.

41. Ibid., 89.

42. Ibid., 104.

43. Al-Bayātī, *Al-Aʿmāl al-Shiʿriyya*, 2:319.

44. Ibid., 2:321.

45. Ibid., 2:322.

46. Ibid., 2:317–24.

47. Ibid., 2:324.

48. ʿAbd al-Wahhāb al-Bayātī, *Yanābīʿ al-Shams: Al-Sīra al-Shiʿriyya* (Damascus: Dar al-Farqad, 1999), 146.

49. Azouqa, "Defamiliarization," 176–77.

50. Al-Bayātī, *Al-Aʿmāl al-Shiʿriyya*, 2:395–97.

51. Ibid., 2:389–402.

52. Ibid., 2:405–8.

53. Ibid., 2:409–12.

54. Ibid., 2:417–20.

55. Ibid., 2:434–38.

56. Ibid., 2:402–4.

57. Ibid., 2:421–25.

58. Ibid., 2:430–33.

59. Ibid., 2:439–42.

60. Ibid., 2:425–30.

61. Azouqa, "Metapoetry," 38–40.

62. Al-Bayātī, *Al-Aʿmāl al-Shiʿriyya*, 2:395–97.

63. Akiko Motoyoshi Sumi, *Description in Classical Arabic Poetry: Waṣf, Ekphrasis, and Interarts Theory* (Leiden: Brill, 2004), 92.

64. Al-Bayātī, *Al-Aʿmāl al-Shiʿriyya*, 2:395–96.

65. Al-Bayātī, *Love, Death, and Exile*, 235 (with emendation).

66. Boullata, "Abd al-Wahhab al-Bayati," 49.

67. Al-Bayātī, *Al-Aʿmāl al-Shiʿriyya*, 2:397.

68. Al-Bayātī, *Love, Death, and Exile*, 239 (with emendation).

69. Al-Bayātī, *Al-Aʿmāl al-Shiʿriyya*, 2:396; Al-Bayātī, *Love, Death, and Exile*, 239.

70. Yair Huri, "The Queen Who Serves the Slaves: From Politics to Metapoetics in the Poetry of Qāsim Ḥaddād," *Journal of Arabic Literature* 34, no. 3 (2003): 258.

71. Al-Bayātī, *Love, Death, and Exile*, 241.

72. Ibid., 235–37.

73. Azouqa, "Metapoetry," 39.

74. Huri, "Queen Who Serves," 270.

75. Ibid.

76. Ibid.

77. Mohammad R. Salama, "The Mise-en-Scène of Writing in al-Bayātī's 'Al-Kitābah ʿAlā Al-Ṭīn,'" *Journal of Arabic Literature* 32, no. 2 (2001): 149.

78. Al-Bayātī, *Al-Aʿmāl al-Shiʿriyya*, 2:409–12.

79. Al-Bayātī, *Yanābīʿ al-Shams*, 163.

80. Al-Musawi, *Arabic Poetry*, 151.

81. Al-Bayātī, *Yanābīʿ al-Shams*, 166.

82. Ibid., 164.

83. Ibid., 143.

84. Al-Bayātī, *Yanābīʿ al-Shams*, 172.

85. Ibid.

86. Ibid., 174.

87. Ibid.

88. Al-Bayātī, *Love, Death, and Exile*, 253.

89. Al-Bayātī, *Al-Aʿmāl al-Shiʿriyya*, 2:434.

90. Ibid., 2:433.

91. Ibid., 2:438.

92. Ibid., 2:435.

93. Ibid., 2:442.

94. Ibid., 2:439.

95. Ibid., 2:440.

96. Al-Bayātī, *Yanābīʿ al-Shams*, 176.

97. Al-Bayātī, *Al-Aʿmāl al-Shiʿriyya*, 2:425–30.

98. Ibid., 2:425.

99. Ibid., 2:425–26.

100. Ibid., 2:426–27.

101. Jabra, "Rebels," 195.

102. Al-Bayātī, *Al-Aʿmāl al-Shiʿriyya*, 2:427.

103. Ibid., 2:427–29.

104. Al-Bayātī, *Yanābīʿ Al-Shams*, 153.

105. Ibid., 156.

106. Ibid.
107. Ibid.
108. Ibid.
109. Aida Azouqa, "Al-Bayātī and W. B. Yeats as Mythmakers: A Comparative Study," *Journal of Arabic Literature* 30, no. 3 (1999): 275.
110. Al-Bayātī, *Yanābī' al-Shams*, 145.
111. Ibid., 163.
112. Ibid.
113. Ibid., 166–67.

CHAPTER 3 From *Iltizām* to the Arab Uprising

1. Usama Urabi, "Masīrat Ḥijāzī al-Ibdā'iyya" (Ḥijāzī's Creative Journey), in *Aḥmad 'Abd al-Mu'ṭī Ḥijāzī: Sab'ūn 'Āman min al-Riyāda wa-al-Tajdīd*, ed. Ḥasan Ṭilib et al., 327–35 (Cairo: al-Majlis al-A'lā lil-Thaqāfa, 2005), 333.
2. Issa J. Boullata, *Modern Arab Poets, 1950–1975* (Washington, DC: Three Continents, 1976), 163.
3. Aḥmad 'Abd al-Mu'ṭī Ḥijāzī, *Al-A'māl al-Kāmila* (The Complete Works) (Kuwait: Dār Su'ād al-Ṣabāh, 1993), 85–87. This poem's title is "al-Baṭal" (The Hero) in a collection of Ḥijāzī's complete works published in 1982.
4. Ibid., 86–87.
5. Aḥmad 'Abd al-Mu'ṭī Ḥijāzī, *Al-Shi'r Rafīqī* (Poetry Is My Companion) (Riyadh: Dār al-Marrīkh lil-Nashr, 1988), 163.
6. Aḥmad 'Abd al-Mu'ṭī Ḥijāzī, "Al-Shi'r wa-'Abd al-Nāṣir" (Poetry and Abd al-Nasser), in *Kitābāt 'alā Qabr 'Abd al-Nāṣir* (Writings on the Tomb of Nasser), ed. Aḥmad 'Abd al-Mu'ṭī Ḥijāzī et al. (Beirut: Dār al-'Awda, 1971), 9.
7. Ḥijāzī, *Al-A'māl al-Kāmila*, 105–9.
8. Ḥijāzī, "Al-Shi'r wa-'Abd al-Nāṣir," 8.
9. Ḥijāzī, *Al-A'māl al-Kāmila*, 153–207.
10. Ibid., 153–72.
11. Ibid., 197–99.
12. Ibid.
13. Jaroslav Stetkevych, "Al-Ḥadātha fī Shi'r Aḥmad 'Abd al-Mu'ṭī Ḥijāzī" (Modernism in the Poetry of Aḥmad 'Abd al-Mu'ṭī Ḥijāzī), in *Mamlakat Aḥmad 'Abd al-Mu'ṭī Ḥijāzī*, ed. Ḥasan Ṭilib (Cairo: al-Hai'a al-Miṣriyya al-'Āmma lil-Kitāb, 2006), 50.
14. Ibid., 177–80.
15. Aḥmad 'Abd al-Mu'ṭī Ḥijāzī, *Qaṣidat al-Nathr aw al-Qaṣida al-Kharsā'* (The Prose Poem or the Mute Poem), (Dubai: Majallat Dubai al-Thaqfiyya, 2008), 90.
16. Shmuel Moreh, *Modern Arabic Poetry, 1800–1970: The Development of Its Forms and Themes under the Influence of Western Literature* (Leiden: Brill, 1976), 282.

17. Ḥijāzī, *Al-Shi'r Rafīqī*, 6.

18. Badawi, *Critical Introduction*, 219.

19. Ibid., 218.

20. Ḥijāzī, *Al-A'māl al-Kāmila*, 265–68.

21. Ibid., 85–87.

22. Ḥijāzī, *Al-A'māl al-Kāmila*, 371–75.

23. Ibid., 289–90. This poem's title is given as "Ughniya lil Itiḥād al-'Arabī al-Ishtirākī" (A Song to the Arab Socialist Union) in a collection of Ḥijāzī's complete works published in 1982. *Ḥizb* means "party," and in this context it refers to Nasser's party. However, I use "party" and "union" interchangeably to refer to Nasser's Socialist Union.

24. Ḥijāzī, *Al-A'māl al-Kāmila*, 269.

25. Ibid., 233–40.

26. Ibid., 240.

27. El-Azma, "Tammūzī Movement," 671.

28. Gelvin, *Modern Middle East*, 242.

29. Ḥijāzī, *Al-A'māl al-Kāmila*, 239–40.

30. For example, see ibid., "My Beloved," 259–64, and "The Birthday Gift," 323–25.

31. Ḥijāzī, e-mail interview with Yāsir Ḥijāzī and Waed Athamneh, January 10, 2012.

32. David Dean Commins, *Historical Dictionary of Syria* (Lanham, MD: Scarecrow, 1996), 232.

33. Ḥijāzī, *Al-A'māl al-Kāmila*, 271–77.

34. Ibid., 391–92.

35. Aḥmad 'Abd al-Mu'ṭī Ḥijāzī, "As If a Voice Were Calling: Ahmed Abdel Mu'ti Hijazi," trans. Omnia Amin and Rick London, *Big Bridge* (Spring 2011), 6. Available at http://www.bigbridge.org/BB15/toc.html.

36. Ḥijāzī, *Al-A'māl al-Kāmila*, 353–55. This poem's title is given as "Al-Shā'ir wa-al-Baṭal" (The Poet and the Hero) in a collection of Ḥijāzī's complete works published in 1982.

37. Ḥijāzī, *Al-A'māl al-Kāmila*, 265–68.

38. Ibid., 353.

39. Ibid., 354.

40. Majdi Shandi, "Ḥijāzī Yastarji' al-Dhākira" (Ḥijāzī Recalls Memories). *Al-Mashhad*. Mu'assasat al-Mashhad lil-Nashr Wa-al-Tawzī', October 5, 2011. Available at http://www.masress.com/almashhad/22173.

41. Ḥijāzī, *Al-A'māl al-Kāmila*, 411–21.

42. Ibid., 411.

43. Ibid., 412.

44. Ibid., 414.

45. Ibid., 412.

46. Ibid., 413.

47. Ibid., 421.

48. Ibid.

49. Ibid.

50. Ibid., 357–67.

51. Ḥijāzī, *Al-Shi'r Rafīqī*, 201.

52. Saad Al-Bazei, "Realms of the Wasteland: Hijazi and the Metropolis," *World Literature Today* 67, no. 2 (1993): 307.

53. Ḥijāzī, *Al-A'māl al-Kāmila*, 465.

54. Ibid., 468.

55. Ḥijāzī, *Al-Shi'r Rafīqī*, 199.

56. Ibid., 201–2.

57. Al-Bazei, "Realms of the Wasteland," 307.

58. Melvin E. Becraft, *Picasso's Guernica: Images within Images* (Rohnert Park, CA: M. E. Becraft, 1986), viii.

59. Ḥijāzī, *Al-Shi'r Rafīqī*, 218.

60. Shandi, "Ḥijāzī Yastarji' al-Dhākira."

61. Ḥijāzī, *Al-A'māl al-Kāmila*, 517–18.

62. Ḥijāzī, "As If a Voice Were Calling," 23.

63. Ḥijāzī, *Al-A'māl al-Kāmila*, 519–20.

64. Ḥijāzī, "As If a Voice Were Calling," 23–24.

65. Ḥijāzī, *Al-A'māl al-Kāmila*, 521–22.

66. Ḥijāzī, "As If a Voice Were Calling," 24–25.

67. Silvano Levy, *Surrealism: Surrealist Visuality* (Edinburgh: Edinburgh University Press, 1996), 137.

68. Ibid., 144.

69. Ḥijāzī, *Al-A'māl al-Kāmila*, 523–24.

70. Ḥijāzī, "As If a Voice Were Calling," 25–26.

71. Stephen Hart, *"No Pasarán": Art, Literature and the Spanish Civil War* (London: Tamesis, 1988), 45.

72. Ḥijāzī, *Al-A'māl al-Kāmila*, 468.

73. Levy, *Surrealism*, 137.

74. Pablo Picasso and Dore Ashton, *Picasso on Art: A Selection of Views* (New York: Da Capo, 1988), 143.

75. Ḥijāzī, *Al-A'māl al-Kāmila*, 549–65.

76. Ibid., 600.

77. Ibid., 601.

78. Ḥijāzī, "Al-Shi'r wa-'Abd al-Nāṣir," 5–8.

79. Edward William Lane, *Arabic–English Lexicon*, vol. 5 (New Delhi: Asian Educational Services, 2003), 1863.

80. Aḥmad 'Abd al-Mu'ṭī Ḥijāzī, *Ṭalal al-Waqt* (The Standing Ruins of Time) (Cairo: Al-Hay'a al-Miṣriyya al-'āmma lil-Kitāb, 2011), 7.

81. Ibid., 33–35.

82. Joseph P. Byrne, *Encyclopedia of Pestilence, Pandemics, and Plagues* (Westport, CT: Greenwood, 2008), 70.

83. Thomas J. Mooney, *Live Forever or Die Trying: The History and Politics of Life Extension* (Xlibris, 2011), 81.

84. Ḥijāzī, *Ṭalal al-Waqt*, 113–15.

85. Ibid., 117.

86. Ibid.

87. Ibid., 102–6.

88. "Seventy centuries" might be an allusion to Napoleon's Battle of the Pyramids.

89. Ḥijāzī, *Ṭalal al-Waqt*, 29–31.

90. *Muʿāraḍa* in poetry is when "a later poet wants to compete with his predecessor and thus writes a *muʿāraḍah*, or a later poet wants to create a poem that resembles in some respect his predecessor's poem and thus writes a *muʿāraḍah*." Mishari Almusa, "The Andalusian Panegyric Muʿāraḍah: Rhetorical Strategy and Speech Act Theory" (Ph.D. dissertation, Indiana University, 2010), 8.

91. Ḥijāzī, *Ṭalal al-Waqt*, 36–9.

92. Ḥijāzī, *Qaṣidat al-Nathr aw al-Qaṣida al-Kharsā'*, 90.

93. Ibid.

94. Ibid., 570.

95. Ḥijāzī, *Ṭalal al-Waqt*, 48–49.

96. Ibid., 123–29.

97. Ḥijāzī, interview by Ḥijāzī and Athamneh, January 10, 2012.

98. Ibid., 87–98.

99. Al-Musawi, *Arabic Poetry*, 139.

100. Ibid., 143.

101. Ibid.

102. J. Stetkevych, "Al-Ḥadātha," 45.

103. Al-Musawi, *Arabic Poetry*, 138.

104. Ibid., 9.

105. Azouqa, "Metapoetry," 63.

106. Jayyusi, *Trends and Movements*, 270.

107. Ibid., 261.

108. Jabra, "Rebels," 194.

109. Aḥmad ʿAbd al-Muʿṭī Ḥijāzī, "The Sun and the Dark Ones," *Al-Ahram*, October 8, 2013.

110. Aḥmad ʿAbd al-Muʿṭī Ḥijāzī, "Only Now, We Left the Middle Ages," *Al-Masry al-Youm*, August 29, 2013.

111. Ibid.

112. Ḥijāzī, "The Sun and the Dark Ones."

113. Aḥmad ʿAbd al-Muʿṭī Ḥijāzī, "Revolution or Coup?" *Al-Ahram*, July 23, 2014.

114. Ibid.

115. Ibid.

116. Ḥijāzī, "Only Now, We Left the Middle Ages."

117. Aḥmad ʿAbd al-Muʿṭī Ḥijāzī, "We Have Not Revolted Yet," *Al-Ahram*, April 6, 2016.

118. Ibid.

119. Ibid.

CHAPTER 4 From Militant *Iltizām* to Humanist

1. Maḥmūd Darwīsh, *Psalms: Poems by Mahmoud Darwish*, trans. Ben Bennani (Colorado Springs, CO: Three Continents, 1994), 9.

2. Ibid., 9–10.

3. Quoted in Rajā' al-Naqqāsh, *Maḥmūd Darwīsh: Shāʿir al-Arḍ al-Muḥtalla* (Mahmoud Darwish: Poet of the Occupied Land), 2nd ed. (Cairo: Dār al-Hilāl, 1971), 268–70. My translation.

4. Maḥmūd Darwīsh, *Unfortunately, It Was Paradise: Selected Poems*, trans. Munir Akash and Carolyn Forché (Berkeley: University of California Press, 2003), xvii.

5. Fady Joudah, "Mahmoud Darwish's Lyric Epic," *Human Architecture: Journal of the Sociology of Self-Knowledge* 7, no. 5 (2009): 12.

6. Ibid.

7. Darwīsh, *Al-ʿAmāl al-Kāmila*, vol. 3 (Jerusalem: Wizarat al-Thaqafa, 2010), 341.

8. Ibid., 340.

9. Ibid., 342.

10. Jacqueline Rose, *Proust among the Nations: From Dreyfus to the Middle East* (Chicago: University of Chicago Press, 2011), 102–3.

11. Darwīsh, *Al-ʿAmāl al-Kāmila*, 336.

12. Ibid., 337.

13. Darwīsh, *Unfortunately*, 25.

14. Darwīsh, *Psalms*, 4.

15. Maḥmūd Darwīsh, *Awrāq al-Zaytūn* (Olive Leaves) (Haifa: Maṭbaʿat al-ittiḥād al-Taʿāwuniyya, 1964), 5–10.

16. It is worth noting that this line was eliminated from later editions of the poem. Rajā' al-Naqqāsh maintains that this line is a historic error because people living in the Occupied Territories included both communists and noncommunists, so Darwīsh should not say that all people there love communism. See al-Naqqāsh, *Maḥmūd Darwīsh*, 287.

17. Maḥmūd Darwīsh, *The Music of Human Flesh: Maḥmūd Darwīsh*, trans. Denys Johnson-Davies (London: Heinemann, 1980), 10–12 (with emendation).

18. Martin S. Kramer, *Arab Awakening and Islamic Revival: The Politics of Ideas in the Middle East* (New Brunswick, NJ: Transaction, 2008), 19.

19. Al-Naqqāsh, *Maḥmūd Darwīsh*, 292.

20. Ibid., 290.

21. Ibid., 291.

22. Ibid., 296.

23. Maḥmūd Darwīsh, Ākhir al-Layl (Beirut: Dār al-ʿAwda, 1969), 36–43.

24. At Darwīsh's request, the title of this poem in English was changed from "A Soldier Dreams of White Tulips" to "A Soldier Dreams of White Lilies." Perhaps it is because white tulips symbolize peace, while white lilies symbolize purity of intention. As the translation treats the Arabic lines as phrases, line numbers below refer only to the English version.

25. Darwīsh, *Unfortunately*, 165–68 (with emendation).

26. Adam Shatz, "A Love Story between an Arab Poet and His Land," in *The Struggle for Sovereignty: Palestine and Israel, 1993–2005*, ed. Joel Beinin and Rebecca L. Stein (Stanford, CA: Stanford University Press, 2006), 224.

27. Ibid.

28. Ibid.

29. Al-Naqqāsh, *Maḥmūd Darwīsh*, 284. This refers to Darwīsh's poetry up to 1971, when the second edition of the book was published.

30. R. Victoria Arana, *The Facts on File Companion to World Poetry: 1900 to the Present* (New York: Facts on File, 2008), 127.

31. Khalid A. Sulaiman, *Palestine and Modern Arab Poetry* (London: Zed, 1984), 199.

32. Issa J. Boullata, "An Arabic Poem in an Israeli Controversy: Maḥmūd Darwīsh's 'Passing Words,'" in *Humanism, Culture, and Language in the Near East: Studies in Honor of Georg Krotkoff*, ed. Asma Afsaruddin and A. H. Mathias Zahniser (Winona Lake, IN: Eisenbrauns, 1997), 119.

33. Ibid., 120.

34. Alcalay, *Memories of Our Future*, 100.

35. Maḥmūd Darwīsh, *ʿĀbirun fī Kalām ʿĀbir* (Beirut: Dār al-ʿAwda, 1994), 51–53.

36. Zachary Lockman and Joel Beinin, *Intifada: The Palestinian Uprising against Israeli Occupation* (Boston: South End, 1989), 26–27 (with emendation).

37. Mike Evans, *Jerusalem Betrayed: Ancient Prophecy and Modern Conspiracy Collide in the Holy City* (Dallas: Word Publishing, 1997), "The Crucible of Faith."

38. Elad-Bouskila, *Modern Palestinian Literature*, 113.

39. Ibid.

40. Najat Rahman, "Interview with Mahmoud Darwish: On the Possibility of Poetry at a Time of Siege," in *Mahmoud Darwish, Exile's Poet: Critical Essays*, ed. Hala Khamis Nassar and Najat Rahman (Northampton, MA: Olive Branch, 2008), 320.

41. Ibid., 322–23.

42. James L. Gelvin, *The Israel–Palestine Conflict: One Hundred Years of War* (Cambridge: Cambridge University Press, 2007), 161.

43. Sinan Antoon, "Mahmud Darwish's Allegorical Critique of Oslo," *Journal of Palestine Studies* 31, no. 2 (2002): 76.

44. Quoted in Gelvin, *Israel–Palestine Conflict*, 162.

45. Muna Abu Eid, *Mahmoud Darwish: Literature and the Politics of Palestinian Identity* (New York: I. B. Tauris, 2016), 60.

46. Maḥmūd Darwīsh, *Ḥālat Ḥiṣār* (State of Siege) (Beirut: Riyāḍ al-Rayyis lil-Kutub wa-al-Nashr, 2002), 18.

47. Maḥmūd Darwīsh, *State of Siege [Ḥālat Ḥiṣār]*, trans. Munir Akash and Daniel Moore (Syracuse, NY: Jusoor and Syracuse University Press, 2010), 21.

48. Darwīsh, *Ḥālat Ḥiṣār*, 29.

49. Darwīsh, *State of Siege*, 43.

50. Muhammad Siddiq, "Significant but Problematic Others: Negotiating 'Israelis' in the Works of Mahmoud Darwish," *Comparative Literature Studies* 47, no. 4 (2010): 501–2.

51. Darwīsh, *Ḥālat Ḥiṣār*, 86.

52. Darwīsh, *State of Siege*, 161.

53. Darwīsh, *Ḥālat Ḥiṣār*, 81.

54. Ibid., 151.

55. Gelvin, *Israel–Palestine Conflict*, 162.

56. Darwīsh, *State of Siege*, 175.

57. Darwīsh, *Ḥālat Ḥiṣār*, 83.

58. Darwīsh, *State of Siege*, 155.

59. Darwīsh, *Ḥālat Ḥiṣār*, 9.

60. Darwīsh, *State of Siege*, 3.

61. Patrick Sylvain, "Darwish's Essentialist Poetics in a State of Siege," *Human Architecture: Journal of the Sociology of Self-Knowledge* 7, no. 5 (2009): 143.

62. Darwīsh, *Ḥālat Ḥiṣār*, 72.

63. Darwīsh, *State of Siege*, 133. *They* in the translation refers to the Zionists, but in the original Arabic text, the *she* refers to the State of Israel.

64. Darwīsh, *Ḥālat Ḥiṣār*, 73.

65. Darwīsh, *State of Siege*, 72.

66. Darwīsh, *Ḥālat Ḥiṣār*, 48.

67. Darwīsh, *State of Siege*, 83 (with emendation).

68. Klemm, "Different Notions," 57.

69. Herbert C. Kelman, "Nationalism, Patriotism, and National Identity: Social-Psychological Dimensions," in *Patriotism in the Lives of Individuals and Nations*, ed. Daniel Bar-Tal and Ervin Staub (Chicago: Nelson-Hall, 1997), 184.

70. Quoted in Alcalay, *Memories of Our Future*, 103.

71. Edward Said, *Peace and Its Discontents: Essays on Palestine in the Middle East Peace Process* (New York: Vintage, 1995), 163.

72. Anat Matar, "Postmodernism and the Oslo Agreement," in *Looking Back at the June 1967 War*, ed. Hayim Gordon (Westport, CT: Praeger, 1999), 127–28.

73. Homi Bhabha, "Remembering Fanon: Self, Psyche and the Colonial Condition," in *Colonial Discourse and Post-Colonial Theory: A Reader*, ed. Patrick Williams and Laura Chrisman (New York: Columbia University Press, 1994), 117.

74. Maḥmūd Darwīsh, *Lā Taʿtadhir ʿAmmā Faʿalt* (Do Not Apologize for What You Did), 2nd ed. (Beirut: Riyāḍ al-Rayyis lil-Kutub wa-al-Nashr, 2004), 87–88.

75. Maḥmūd Darwīsh, *Now, As You Awaken*, trans. Omnia Amin and Rick London, *Big Bridge* (2006). Available at http://www.bigbridge.org/DARWISH.HTM.

76. Herbert C. Kelman, "The Interdependence of Israeli and Palestinian National Identities: The Role of the Other in Existential Conflicts," *Journal of Social Issues* 55, no. 3 (1999): 588.

77. Julia DiGangi, "Homeland, Hopelessness, Hate, and Heroes: Psychological Dynamics in the Israeli–Palestinian Conflict," in *Terror in the Holy Land: Inside the Anguish of the Israeli–Palestinian Conflict*, ed. Judith Kuriansky (Westport, CT: Praeger, 2006), 4.

78. Quoted in Khaled Mattawa, *Mahmoud Darwish: The Poet's Art and His Nation* (Syracuse, NY: Syracuse University Press, 2014). Kindle edition.

79. Darwīsh, *Lā Taʿtadhir ʿAmmā Faʿalt*, 105–7.

80. Fady Joudah, trans., "Wedding Song, and: She's Alone in the Evening, and: While Waiting," *Prairie Schooner* 80, no. 2 (2006): 27–28 (with emendation).

81. Bhabha, "Remembering Fanon," 117.

82. Jeremy Bowen, *Six Days: How the 1967 War Shaped the Middle East* (New York: St. Martin's Press/Thomas Dunne, 2005), 6.

83. Bhabha, "Remembering Fanon," 117.

84. Julia DiGangi, "Homeland," 4.

85. Rahman, "Interview," 323.

86. Sylvain, "Darwish's Essentialist Poetics," 148.

87. Maḥmūd Darwīsh, *Almond Blossoms and Beyond*, trans. Mohammad Shaheen (Northampton, MA: Interlink Books, 2009), 3.

88. Ibid., 28.

89. Maḥmūd Darwīsh, *Kazahr al-Lawz aw Ab'ad* (Almond Blossoms and Beyond) (Beirut: Riyāḍ al-Rayyis lil-Kutub wa-al-Nashr, 2005), 33.

90. Darwīsh, *Almond Blossoms*, 7 (with emendation).

91. Darwīsh, *Athar al-Farasha* (The Butterfly Effect), 2nd ed. (Beirut: Riyāḍ al-Rayyis lil-Kutub wa-al-Nashr, 2009), 62–63.

92. Ibid., 269–75.

93. Ibid., 45–46.

94. Ibid., 56–57.

95. Ibid., 45–46.

96. Ibid.

97. Quoted in Mattawa, *Mahmoud Darwish.*

98. Ibid.

99. Ibid.

100. Ibid.

101. Darwīsh, *Athar al-Farasha*, 269–75.

102. Mattawa, *Mahmoud Darwish.*

103. Morani Kornberg-Weiss, *Dear Darwish* (Buffalo, NY: BlazeVox, 2014). Kindle edition.

104. Ibid.

105. Mattawa, *Mahmoud Darwish.*

106. Ibid.

107. Darwīsh, *Lā Urīdu li-Hāthī al-Qaṣīda ʿan Tantahī* (I Do Not Want for This Poem to End) (Beirut: Riyāḍ al-Rayyis lil-Kutub wa-al-Nashr, 2009), 56–58.

CONCLUSION

1. Yair Huri, "Perhaps I Disappointed You: On a Metapoetic Poem by Saʿdī Yūsuf," *Middle Eastern Literature* 7, no. 1 (2004): 82.

2. *ʿAl-ʿAmā* translates literally to "blindness." It is also a variation of "damn" in Arabic. However, I choose to translate it literally as "blindness" because I believe the poet could have repeated "damn" twice, if this is the meaning he wanted to deliver. "Blindness" in this context may suggest turning a blind eye to what is happening on the political front in the Arab world.

3. Saʿdī Yūsuf, "Slaves Are More Fierce Than Masters," *Saadi Yousif* (blog), September 7, 2013, http://www.saadiyousif.com/home/index.php?option=com_content&task=view&id=1657&Itemid=1.

4. Saʿdī Yūsuf, "Egypt Nearly Lost Its Independence at the Hands of the Muslim Brotherhood," *Saadi Yousif* (blog), October 8, 2013, http://www.saadiyousif.com/home/index.php?option=com_content&task=view&id=1672&Itemid=1.

5. Ibid.

6. Ibid.

7. Ibid.

8. Ibid.

9. Ibid.

10. Adūnīs, *Zaman al-Shiʿr* (Time of Poetry) (Beirut: Dār al-ʿAwda, 1987), 75.

11. Ibid., 75–76.

12. Ibid., 80.

13. Darwīsh, interview by Abduh Wazin, *Al-Ḥaya al-Landaniyya*, December 14, 2005.

14. Ibid.

15. Ibid.

16. Ibid.

BIBLIOGRAPHY

ʿAbd al-Ṣabūr, Ṣalāḥ. *Wa-tabqā al-Kalima: Dirāsāt Naqdiya*. Beirut: Dār al-Adab, 1970.

Aburish, Said K. *Nasser: The Last Arab*. New York: St. Martin's Press/Thomas Dunne Books, 2004.

Adūnīs. *Zaman al-Shiʿr* (Time of Poetry). Beirut: Dār al-ʿAwda, 1987.

Ajami, Fouad. "The End of Pan Arabism." *Foreign Affairs* 57, no. 2 (Winter 1978): 355–73.

Alcalay, Ammiel. *Memories of Our Future: Selected Essays, 1982–1999*. San Francisco: City Lights, 1999.

Almusa, Mishari. "The Andalusian Panegyric Muʿāraḍah: Rhetorical Strategy and Speech Act Theory." Ph.D. diss., Indiana University, 2010.

Altoma, Salih J. "Postwar Iraqi Literature: Agonies of Rebirth." *Books Abroad* 46, no. 2 (1972): 211–17.

Antoon, Sinan. "Mahmud Darwish's Allegorical Critique of Oslo." *Journal of Palestine Studies* 31, no. 2 (2002): 66–77.

Arana, R. Victoria. *The Facts on File Companion to World Poetry: 1900 to the Present*. New York: Facts on File, 2008.

Aruri, Naseer Hasan, and Edmund Ghareeb. *Enemy of the Sun: Poetry of Palestinian Resistance*. Washington, DC: Drum and Spear, 1970.

el-Azma, Nazeer. "The Tammūzī Movement and the Influence of T. S. Eliot on Badr Shākir al-Sayyāb." *Journal of the American Oriental Society* 88, no. 4 (1968): 671–78.

Azouqa, Aida. "Al-Bayyātī and W. B. Yeats as Mythmakers: A Comparative Study." *Journal of Arabic Literature* 30, no. 3 (1999): 258–90.

———. "Defamiliarization in the Poetry of ʿAbd al-Wahhāb al-Bayātī and T. S. Eliot: A Comparative Study." *Journal of Arabic Literature* 32, no. 2 (2001): 167–211.

———. "Ghassan Kanafani and William Faulkner: Kanafani's Achievement in *All That's Left to You*." *Journal of Arabic Literature* 31, no. 2 (2000): 147–70.

———. "Metapoetry between East and West: ʿAbd al-Wahhāb al-Bayātī and the Western Composers of Metapoetry—A Study in Analogies." *Journal of Arabic Literature* 39 (2008): 38–71.

Badawi, Mohammed Mustafa. "Commitment in Contemporary Arabic Literature." In *Critical Perspectives on Modern Arabic Literature*, edited by Issa J. Boullata, 23–44. Washington, DC: Three Continents, 1980.

———. *A Critical Introduction to Modern Arabic Poetry*. New York: Cambridge University Press, 1975.

Baker, Dorothy. *Mythic Masks in Self-Reflexive Poetry: A Study of Pan and Orpheus*. Chapel Hill: University of North Carolina Press, 1986.

al-Bayātī, ʿAbd al-Wahhāb. *Al-Aʿmāl al-Shiʿriyya* (The Complete Poetic Works). 2 vols. Beirut: Al-Mu'assasa al-ʿArabiyya lil-Dirāsāt wa-al-Nashr, 1995.

———. *Love, Death, and Exile: Poems Translated from Arabic*. Translated by Bassam Frangieh. Washington, DC: Georgetown University Press, 2004.

———. *Yanābīʿ al-Shams: Al-Sīra al-Shiʿriyya*. Damascus: Dar al-Farqad, 1999.

al-Bazei, Saad. "Realms of the Wasteland: Hijazi and the Metropolis." *World Literature Today* 67, no. 2 (1993): 306–9.

Becraft, Melvin E. *Picasso's Guernica: Images within Images*. Rohnert Park, CA: M. E. Becraft, 1986.

Bernard, Suzanne. *Le Poème en prose du Baudelaire jusqu'à nos jours*. Translated by Rawiya Sadeq. Cairo: Dār Sharqiyyāt, 1998.

Bhabha, Homi. "Remembering Fanon: Self, Psyche and the Colonial Condition." In *Colonial Discourse and Post-Colonial Theory: A Reader*, edited by Patrick Williams and Laura Chrisman, 112–23. New York: Columbia University Press, 1994.

Boullata, Issa J. "Abd al-Wahhab al-Bayati." *Contemporary World Writers*, 2nd ed., 47–50. London: St. James Press, 1993.

———. "An Arabic Poem in an Israeli Controversy: Mahmoud Darwish's 'Passing Words.'" In *Humanism, Culture, and Language in the Near East: Studies in Honor of Georg Krotkoff*, edited by Asma Afsaruddin and A. H. Mathias Zahniser, 119–28. Winona Lake, IN: Eisenbrauns, 1997.

———. *Modern Arab Poets, 1950–1975*. Washington, DC: Three Continents, 1976.

Bowen, Jeremy. *Six Days: How the 1967 War Shaped the Middle East*. New York: St. Martin's Press/Thomas Dunne, 2005.

Bresheeth, Haim. "Self and Other in Zionism: Palestine and Israel in Recent Hebrew Literature." In *Palestine: Profile of an Occupation*, edited by the Khamsin Collective, 120–52. London: Zed Books, 1989.

Brugman, Johannes. *An Introduction to the History of Modern Arabic Literature in Egypt*. Leiden: Brill, 1984.

Budairi, Musa. "Defeat and Victory: Thirty Years since the June 1967 War." In *Looking Back at the June 1967 War*, edited by Ḥayim Gordon, 51–58. Westport, CT: Praeger, 1999.

Byrne, Joseph P. *Encyclopedia of Pestilence, Pandemics, and Plagues*. Westport, CT: Greenwood, 2008.

Choueiri, Youssef M. *Arab Nationalism—A History: Nation and State in the Arab World*. Oxford: Blackwell, 2000.

Commins, David Dean. *Historical Dictionary of Syria*. Lanham, MD: Scarecrow, 1996.

Darwīsh, Maḥmūd. *ʿĀbirun fī Kalām ʿĀbir*. Beirut: Dār al-ʿAwda, 1994.

———. *Ākhir al-Layl* (End of Night). Beirut: Dār al-ʿAwda, 1969.

———. *Almond Blossoms and Beyond*. Translated by Mohammad Shaheen. Northampton, MA: Interlink Books, 2009.

———. *Al-ʿAmāl al-Kāmila* (Complete Works). Vol. 3. Jerusalem: Wizarat al-Thaqafa, 2010.

———. *Athar al-Farasha* (The Butterfly Effect). 2nd ed. Beirut: Riyāḍ al-Rayyis lil-Kutub wa-al-Nashr, 2007.

———. *Awrāq al-Zaytūn* (Olive Leaves). Haifa: Maṭbaʿat al-ittiḥād al-Taʿāwuniyya, 1964.

———. *Ḥālat Ḥiṣār* (State of Siege). Beirut: Riyāḍ al-Rayyis lil-Kutub wa-al-Nashr, 2002.

———. Interview by Abduh Wazin. *Al-Ḥaya al-Landaniyya*. December 14, 2005.

———. *Kazahr al-Lawz aw Ab'ad* (Almond Blossoms and Beyond). Beirut: Riyāḍ al-Rayyis lil-Kutub wa-al-Nashr, 2005.

———. *Lā Taʿtadhir ʿAmma Faʿalt* (Do Not Apologize for What You Did). 2nd ed. Beirut: Riyāḍ al-Rayyis lil-Kutub wa-al-Nashr, 2004.

———. *Lā Urīdu li-Hāthī al-Qaṣīda ʿan Tantahī* (I Do Not Want for This Poem to End). Beirut: Riyāḍ al-Rayyis lil-Kutub wa-al-Nashr, 2009.

———. *The Music of Human Flesh: Maḥmūd Darwīsh*. Translated by Denys Johnson-Davies. London: Heinemann, 1980.

———. *Now, As You Awaken*. Translated by Omnia Amin and Rick London. *Big Bridge*, 2006. Available at http://www.bigbridge.org/DARWISH.HTM.

———. *Psalms: Poems by Mahmoud Darwish*. Translated by Ben Bennani. Colorado Springs, CO: Three Continents, 1994.

———. *State of Siege [Ḥālat Ḥiṣār]*. Translated by Munir Akash and Daniel Moore. Syracuse, NY: Jusoor and Syracuse University Press, 2010.

———. *Unfortunately, It Was Paradise: Selected Poems*. Translated by Munir Akash and Carolyn Forché. Berkeley: University of California Press, 2003.

DiGangi, Julia. "Homeland, Hopelessness, Hate, and Heroes: Psychological Dynamics in the Israeli–Palestinian Conflict." In *Terror in the Holy Land: Inside the Anguish of the Israeli–Palestinian Conflict*, edited by Judith Kuriansky, 3–12. Westport, CT: Praeger, 2006.

Eid, Muna Abu. *Mahmoud Darwish: Literature and the Politics of Palestinian Identity*. New York: I. B. Tauris, 2016.

Elad-Bouskila, Ami. *Modern Palestinian Literature and Culture*. London: F. Cass, 1999.

Eliot, T. S. "Tradition and the Individual Talent." *Perspecta* 19 (1982): 36–42.

el-Enany, Rasheed. "Poets and Rebels: Reflections of Lorca in Modern Arabic Poetry." *Third World Quarterly* 11, no. 4 (1989): 252–64.

Etman, Ahmed. "Translation at the Intersection of Traditions: The Arab Reception of the Classics." In *A Companion to Classical Receptions*, edited by Lorna Hardwick and Christopher Stray, 141–52. Malden, MA: Blackwell, 2008.

Evans, Mike. *Jerusalem Betrayed: Ancient Prophecy and Modern Conspiracy Collide in the Holy City*. Dallas: Word Publishing, 1997.

Frangieh, Bassam. "Modern Arabic Poetry: Vision and Reality." In *Tradition, Modernity, and Postmodernity in Arabic Literature: Essays in Honor of Professor Issa J. Boullata*, edited by Kamal Abdel-Malek and Wael B. Hallaq, 221–49. Leiden: Brill, 2000.

Furani, Khaled. "Rhythms of the Secular: The Politics of Modernizing Arab Poetic Forms." *American Ethnologist* 35, no. 2 (2008): 290–307.

Gamal, Adel S. "A City without a Heart: The Predicament of Man." In *Investigating Arabic*, edited by R. Rammuny and D. Parkinson, 257–77. Columbus, OH: Greyden Press, 1994.

Gawrych, G. W. "The Egyptian Military Defeat of 1967." *Journal of Contemporary History* 26, no. 2 (1991): 277–305.

Gelvin, James L. *The Israel–Palestine Conflict: One Hundred Years of War*. Cambridge: Cambridge University Press, 2007.

———. *The Modern Middle East: A History*. New York: Oxford University Press, 2008.

Gohar, Saddik. "The Image of Cairo in Hejazi's 'A City without a Heart.'" *Nebula* 8, no. 1 (2011): 137–58.

———. "The Integration of Western Modernism in Postcolonial Arabic Literature: A Study of Abdul-Wahhab al-Bayati's Third World Poetics." *Third World Quarterly* 29, no. 2 (2008): 375–90.

Goode, Stephen. *The Prophet and the Revolutionary: Arab Socialism in the Modern Middle East*. New York: Watts, 1975.

Gordon, Joel. *Nasser's Blessed Movement: Egypt's Free Officers and the July Revolution*. New York: Oxford University Press, 1992.

Hart, Stephen. *"No Pasarán": Art, Literature and the Spanish Civil War*. London: Tamesis, 1988.

Ḥijāzī, Aḥmad ʿAbd al-Muʿṭī. *Al-Aʿmāl al-Kāmila* (The Complete Works). Kuwait: Dār Suʿād al-Ṣabāh, 1993.

———. "As If a Voice Were Calling: Ahmed Abdel Muʿti Hijazi." Translated by Omnia Amin and Rick London. *Big Bridge* (Spring 2011). Available at http://www.bigbridge.org/BB15/toc.html.

———. E-mail interview with Yāsir Ḥijāzī and Waed Athamneh. January 10, 2012.

———. "Only Now, We Left the Middle Ages." *Al-Masry al-Youm*. August 29, 2013.

———. *Qaṣīdat al-Nathr aw al-Qaṣīda al-Kharsāʾ* (The Prose Poem or the Mute Poem). Dubai: Majallat Dubai al-Thaqfiyya, 2008.

———. "Revolution or Coup?" *Al-Masry al-Youm*. July 23, 2014.

———. *Al-Shiʿr Rafīqī* (Poetry Is My Companion). Riyadh: Dār al-Marrīkh lil-Nashr, 1988.

———. "Al-Shi'r wa-'Abd al-Nāṣir" (Poetry and Abd al-Nasser). In *Kitābāt 'alā Qabr 'Abd al-Nāṣir* (Writings on the Tomb of Nasser), edited by Aḥmad 'Abd al-Mu'ṭī Ḥijāzī et al., 5–12. Beirut: Dār al-'Awda, 1971.

———. "The Sun and the Dark Ones." *Al-Ahram*. October 8, 2013.

———. *Ṭalal al-Waqt* (The Standing Ruins of Time). Cairo: Al-Hay'a al-Miṣriyya al-'āmma lil-Kitāb, 2011.

———. "We Have Not Revolted Yet." *Al-Ahram*. April 6, 2016.

Hourani, Albert Habib. *Arabic Thought in the Liberal Age, 1798–1939*. London: Oxford University Press, 1962.

———. *A History of the Arab Peoples*. Cambridge, MA: Belknap Press, 1991.

Huri, Yair. "Perhaps I Disappointed You: On a Metapoetic Poem by Sa'dī Yūsuf." *Middle Eastern Literature* 7, no. 1 (2004): 77–83.

———. "The Queen Who Serves the Slaves: From Politics to Metapoetics in the Poetry of Qāsim Ḥaddād," *Journal of Arabic Literature* 34, no. 3 (2003): 252–79.

Ismael, Tareq Y. *The Communist Movement in the Arab World*. London: Routledge Curzon, 2005.

Ismael, Tareq Y., and Rifa'at El-Sa'id. *The Communist Movement in Egypt, 1920–1988*. Syracuse, NY: Syracuse University Press, 1990.

Ismā'īl, Ṣidqī. "Niqāṭ Asāsiyya fī Masāi'l al-Iltizām wa-al-Adā' al-Fannī" (Fundamental Issues in Commitment and Performative Art). *Al-Mawqif al-Adabī* 9–10 (1972): 5–16.

Isstaif, Abdul-Nabi. "Forging a New Self, Embracing the Other: Modern Arabic Critical Theory and the West—Luwīs 'Awaḍ." *Middle Eastern Literatures* 5, no. 2 (2002): 161–80.

Jabra, Jabra Ibrahim. "Modern Arabic Literature and the West." *Journal of Arabic Literature* 2, no. 1 (1971): 76–91.

———. "The Rebels, the Committed, and Others: Transitions in Arabic Poetry Today." In *Critical Perspectives on Modern Arabic Literature*, edited by Issa J. Boullata, 191–205. Washington, DC: Three Continents, 1980.

Jankowski, James P. *Nasser's Egypt, Arab Nationalism, and the United Arab Republic*. Boulder, CO: Lynne Rienner, 2002.

Jayyusi, Salma Khadra. *Modern Arabic Poetry: An Anthology*. New York: Columbia University Press, 1987.

———. *Trends and Movements in Modern Arabic Poetry*. Leiden: Brill, 1977.

Joudah, Fady. "Mahmoud Darwish's Lyric Epic." *Human Architecture: Journal of the Sociology of Self-Knowledge* 7, no. 5 (2009): 6–18.

———, trans. "Wedding Song, and: She's Alone in the Evening, and: While Waiting." *Prairie Schooner* 80, no. 2 (2006): 26–29.

Kadhim, Hussein N. *The Poetics of Anti-Colonialism in the Arabic Qaṣīdah*. Leiden: Brill, 2004.

Kassab, Elizabeth Suzanne. *Contemporary Arab Thought: Cultural Critique in Comparative Perspective*. New York: Columbia University Press, 2010.

Kelman, Herbert C. "The Interdependence of Israeli and Palestinian National Identities: The Role of the Other in Existential Conflicts." *Journal of Social Issues* 55, no. 3 (1999): 581–600.

———. "Nationalism, Patriotism, and National Identity: Social-Psychological Dimensions." In *Patriotism in the Lives of Individuals and Nations*, edited by Daniel Bar-Tal and Ervin Staub, 166–89. Chicago: Nelson-Hall, 1997.

Khouri, Mounah A., and Hamid Algar. *An Anthology of Modern Arabic Poetry*. Berkeley: University of California Press, 1975.

Kimche, David. *The Last Option: After Nasser, Arafat, and Saddam Hussein; the Quest for Peace in the Middle East*. New York: Charles Scribner's Sons, 1991.

Klemm, Verena. "Different Notions of Commitment (Iltizām) and Committed Literature (al-Adab al-Multazim) in the Literary Circles of the Mashriq." *Arabic and Middle Eastern Literature* 3, no. 1 (2000): 51–62.

Kornberg-Weiss, Morani. *Dear Darwish*. Buffalo, NY: BlazeVox, 2014. Kindle edition.

Kramer, Martin S. *Arab Awakening and Islamic Revival: The Politics of Ideas in the Middle East*. New Brunswick, NJ: Transaction, 2008.

Lane, Edward William. *Arabic–English Lexicon*. Vol. 5. New Delhi: Asian Educational Services, 2003.

Levy, Silvano. *Surrealism: Surrealist Visuality*. Edinburgh: Edinburgh University Press, 1996.

Lockman, Zachary, and Joel Beinin. *Intifada: The Palestinian Uprising against Israeli Occupation*. Boston: South End, 1989.

Makdisi, Saree. "Postcolonial Literature in a New Colonial World: Modern Arabic Culture and the End of Modernity." In *The Pre-Occupation of Postcolonial Studies*, edited by Fawzia Afzal-Khan and Kalpana Seshadri-Crooks, 266–91. Durham, NC: Duke University Press, 2000.

Malik, Charles. "The Near East: The Search for Truth." In *Arab Nationalism: An Anthology*, edited by Sylvia G. Haim, 188–224. Berkeley: University of California Press, 1964.

Massad, Joseph Andoni. *Desiring Arabs*. Chicago: University of Chicago Press, 2007.

Matar, Anat. "Postmodernism and the Oslo Agreement." In *Looking Back at the June 1967 War*, edited by Hayim Gordon, 123–31. Westport, CT: Praeger, 1999.

Mattawa, Khaled. *Mahmoud Darwish: The Poet's Art and His Nation*. Syracuse, NY: Syracuse University Press, 2014. Kindle edition.

Meisami, Julie Scott, and Paul Starkey. *Encyclopedia of Arabic Literature*. Vol. 1. London: Routledge, 1998.

Mikhail, Mona. "Iltizam: Commitment and Arabic Poetry." *World Literature Today* 53, no. 4 (1979): 595–600.

Monshipouri, Mahmood. *Islamism, Secularism, and Human Rights in the Middle East*. Boulder, CO: Lynne Rienner Publishers, 1998.

Mooney, Thomas J. *Live Forever or Die Trying: The History and Politics of Life Extension*. Xlibris, 2011.

Moreh, Shmuel. *Modern Arabic Poetry, 1800–1970: The Development of Its Forms and Themes under the Influence of Western Literature*. Leiden: Brill, 1976.

———. *Studies in Modern Arabic Prose and Poetry*. Leiden: Brill, 1988.

al-Musawi, Muhsin Jassim. *Arabic Poetry: Trajectories of Modernity and Tradition*. London: Routledge, 2006.

———. "Dedications as Poetic Intersections." *Journal of Arabic Literature* 31, no. 1 (2000): 1– 37.

———. "Engaging Tradition in Modern Arab Poetics." *Journal of Arabic Literature* 33, no. 2 (2002): 172–210.

al-Naqqāsh, Rajā'. *Maḥmūd Darwīsh, Shāʿir al-Arḍ al-Muḥtalla* (Mahmoud Darwish: Poet of the Occupied Land). 2nd ed. Cairo: Dār al-Hilāl, 1971.

Oren, Michael B. "The Revelations of 1967: New Research on the Six Day War and Its Lessons for the Contemporary Middle East." *Israel Studies* 10, no. 2 (2005): 1–14.

Picasso, Pablo, and Dore Ashton. *Picasso on Art: A Selection of Views*. New York: Da Capo, 1988.

Pinault, David. "Images of Christ in Arabic Literature." *Die Welt Des Islams* 27, no. 1 (1987): 103–25.

Rahman, Najat. "Interview with Mahmoud Darwish: On the Possibility of Poetry at a Time of Siege." In *Mahmoud Darwish, Exile's Poet: Critical Essays*, edited by Hala Khamis Nassar and Najat Rahman, 319–26. Northampton, MA: Olive Branch, 2008.

Rizk, Khalil Shukrallah. "The Poetry of ʿAbd al-Wahhāb al-Bayātī: Thematic and Stylistic Study." Ph.D. diss., Indiana University, 1981.

Rose, Jacqueline. *Proust among the Nations: From Dreyfus to the Middle East*. Chicago: University of Chicago Press, 2011.

Said, Edward. *Peace and Its Discontents: Essays on Palestine in the Middle East Peace Process*. New York: Vintage, 1995.

Salama, Mohammad R. "The Mise-en-Scène of Writing in al-Bayātī's 'Al-Kitābah ʿAlā al-Ṭīn.'" *Journal of Arabic Literature* 32, no. 2 (2001): 142–66.

Sartre, Jean-Paul. *What Is Literature?* New York: Philosophical Library, 1949.

al-Sayyāb, Badr Shākir. *Dīwān* (Collected Poems). 2 vols. Beirut: Dar al-ʿAwda, 2005.

Shandi, Majdi. "Ḥijāzī Yastarjiʿ al-Dhākira" (Ḥijāzī Recalls Memories). *Al-Mashhad*. Mu'assasat al-Mashhad lil-Nashr wa-al-Tawzīʿ, October 5, 2011. Available at http://www.masress.com/almashhad/22173.

Shatz, Adam. "A Love Story between an Arab Poet and His Land." In *The Struggle for Sovereignty: Palestine and Israel, 1993–2005*, edited by Joel Beinin and Rebecca L. Stein, 219–29. Stanford, CA: Stanford University Press, 2006.

Shaw, Joey. "Butrus al-Bustani and the American Missionaries: Towards a Harmony of Understanding of the Advent of the Nahdah." *St. Francis Magazine* 5, no. 3 (2009): 75–99.

Siddiq, Muhammad. "Significant but Problematic Others: Negotiating 'Israelis' in the Works of Mahmoud Darwish." *Comparative Literature Studies* 47, no. 4 (2010): 487–503.

Simawe, Saadi A. "The Lives of the Sufi Masters in Abd al-Wahhāb al-Bayātī's Poetry." *Journal of Arabic Literature* 32, no. 2 (2001): 119–41.

Stetkevych, Jaroslav. "Al-Ḥadātha fī Shi'r Aḥmad 'Abd al-Mu'ṭī Ḥijāzī" (Modernism in the Poetry of Aḥmad 'Abd al-Mu'ṭī Ḥijāzī). In *Mamlakat Aḥmad 'Abd al-Mu'ṭī Ḥijāzī*, edited by Ḥasan Ṭilib, 33–85. Cairo: al-Hai'a al-Miṣriyya al-'Āmma lil-Kitāb, 2006.

Stetkevych, Suzanne Pinckney. *The Mute Immortals Speak: Pre-Islamic Poetry and the Poetics of Ritual*. Ithaca, NY: Cornell University Press, 2011.

Sulaiman, Khalid A. *Palestine and Modern Arab Poetry*. London: Zed, 1984.

Sumi, Akiko Motoyoshi. *Description in Classical Arabic Poetry: Waṣf, Ekphrasis, and Interarts Theory*. Leiden: Brill, 2004.

Sylvain, Patrick. "Darwish's Essentialist Poetics in a State of Siege." *Human Architecture: Journal of the Sociology of Self-Knowledge* 7, no. 5 (2009): 137–50.

Tagore, Rabindranath. *The English Writings of Rabindranath Tagore*. New Delhi: Atlantic, 2007.

Tamimi, Azzam, and John L. Esposito. *Islam and Secularism in the Middle East*. New York: New York University Press, 2000.

Ṭilib, Ḥasan. "Al-Fāris fī al-Sab'īn ma' Iḥdā Ma'ārikih Ḥawl Qaṣīdat al-Nathr" (The Knight in His Seventies in One of His Battles against the Prose Poem). In *Aḥmad 'Abd al-Mu'ṭī Ḥijāzī: Sab'ūn 'Āman min al-Riyāda wa-al-Tajdīd*, edited by Ḥasan Ṭilib et al., 15–25. Cairo: al-Majlis al-A'lā lil-Thaqāfa, 2005.

Torstrick, Rebecca L. *The Limits of Coexistence: Identity Politics in Israel*. Ann Arbor: University of Michigan Press, 2000.

Urabi, Usama. "Masīrat Ḥijāzī al-Ibdā'iyya" (Ḥijāzī's Creative Journey). In *Aḥmad 'Abd al-Mu'ṭī Ḥijāzī: Sab'ūn 'Āman min al-Riyāda wa-al-Tajdīd*, edited by Ḥasan Ṭilib et al., 327–35. Cairo: al-Majlis al-A'lā lil-Thaqāfa, 2005.

Watson, George. *The Lost Literature of Socialism*. Cambridge, UK: Lutterworth, 1998.

Wellek, Rene. *Discriminations*. New Haven, CT: Yale University Press, 1971.

Wu, Bingbing. "Secularism and Secularization in the Arab World." *Journal of Middle Eastern and Islamic Studies* 1, no. 1 (2007): 55–65.

Yaqub, Salim. "Contesting Arabism: The Eisenhower Doctrine and the Arab Middle East, 1956–1959." *Middle East Studies Online Journal* (2009): 111–23.

Yūsuf, Sa'dī. *Saadi Yousif* (blog). http://www.saadiyousif.com.

Zurayq, Qustantin. "Arab Nationalism and Religion." In *Arab Nationalism: An Anthology*, edited by Sylvia G. Haim, 167–88. Berkeley: University of California Press, 1964.

INDEX

WAED ATHAMNEH
is assistant professor of Arabic studies at Connecticut College.

CPSIA information can be obtained
at www.ICGtesting.com
Printed in the USA
LVOW12*0923080217
523527LV00004B/5/P

9 780268 101541